M000112974

ELUCIDATIONS

ELUCIDATIONS

Hans Urs von Balthasar

TRANSLATED BY
JOHN RICHES

IGNATIUS PRESS SAN FRANCISCO

Title of the German original:
Klarstellungen: zur Prüfung der Geister
© 1971 Verlag Herder KG, Freiburg-im-Breisgau

First published in English in 1975
by S.P.C.K., London
Translation by S.P.C.K., © 1975
Reprinted with permission

Biblical quotations taken from the
Revised Standard Version of the Bible,
© 1946, 1952, and 1957 by the Division of Christian Education
of the National Council of the Churches of Christ
are used by permission.

Cover by Roxanne Mei Lum

This edition by permission of Johannes Verlag, Freiburg-im-Breisgau
Published in 1998 Ignatius Press, San Francisco
ISBN 0–89870–621–1
Library of Congress catalogue number 98–78007
Printed in the United States of America ∞

CONTENTS

Preface

The object of these "elucidations" is to offer a concise and summary treatment of a few essential questions concerning the substance of the Christian life, experience, and faith, which today are in dispute or—as is true of the majority—are disappearing into oblivion. Each chapter stands on its own; the order is of no importance. Together they bear witness to an underlying view of things; they are a few rays which all radiate from the same center. Much which today arouses passion remains untreated, not because one is afraid to get involved at close quarters, preferring to take his stand behind less dangerous positions, but for a variety of reasons. In some cases the question would require a more detailed treatment; in others it could only be decided by a positive decision of the Church; in yet others it has only been artificially turned into a burning problem and that perhaps because one avoids the true burning center oneself. It is often the case that what fires me, the lukewarm Christian, does not touch the one who is truly afire, and what nearly destroys the latter does not disturb me in any manner.

If these few rays do indeed proceed from the true sun, then perhaps one could on that basis calculate the center of the fire from which our questions would be shown to be truly burning and often would nearly be solved. Much, however, which seemed to me simple and unquestionable could perhaps, unheeded, turn itself into a question mark.

Much is offered in a concentrated form. Those who find pieces like "Trinity and Future" or "Christianity as Utopia" too compressed should pass them over. There are, however, many things which become clearer by compression. I would ask you, then, not simply to read over difficult passages but to resolve them in subsequent reflection. There is much which overlaps, but one should exercise patience, for there are Christian things which only come home to one through repetition.

Certain problems today are given excessive publicity; men try to exalt them by force into "articles by which the Church stands or falls". They are practically all problems which men try to solve by smoothing over or playing down the difficulties, by suggesting, supposedly out of sympathy for men's needs, the easier way. And yet in the long run it is the narrow way which attracts the best men. It is, for example, well known that monasteries which have preserved the strictness of their discipline undiminished today still have new postulants, whereas those who prefer a softer line seem to be despised by God and men. That is only intended to be taken as a symptom. The one who makes demands (but he must also give evidence that he has much to offer and must only make his demands for God and his work) still has a chance of being heard. It is part of the definition of fashion that it will change next year. That which is truly Christian was fortunately never fashionable, not even in the so-called Christian ages.

What little is said here is without pretension. One can only wonder, when reading many present-day books, how much expertise and skill have been squandered on unfruitful matters. But then one may draw comfort from Hofmannsthal's dictum, "the most dangerous sort of stupidity is a sharp understanding." So one can accept it happily enough if one is thought of as simple and a little weak-minded.

A Verse of Matthias Claudius

If someone receives a present from a friend, what should he then *not* do? There are a hundred ways of saying the wrong thing, and so it is best to get it right straightaway. "Thank you! It makes me very happy! I am so pleased to have it! I think it's beautiful! It will remind me of you!" Then the recipient too causes joy and happiness. Nothing could be simpler than that, and without question it is right.

If, however, one departs from this simplicity and begins to divide what is indivisible, then it is remarkable what a variety of false reactions can be discovered and developed. In the first place, one can pretend not to want it: "Oh, that's much too beautiful for me, and far too good for me. I'd much prefer you to have it, won't you take it back and use it yourself? You've got a much better safe and I might lose it. And my taste is much poorer than yours. You're surely a much better judge of its value than I am." Or one might sound a note of mistrust: "Why on earth did he give that to me? What's behind it? Does he want to make me feel indebted to him? Is he trying to entangle me with his presents? Or does he want to humiliate me, because he knows that I can't give him anything of equivalent worth in return? How difficult it is to be so indebted without being able to make adequate return!" We can, however, try to get rid of this rather oppressive sense of obligation by indulging in more fantastic speculations: "What if the present doesn't come from him at all? If someone or other has sent it under a false name in order to play me a malicious trick and will die laughing when he gets my moving letter of thanks? I must first examine the matter thoroughly and find out who really has sent it." One can also subject the present to a really thorough examination. Is it really genuine? Is it silver or plate or merely a cheap imitation? Is it an original or mass-produced? Has it been cast in one piece, or has it been stuck together? And if the latter, from how many parts and elements? Then one breaks up the thing into its individual components, and in this state it no longer looks like anything at all and only confirms one's suspicion. If one looks at the matter more closely, more soberly, more critically, then the whole thing (but now, of course, it is not a whole thing any longer) is revealed as a fraud. "I wonder what he paid for it?" At first sight it gave the impression—as was, of course, intended—of being a very valuable, indeed almost priceless, piece. It was intended to create such a belief and that such belief should lead to a corresponding gratitude. One can see the intention. But something simpler would have rung more true. Next time I go shopping I will take the piece along and go into a few shops and ask how much they are worth. Unfortunately, probably very little. I can't sell it back. But at least I can work out how much the giver has been prepared to lay out on me. And then, at last, I will find out what his loudly proclaimed love is really worth.

Do you see there stands the moon?—
It is but half in view,

And yet is round and beautiful!
So too are many things
We lightly laugh to scorn,
Because our eyes fail to see. (*Matthias Claudius*)

The criticism of Christianity is a highly exasperating matter. The nearer one gets to the details, the stronger the lens one takes to examine them, the more incredibly banal and cheap everything appears. And yet criticism is such an invaluable instrument, indeed the most reliable which God (or "God-nature") has given to us men that we might work our way up from a state of primitive humanity to the highest state of the superman. As soon as any of the accepted criticism of our day is labelled "uncritical", then it is simply out of date. If you can prove that a professor has accepted something "uncritically", he will have forfeited a large measure of the brightness of his halo.

Now it is a fact that that which is truly Christian only comes in view when it is "accepted". "Take, eat, this is my body which is given for you." And so we are brought back to the beginning. There is only one proper way of receiving a present—if indeed it is a present at all. That is the uncritical way. Then everything is round and beautiful. It is in truth a present if it mediates the immediacy of love to love. For a moment a ray bursts forth and bears witness to the light which endures. The character of the present is as such not uppermost, not the real subject; it only points to the heart of the one who gives and appeals to the heart of the one who receives. It makes a genuine appeal, in an act of trust. It wants not to be misunderstood as a present, to possess no value of its own, only to be grasped as a sign of love. It does not wish to put a burden on the receiver. For the lover the best thing would be if he did not need to make his offering in the form of a present but could give his love itself this form so that he could visibly lay it in the hands of the loved one. Then, indeed, everything would be so transparent that there would be no need to "look behind it", because then the wholeness (the "catholicity") of love would have been portrayed in the wholeness of the present as in a crystal. This wholeness could, of course, only be perceived by those who know how to see things whole and only be received by a heart which is itself whole. One can see already that "critical catholicism" is a contradiction in terms.

For the first thing about Christianity is that it is a gift of God to men, and, because God is not a mean giver, it is the most beautiful gift possible. Only the man who accepts it in the manner in which it is given will not "lightly laugh it to scorn". "See, I proclaim to you a great joy." The man who listens to that in a critically morose and mistrusting frame of mind will naturally be no more ready to hear the proclamation of great joy than to receive the gift which would bring such joy. If one does indeed want to use the word "critical"—and perhaps one only means by that "appropriate"—then the only critical attitude to this gift would be a lightness of heart which, without reflecting about itself, says "thank you". And this all the more so because, according to the Christian message, the gift which is offered is indeed truly the crystallized (and at the same time liquefied) love of the giver: God in the form of his given-ness. There is only one man who may receive such a present as it is intended: he who himself is transformed into the form of given-ness, conformed to it by virtue of his own whole-hearted assent, thanks, and acceptance.

And so, incidentally, we have reached our goal. The process of purifying, and consequently of elucidating, clarifying, our troubled and infested Christian effluent can be nothing else than that of converting it back into the pure transparent whole. Not, that is, its detailed microscopic examination and treatment with chemical ingredients. For the cloudiness and discoloration all come from the fact that certain problems relating only to partial aspects of Christianity have been taken out of their context within the whole and treated "critically" on their own, whereas they can receive meaning and gain their proper form and exhaustive treatment only through integration into the whole and by being plotted out in relation to the overall unity. We are becoming submerged in a superfluity of such "partial" problems; as such they are becoming more and more confused; each receives for itself a leaden weight which makes it weigh more than the united whole. Not only does one no longer see the whole in its external appearance—that is not surprising—but also one no longer sees it in its inner essence, and so whole peoples and continents emigrate from a lost inner essence toward an undiscoverable outward appearance. Men rack their brains and at the same time threaten to beat each other's out over the "structural problems" of the Church, as if the Church were in any sense a structure alone and not rather in her essence the transparent gift which God gives us of himself, long before it becomes our answer, which is appropriate only when it gives expression to the assent and thanksgiving and amen of love. We can gaze as intensely as we will at individual structures and examine them from all sides critically, but we shall still totally fail to understand them if we do not grasp them as that which they are of themselves: "because our eyes fail to see".

There are here and there Christians whom one calls "saints" (they do not all turn out equally well). They allow us to see in their existence, as it were in a small model, what the large model of Christianity truly means. They are the best clarifiers there are in the Church. They are transparent to the whole, the gift of God to us. Their whole lives are lived out of this gift, are an attempt to respond to it in gratitude. It makes such total demands on them that for them there is neither time nor place for critical reflection from a neutral standpoint. At least they know so much of God that they constantly trust him to perform the greatest work, which is also the most difficult and most beautiful, and consequently from the start they sense falsehood wherever there is any attempt to chip away at the substance of Christianity, to reduce it or to equate it with other philosophies. It is this vision, this way of looking at things and this way of thinking common to the saints that we wish at least to take as our guide in what follows.

This will doubtless disappoint many expectations. In the first place, one will be able constantly to offer as an objection to the method that it presupposes in every case what ought to be proved—if of course one can in any way ever prove a "whole", for that is something which seems beyond the reach of critical reason, something which it can only approach (or alternatively move away from) asymptotically by treatment of individual aspects. To continue to presuppose the existence of the whole and to attempt to resolve all the obscurities of the individual problems simply by letting every river run out into the sea seems offensive in view of the efforts which are being made on so many sides today, and ultimately it seems to clarify nothing. But we must also at this time put this objection to one side. For in these little essays we shall be following no other method than that which has been used from time immemorial, namely, that of starting by seeing and weighing and recognizing the whole.

Second, everything will remain quite fragmentary and unsystematic. If one tried with every cut to bisect the center of an apple, how many such cuts would be possible? The question shows that the answer is irrelevant. The important thing is to prove that one can in every case, as often as one likes, really hit the middle. Once one has grasped the principle by being shown a few examples, then one can do it oneself. In what sense can one speak of "systematics" with reference to a divine gift? In order to achieve a "system" (which means precisely a "placing together"), one would have to start from the horizontal inter-relationship of the parts and so to proceed from below gradually to construct or, indeed, to reconstruct the whole. But that is impossible precisely because God's gift as a whole is reached only from above.

And so I ask the reader not to attempt to find an internal and consecutive relationship between these sketches. There is no such thing. Everything is related only by reference to the center.

Third and worst. We cannot afford, if we are concerned with God's gift to us, to think toward God from the point of view of man, particularly from the point of view of "modern man". We must not think from the point of view of what we need; of that to which the gift would most reasonably have to adjust itself; of what we still believe and can reasonably answer for; and of what can no longer be demanded of us critical and enlightened men. With such a priori postulates we shall indeed make it precisely impossible for ourselves to distinguish between the kernel and the husk, between historical wrapping and the eternal valid content, and then it happens that we by mistake throw away the kernel with the husks and are simply left with husks. If we take a single passage of the Bible, then criticism can ask what it means in a historical, in a national, in a Near Eastern context, can ask from what sources it comes, what outlook and views it presupposes in the speaker, the writer, and the hearer. All that is well and good. But there simply are no "single passages of the Bible", but only a total complex which is the event of revelation, which through the centuries has used very many words in order to say one thing from many sides and points of view. The meaning of a word in a sentence or a paragraph depends in each case on the context. Everybody knows that. The relative importance of a phase in the development of New Testament Christology is decided by the synthesis within which it is integrated. Now unfortunately not everybody considers this. The final, definitive meaning of a dogma which the Church has on occasion defined is decided by her total understanding of revelation, which is expressed in the particular statements but which also transcends them. The standpoint from which one views something, from which one attempts to cast light on it, can change, precisely because the object around which one moves is always the same. In order that critical reason may begin to get to work on this object at all, one thing is necessary: namely, that it first gets it in its sights (instead of always first thinking of itself) and then, when it has seen, asks itself with what method one can approach it in order to do justice to it. This is the manner of approach in every science which has pretensions to respectability. Again, in this case the whole has priority over the part, and it is from the whole that the part is to be understood and elucidated; again and again we return to the same point.

Not, of course, as if all questions which press on us today can be solved by the magic means of integration. And yet a clarification, where possible, can only be hoped for if we attempt to answer questions by thinking them out from their center and, as it were, thus decontaminating them. The center does not offer any oracles which would absolve us from the task of understanding; and, of course, individual questions within the context of the whole may always be treated quite separately, according to the context within which they are placed. Is polygenism theologically assimilable? How far is inter-communion to be encouraged ecclesiastically or to be forbidden? What legal arrangements are to be made in the question of mixed marriages? What is the precise meaning of the sacrament of holy orders? Such and a hundred other similar questions demand extensive investigation, the weighing up of the advantages and disadvantages of many different points of view. But whence can we expect clarifying light to be shed on such problems if not from the total meaning of the Christian revelation? It is before this light, and not primarily before the light of reason or of humanity, that one will have to answer for the decisions which one makes. This demands of all who take part in the discussion the ability to hold in view contemplatively the whole and not the half moon: a contemplative ability. Questions which embrace the immense space between heaven and earth, life and death, nature and grace, cannot be clarified from purely earthly and natural points of view. One can see this best if one tries the alternative approach. How insoluble such problems then seem and indeed are in the restricted space which is allowed to them, if one honestly allows them to retain all their questionableness and does not instead violently explain them away.

We cannot hope in the following pieces to arouse the contemplative sense in men, but merely, where it is present, to encourage its exercise a little. And, perhaps, to fire the reader with a desire to continue such exercises himself. Above all, to remind him that no Christian question can be clarified or elucidated unless in faith. "And yet is round and beautiful."

Criteria

What is clouded and confused can only be clarified by discernment. Where, however, what is to be discerned is of final, ultimate importance, where we are concerned with the being and non-being of man before God, who would be bold enough to make distinctions there unless in the Holy Spirit? This is a sharp, cutting wind which can set our teeth chattering. And it is also a scorching fire which would sear out the brain of many a man if it descended on him as tongues of fire. And who will so overreach himself as to claim that he has the Spirit? Parties cannot lay claim to him for themselves; he sweeps through proposition and counter-proposition. Defenders of tradition may be parched and spiritless; defenders of progressiveness may march on into empty spaces. No one group can capture the heavenly dove for itself. It comes and goes. It descends, but it does not settle. "The tumult of the spirit storms where it will." Is this, then, merely the arbitrary exercise of the divine will, beyond all our confused and embittered struggles for faith, for the Church, for Christian existence? Does our despair not trouble him? But how would he then be the Spirit who with "unutterable groaning" sighs from within our hearts? And if he who is "sharper than any two-edged sword" pierces us until "he has divided soul and spirit, joint and marrow one from the other", should we think of him more as a butcher or perhaps more as an experienced surgeon who can cut so deep only because of his responsibility and skill? Are we simply the objects on which he works, or does he not perhaps also teach us something of his skill? Paul at least maintains that "we have received the Spirit which is from God" and continues: "The purely natural man does not understand what is of the Spirit of God. It is for him as folly and he cannot understand it because it must be understood spiritually. The spiritual man on the other hand judges all, whereas he himself is judged by no man. 'For who knows the mind of the Lord that he might be able to teach him?' We however possess the Spirit of Christ." Great words, high claims. But what here appears as a claim stands in the gospel as a demand, a demand that we should interpret signs and discern spirits. "The Spirit of Christ": that is a clue which may help us to understand this freely blowing, indomitable Spirit. Here criteria are sensed, criteria to indicate whether the Spirit moves in a man, empowering him to clarify what is unclarified.

If the Spirit descended on Jesus at his humiliation in the baptism of sinners in the Jordan, then this means that one cannot gain possession of the dove by reaching up to the skies. The Spirit reaches out to us, not we to him. And he descends where he finds room, readiness, listening, recognition, and acceptance. The less resistance he finds from preconceived views, ready-made systems, categorical principles, definitive plans, the more clearly he can express himself, the more clearly he can discern. And thus he lends to us something of his power to discern; we receive a share of his criteria. There are four which we might list, but which are only different sides of the same thing: namely, of the Spirit, who as fire, tumult, and sword makes his discernment by himself. In the humiliation of the "critical reason" he raises our spirit up to the place where, as Lord of the whole, he judges the parts.

1. "He who speaks on his own authority seeks his own glory; but he who seeks the glory of him who sent him is true and in him there is no falsehood" (Jn 7:18 RSV). An alternative which allows for no in-betweens and so provides a sharp criterion. Christians who from their baptism have received a sense for the language of the Spirit, even non-Christians who know what it is to carry out a positive task, may use it. Indeed, they are often in the process of doing precisely that when the other spirit throws dust into their eyes, with the consequence that they overlook what is most blatantly obvious. A name, something which is going to gain publicity, something which seems modern, stands in their way and distorts such a simple view of things. Take, for example, a preacher or a professor of theology: Is it really so very difficult to distinguish whether he is seeking his own honor or the honor of him who has sent him? You can smell the pride which seeks its own honor; as is well known, it stinks. Or has our modern sense of smell become so entirely dulled that we no longer have any sense organ which can detect this most powerful and unpleasant of all scents? The human spirit can be developed in two directions. In the one it offers its help without consideration of self and takes its place among the ranks of those who wish to shift the great burden of the commonplace, at least at one small point. In the other

it seeks to dominate, under the pretext of carrying things a stage farther; the voice becomes commanding, the language magical, the gestures compelling, the thought sweeps you along. It is precisely this element of violence in all its forms—from the violent enthusiasm which it engenders to the violent disruptions which it creates—which enables one to recognize this spirit. The breast is puffed out. A great wave of popular enthusiasm raises its head. The lecture hall thunders with applause (in its enthusiasm). At last things are beginning to move! One has had enough of theologians endlessly treading water; one smells the morning air and the future. And if his enthusiastic hearers are swept on farther than the speaker had foreseen, there is still time for him to absolve himself: "This is not what I intended." But such disclaimers are defeats; for the manner in which he set out is what counts. The style of thinking. The sense of doing battle. There are overpowering proofs, irresistible arguments; subjects are illuminated by harsh searchlights, breaches are made in defenses, and the reward is reaped in banner headlines. A saying is wrested from the Gospel, the claims of Christian existence are stamped out, tempered into a slogan, borne forward on a pikestaff like a severed head. One can turn up the volume on something which by nature is quiet in such a manner that its nature becomes unrecognizable. It is remarkable and surprising how the same word, whispered or shouted, can express two quite contradictory things. The Holy Spirit always has his own particular atmosphere. The truth "is in the air". Even in theology and proclamation, in the manner in which Christians live their faith, the climate is decisive.

"Beloved, do not trust in every spirit, but test the spirits to see whether they are of God. For many false prophets have gone out into the world" (1 Jn 4:1).

2. Perhaps, it may be thought, human knowledge consists in relating that which we encounter back to something which we already know, in subsuming what is new and apparently unique under already prepared categories. We then arrive at a mode of thinking which takes the form: "Christ is nothing but ..." Life is nothing but a more complicated combination of chemical elements. Thought is nothing but the appropriation of particular modes of behavior as we are confronted by sensory phenomena. Morality is nothing but biological behavior and consequently takes different forms according as the individual is physically strong or weak. Evil (so-called) is nothing but a mode of reaction conditioned by biological selection. The state is nothing but the product of an agreement between individual egoisms which, were they left to themselves, would pursue the struggle of all against all and would thus destroy themselves. A work of art is nothing but a symptom of social relationships; changing forms and styles are conditioned by alterations in these relationships and are to be judged from that point of view. Christianity is nothing but a world religion; more precisely, one of the "revelation" and "redemption" religions: it belongs to the theistic type; in its peculiarities it can be explained in terms of the constellation of cultural and religious factors at the time of its origin. The eschatological claim of the founder is nothing but a particular form of the messianic and apocalyptic move-

ments and claims which we find widely spread throughout pre- and post-Christian Judaism. Pauline religion is nothing but a remarkable and idiosyncratic combination of Jewish and Hellenistic forms of thought which by their conjunction have produced this fantastic, fascinating construct. The history of the Church is nothing but the usual history of misunderstandings and distortions of an ideal originally great in its conception, fascinating, but unusable for the mass of the people. According to well-known laws of psychology (in particular the power-psychology of the priest classes) this had to be altered in such a manner that it could be handed on and have a pacifying effect (like opium) on self-estranged humanity.

More especially, the Church is nothing but a sociological construction, which consequently can and must be steered out of the straits in which she presently finds herself by sociological methods. The perplexing situations with which the Christian is confronted in our present world are nothing but blocks which can be resolved with the approved methods of depth psychology; it is these latter which can free the Christian from his embarrassing isolation and can transform him into a useful member of society, open to the world. The sacraments are nothing but the remains of a mythical understanding of the world and must be driven out of the Christian congregations along with many other things, like prayer, penance, pilgrimages, and so on, as a magical remainder from another age. The priest is nothing but a functionary of the group, which endows him with the appropriate tasks and authority. The Pope is nothing but the president of the universal assembly of the Church and ideally should be elected for a limited period of office. And so on, *ad libitum in saecula.*

There is a great desire to take refuge in generalities. For the "nothing-but" thinker, the unique, the other, the unclassifiable does not exist. Anything that stands out is immediately cut down to size. If Jesus was a man, why then should he have been anything other than a man? If he came into the world, why then not by the normal means of sexual intercourse between a man and a woman? If indeed he was prophetically inclined, why is it not possible to classify him satisfactorily by means of the religio-historical category of the prophetically gifted? And if the Church must take his name, what reason is there for taking the Church as anything more than a union of those who band together in his spirit and in memory of him, perhaps with the aim of vigorously putting into practice his idea of the kingdom of God?

And so we see a second criterion for the discernment of spirits: There is a spirit of banalization which does not rest until it has brought things down to its own level, until it has reduced the extraordinary, which in the first place does not belong to me, which I must be given, to something ordinary which always belonged to everybody (for that is what "banal" means: that which commonly belongs to a group; in feudal terms, the "common mill"). In the world there is that which is relatively unique, which can only be indirectly classified by means of categories. Thus, for instance, men as subjects are similarly structured but as persons are not interchangeable. And for the Christian there is that which is absolutely unique: the existence and event of Jesus Christ, and whatever proceeds from him which bears witness to and represents him, whether officially or existentially. It is here that occurs the division of spirits. "By this you know the Spirit of God: every spirit which confesses that Jesus Christ has come in the flesh is of God, and the spirit which does not confess Jesus [as the Son of God] is not of God" (1 Jn 4:2–3 RSV).

3. The criteria which we are listing all spring from a common root; this cannot be otherwise, if indeed the Holy Spirit sets his signature under his works for all to read. The principle of "success" is a variation and no more. Fruit trees are grown to bear fruit; they are grafted, fertilized, sprayed, and treated by every means available in order that they should bear more and better fruit. This is the only point of any technology: that one should achieve greater success with less expenditure of time and energy. A good school is one in which a pupil receives in a short time the best training. A good job is one in which a not excessively taxing task is paid for at the best rates. Progress is an increase in output, a more effective exploitation of existing forces, and the bringing into play of as yet untapped resources. Ever-increasing attempts must be made to cut back the realm of useless, wasted, and unproductive effort. Everything must be worthwhile. It is surely more worthwhile to have an audience of a million in front of one on the television than to preach to a mere handful in a half-empty church. "Let your light shine before men."

It would be wrong to say that all success is of the devil. There are also, as we have just seen, sayings in the Bible which take it into account. Where one meets with no success, one may "shake off the dust from one's feet" and try elsewhere. And, above all, the Bible knows the difference between what is fruitful and what is fruitless. The tree which did not bear fruit is given a chance for another year; if it then bears nothing, it is cut down. The branches of the vine which bear no fruit are cut back and thrown into the fire. The fruit-bearing branches are cleansed in order that they may bear more fruit. The servants must see to it that the money of their master is doubled by their work or at least gains interest. On the other hand, this fruitfulness of the believers is something quite different from earthly success. Such success is nowhere envisaged, but: "The disciple is not greater than his master. The disciple must be content to receive the same treatment as his master. If one has called the master of the house a devil, how much more the members of his household!" (Mt 10:24f.). Jesus lived without success and was certainly not driven along by the spirit of success or otherwise he would have acted more wisely. "Success", says Martin Buber, "is not one of the names of God." Indeed the point of Christianity lies precisely in the fact that lack of worldly success, bankruptcy on the Cross, was the highest point of Christian fruitfulness. In the abandonment of all one's own plans to the incomprehensible will of the Father, in obedience in the midst of the spiritual night, in being led "where thou wouldest not", in the falling of the grain of wheat into the earth, lies the principle of a new fruitfulness, incomprehensible to the world, which cannot be calculated according to any scale of success. "Gratis", "for nothing", "in vain": the shades vary even within the Christian sphere from light to dark, from aimless play to failure—but it is always the same principle: the transcending of the goals which one has set oneself, the offering of the whole personal sphere to God's disposing. Here is Christian fruitfulness, linked to the fruitfulness of the crucified Christ: "Without me you can do nothing", and what you can do will, if it is genuine, always somewhere bear the mark of my earthly failure. We may without qualms apply the standard to the great social and political programs of the Christian Church today and also to the attitudes of individuals—laymen, priests, theologians—whose hearts have been hardened by the god "success", who is a god of this world. Many (for example, members of religious orders, contemplative monasteries) are today exchanging fruitfulness for success. And in many theological lectures truth is measured in accordance with and tailored to what pleases "eager ears" (and that changes very quickly). Mostly, what pleases is what is easy. And so we pass on from the third to the fourth of our criteria.

4. The spirit, or what one takes for the spirit, ideology, wild ideas, is light, without weight. A body is heavy. But the word has become flesh, and thus weighty. This is intended as a parable: That which is Christian has a weight, a degree of reality, a seriousness which cannot be outdone. If it could be brought into a manageable system, then it would be less heavy, less difficult, one would be able to breathe again, one would have overcome it in

some way. Then man would have got to the bottom of God and would have reduced him to his own terms; to put it quite simply: He would have penetrated rationally the love of God which has embarked on the incomprehensible mystery of being obedient unto the Cross and to the descent into hell. "Absolute knowledge" would have domesticated the mystery of love. Two sayings warn us against this attempt to make love easy, to make it light, by converting it into knowledge: "Knowledge puffs up, love on the other hand builds up" (1 Cor 8:1). But lest we should forget that our knowledge is not despised by God, we are to "know the love of Christ, which passes all knowledge, that you might be filled with all the fulness of God" (Eph 3:19). In the event of Christ the fulness of the divine love is revealed with true eschatological force and weight. It is impossible to conceive of anything in any direction which could be more weighty, more rich in content, more fulfilling. Here the distinction and the union between God and the world occur perfectly. God's grace and man's freedom are combined in a perfect interplay. God receives the full honor due to the absolute, while at the same time man loses no fragment of his dignity. In Christ love of God and neighbor are perfectly one, because he himself (in his love for the Father) is the perfect expression of the love of the Father for us and because he gives himself for us all, entering even into the depths of our hellish despair. The other "Christian mysteries" which cluster around the central configuration—for example, the divine Trinity (stretched to the breaking point on the Cross) or the Resurrection as the affirmation of the whole man, body and soul, in God, in all his personal, social, and historical aspects, or the Eucharist in its necessarily incarnate, realist understanding, or even the Virgin Birth (whose consistency with the other mysteries we shall not here attempt to demonstrate), or the Church as the real body and "bride" of Christ—all this and much else besides belong to the eschatological weight of the active self-giving of God to the world. Here we may find our last criterion. A spirit which, in its reflection on the content of Christian revelation, in its attempts to translate, to demythologize, and to accommodate that content to the spirit of the age, makes what is heavy light, what is difficult easy, attenuates its substance, casts it overboard as so much ballast, in order to be able to journey out into the future less heavily laden or quite simply in order to gain a hearing, this spirit is not of God.

There is no denying that Christian dogmatics and catechetics need a thorough clearing out, for their hallways are full of all sorts of useless bits and pieces which take up far too much room and are of no service to anyone. But who is to do the sorting out? Only someone who has experienced the absolute weight of the original revelation can lay claim to competence in this matter. And if anyone thinks of clearing out the Bible, then he must have even more experience of this weight to aid him in this task, or else he will throw overboard unsuspectingly all sorts of things which belong to the indivisible (even if multiform) substance. For as soon as this substance loses its eschatological weight or is in any way lightened, it becomes comparable to other facts and ideas within history, to other world views and religions, it becomes part of the stock in trade, part of the goods which are offered for sale in the marketplace of the world, as indeed is often the case in modern religious education. And that of course is quite logical. The dealer displays all his stock in front of his young customers. Look at this Buddhism, a very old and hardy material, though perhaps it doesn't go quite so well with Teilhard de Chardin; or perhaps you might be interested in Islam, which has the advantages of providing a very simple synthesis between biblical and universal human religion; it may very shortly be in fashion again ... And that is how things will be if the preacher no longer knows the true weight of the event of Christ. Such ignorance makes it impossible for schoolchildren, or for anyone else who listens, to catch sight of that which is distinctively Christian, and so it will be lost to this generation. The anti-incarnational spirit, anti-Christ, has won an easy victory by the spirit of easiness, of lightness itself. The results make it plain that one cannot break off any essential part of the organism of Christianity without destroying the whole, without the whole losing its essence. In this Christianity is quite different from any other religion or world view. Platonism, for example, has many aspects; if we were to take away two or three of Plato's dialogues, certain variations of his ideas would be lost, but the outline would still be clear. To take away from the Christian synthesis the Resurrection, the "for us" of the Cross or Jesus' divine Sonship, is to be left with nothing, unless by a misunderstanding, which can only be covered up with the masking tape of historical criticism or by the failure truly to see what is happening, or by a certain religious sentimentality or traditionalism. Nor does the richness of ecumenical forms contradict the either/or of essence or loss of essence, form or loss of form. To degrade Jesus to the level of a "prophet" or of a "wisdom-teacher" is to contradict the basic statement of the gospel, and you can do this only either by cheating yourself or by portraying the authors of the Gospels, and perhaps even their chief character, as frauds.

We hear today on many sides demands for hard and fast, easily recognizable lines to be drawn between faith and unbelief in the Church. Leaving aside the question of how useful such lines might be (according to Augustine, there are many people who appear to be within such boundaries and yet are outside, and vice versa), it is certain that they would not offer any real solution. It would be too easy, in the sense which we have just been discussing. It would not involve the full gravity of the decision for or against faith. We need therefore a distinction between two opposed spirits, which is both more difficult, heavier, and at the same time more clearly recognizable. For these spirits can only be determined "by their fruits" or, if one likes, by the *directions* in which they blow, in which they drive us along. We have to wet our fingers and hold them up to the wind in order to know "whence it comes and whither it blows". In other words, we must be in the Spirit. We must leave room in our spirit for the Holy Spirit which does not allow himself to be carried along whither we will but which carries us along whither he wills. Only so can we practice the discernment of spirits.

The Unknown God

Is not the desire to curb an inflated use of the divine name an indication of a healthy instinct in modern man? Nor is one likely to be mistaken if one places responsibility for this inflation on the shoulders of Christians. For them God has become all at once a continually speaking and acting subject in the midst of the world and among men.

The Jews scarcely dared to utter the word "God" at all. The more deeply they learned to know him, the more unutterable became his name, the more inconceivable he himself became. A more intimate communion with God lay far back in the early period of Judaism, when Moses was allowed to see God face to face and when God tented with his people in the desert. Perhaps the concept of God at that time was still too limited, too much a part of folk religion. Or was it perhaps that the Jews of a later period projected their longing for such a naïve communion with the unutterable on to their portrayal of that primal period? There were, too, times in Christian history, above all at the end of the patristic period, which were epochs marked by an elemental trembling in the face of the total otherness of God, who in his very being transcends every concept and, even more, every statement. Let us leave aside the question of how far such epochs were influenced by Greek philosophy (which we can summarily describe as "natural theology"). We are concerned not with questions of historical influences but with questions of substance and truth.

The question may be put as follows. Does God cease, when he reveals himself in his Son, to be the wholly other, the incomprehensible? If he allows himself to be touched, captured, bound, condemned, and crucified in Jesus of Nazareth, does he then come within the reach of men? Does he then become an element among their rational concepts and calculations? "*Si comprehendis non est Deus*", says Augustine, echoing those Greek Fathers: "If you think you have understood something, then it was certainly not God." In the Eastern Church this sense of awe before the incomprehensibility of the mystery soon led to the liturgys being performed in concealment behind the iconostasis. About the year 500 an unknown figure, probably a Syrian monk, who called himself Dionysius the Areopagite, set the course of Christian theology for a thousand years by placing at its center the total otherness of God and a sense of deep liturgical awe. His influence on the Middle Ages in the West was scarcely less persistent than that of Augustine. The great scholastics wrote commentaries on his writings; he it was who again and again prevented theological speculation from presumptuously forcing its way into the darkness of the divine mystery.

In our times two German thinkers have again taken up this cause. First, Erich Przywara gave positive expression to it, taking as his starting point the formula of the Fourth Lateran Council (1215) and from there formulating his principle of *Analogia Entis as* follows: "That, however great the similarity between creator and creature may be, the dissimilarity always nevertheless remains greater." The "however great" refers not only to the character of the created spirit as "image and likeness of God", but just as much to the supernatural self-revelation of God in Jesus Christ and to the gracious participation in the Divine Being which is offered to man in the outpouring of the Holy Spirit. What Przywara saw clearly was that, even in so intimate a communion between God and man as is portrayed in the Christian doctrines of grace, of the Church, of the "infused virtues", faith, hope, and love (which have their origins in the divine life), of the love of God and one's neighbor, in all this God is still nevertheless always other, the dissimilarity remains always greater. It seems clear that this insight into the best theological tradition had become increasingly strange to modern Christians—with a few exceptions, as, for example, Newman. It was then in our times only by a violent struggle, both in a spirit of reaction and revolution, that the traditional sense of the divinity of God could again be recovered. The second thinker is Gustav Siewerth, who in his book *The Fate of Metaphysics from Thomas to Heidegger* (1959) portrayed negatively the tragic history of the loss of the sense of the divine mystery with a relentless, at times biting, logic. For him the tragedy begins within Christianity and within theology itself. God, so it appeared to Christians and theologians, has destroyed his hiddenness in his self-revelation in Jesus Christ; from now on we know him even in the very depths of his heart. The Holy Spirit which "searches even the depths of God" has also "been bestowed on us" so that we may "understand the gifts bestowed on us by God" (1 Cor 2:10–12). So that, once God in the folly of his love had revealed to us his own deepest secrets, men now armed with the weapons of the spirit which they had received began to advance into the divine arcana and to take possession of his mysteries, with the consequence that for Hegel the divine spirit is no longer distinguishable from the human (for there can only be one single absolute spirit) and that then logically for Feuerbach, Marx, and Freud, the spirit once divine is now replaced by the human spirit, which searches its own psychological and sociological depths.

It is more than instructive to read Siewerth's account of the individual stages of this spiritual development, which led from a theological rationalism that laid claim to precise knowledge about all the mysteries of God, to the final declaration that "God is dead"—a progression which had its own terrible logic. But we may also ask whether it is truly the case that this tragic history goes back only as far as the onset of nominalism after Thomas. For it may be that the dogmatic formulations of the great councils of the first centuries, in which the Trinity and Christology were conceptualized, were at least very dangerous pointers in this direction. The answer is as follows. Even such formulations as these, like any other theological "knowledge" of God, must become dangerous from the very moment when man ceases to know and to be conscious of whom it is he is dealing with. The Catholic tag "Grace presupposes nature, elevates and perfects it" is nowhere more important than here; for the natural man, if he has not already been artificially corrupted, does have a sense of awe in face of the hidden mystery of being, in face of the ultimate origin and destiny of the world, of matter, of life, of evolution, of the fate of the individual and of humanity. Every religion, from the most primitive to the most sophisticated, lives essentially on this awe. Goethe and Albert Schweitzer have given us great examples of such religion, and even the humanitarian world views which today describe themselves as religionless draw their strength, at least in the cases where they do not publicly proclaim their cynicism and demonism, from a primal pathos. They have been gripped by a sense of the urgency of the task of reconciling man with the universal being of the world; hungering and thirsting after ultimate righteousness are not possible without a sense of awe in face of the mystery of being. Religious Judaism which, as we saw, is deeply rooted in this sense of awe, has again and again produced utopian speculations reaching out into the unconditional. That this is so has its grounds in the incomprehensible fact that the eternal incomprehensible God has at a particular time and place in history revealed himself to this people.

But at the moment when the mystery of God bears in upon us so overwhelmingly as it does in the Incarnation, death, and Resurrection of Jesus Christ, a highly dangerous situation arises. On the one hand, those who are confronted with this mystery are enjoined to preach it and consequently to put it into intelligible words and concepts and even, in certain circumstances, to translate it into broadly descriptive formulae in order to *protect* his overwhelming greatness, to frustrate men's attempts to master it with their reason and to fit it into their own forms of thought or to frustrate men's attempts to bring it down to the level of their philosophies of life (as, for example, "being a Christian is nothing other than the brotherhood of man taken seriously"). On the other hand, the wire which is set up round the mystery to protect it can only too easily and almost fatally become a snare to trap men. This, either in the sense that it makes the approaches to the mystery difficult or almost impassable for the man who draws near in a sense of awe (by either a literal or a figurative iconostasis), or in the sense that for educated and uneducated alike, the impression may be created that it is in the wire itself that the mystery has been captured and tamed, that the unknown God has been made known. The "even greater degree of dissimilarity" is then forgotten; for where can one find a work of dogmatics, ancient or modern, which gives it significant expression? Certainly the theological textbooks seem to have lost every trace of such a sense; but do we find it unequivocally in the monumental work of Karl Barth? Or are the texts of the last council formulated primarily on the basis of such a sense? Indeed, may one not have to go to the "liberals" like Paul Tillich in order to find anything approaching such a sense?

It is no easy task to find one's way back from the "all too familiar" God to the truly unknown God. One makes no headway simply by throwing overboard all formulations, by rejecting all the work of theology, of the magisterial office, of the councils as dangerous aberrations. One simply saws through the branch of tradition on which everything historical sits and falls into the void. This can be seen most clearly where attempts have been made to make a clean sweep of things: for instance, where one discards even the earliest expressions of the mystery of Jesus of Nazareth in the formulae of faith of the Early Church (which for the most part make use of Old Testament concepts) and fumbles one's way back into a great darkness. For here one finds nothing on which one can lay firm hold, because all the witnesses to the historical Jesus are formed in part by the Easter faith and confession. If one discards the truth of the way in which in faith the Early Church was overwhelmed by God as of no importance for such an investigation and as not binding on us, then the whole overpowering deed of God was in vain. Nothing remains of it except the fact that Jesus was an "outstanding example",[1] alongside Buddha, Marx, and others. The modern "theology" of secularization and of the "death of God" does in its way open up the way for the old negative theology. Indeed it scarcely needs to open it up but simply points to the fact of its existence as it brushes aside, like so many dead leaves, the withered formulae of a Christianity which would know too much. Even the dogmas of the first ecumenical councils fall victim to this purge; the "unknown God" cannot at the same time also be a known God. But, on the other hand, we must also be quite clear that precisely those Fathers who helped decisively to formulate the trinitarian and christological dogmas—Athanasius, the Cappadocians, Hilary—are full of passages in which they expound the transcendence and

[1] Piet Schoonenberg, in *Die Antworten der Theologen* (Patmos, 1968), p. 54.

unintelligibility of the divine nature in the course of their relentless struggle against the Arian and Eunomian rationalism. It is this which makes it clear that the conciliar definitions of the patristic age are to be taken as attempts to protect the mystery against one-sided "rationalization", attempts repeatedly made always in the consciousness of their inadequacy.

It is true that in Jesus Christ the mystery of the ground of the world burns out more brightly than anywhere. But, on the other hand, it is precisely in this light that for the first time and definitively we grasp the true incomprehensibility of God. It is here that God breaks *for ever* all the "wisdom" of the world by the "folly" of his love, which chooses men without reason, by his entering into the chaos of the history of humanity, by his bearing the guilt of his lost and fallen creatures. This incomprehensible love of the God who acts in the event of Christ raises him far above all the incomprehensibilities of philosophical notions of God which consist simply in the fact of negating all statements about God, which may be ventured on the grounds of our knowledge of the world, out of regard for his total otherness. But this more powerful incomprehensibility of the biblical God only remains in effect so long as the dogmatic formulae protect it against renewed attempts at rationalization. Like the cherubim with their fiery swords, they surround the folly of the love of God, scandalous for both Jews and Greeks, and forestall any cabbalistic or Hegelian attempts to overthrow *agape* with *gnosis*.

John makes the claim that God is love on the basis of the experience which in Jesus Christ we may have of him. However, according to the teaching of the disciple, God is not love because he has found in us an object worthy of his love which before he lacked, in the sense, that is, that we were necessary to him in order that he might be love. Rather, he is love in himself. But one cannot define love even when one meets it in this world. Where it is genuine, it transcends in its sovereign freedom every why and wherefore. It has its necessity only in itself. It can be encompassed by no concept. Even more, the ground of the absolute divine love outstrips immeasurably all human thought. And so, too, the statement that God needs no creature in order to be love, the statement that God is love in himself, begetting and begotten, communing with himself in such a way that from this communion there proceeds again and again the eternal fruit and witness of love: the statement therefore that God is "triune", all this is and remains the expression of an incomprehensible mystery. It is only analogously (where the similarity is overruled by a greater dissimilarity!) that we can speak of persons in God, only analogously (where the similarity is overruled by a greater dissimilarity!) that we can speak of "begetting" and "inspiration", only analogously (where the similarity is overruled by a greater dissimilarity!) that we can speak of "three", for what "three" means in relation to the absolute is in any case something quite other than the innerworldly "three" of a sequence of numbers.

It might then seem that it would be better to abandon any attempt to speak and think of God if he always remains, even when he reveals himself, wholly and then most truly unknown. But we no longer have authority to do this, for he came to us in an event—which had its climax in Jesus Christ—of such self-giving, defenseless, inviting power (or powerlessness) that we understand at least so much: he wants to be *for us*, he wants to gather us into the abyss of his own inner trinitarian love. We do know that this love can in no sense be equated either with individual human beings or with the common humanity of the many; we experience, further, that it addresses us individually and corporately as thou; it is indisputable that Jesus teaches us to reply to this address of love also with thou; throughout the whole Bible there is an increasing demand that we may and must entrust ourselves to it unconditionally, and this demand is based on the "proof" which God has given of his love to the world (Jn 3:16; 1 Jn 4:9).

The Christian centuries and millennia have repeatedly erected towering theological buildings around these mysteries. From time to time it becomes necessary to stress the insufficiency of much that has been thus heaped up in order to make room for new attempts. In the end it is all no more than a start, an attempt, an approximation, just as the life shared between two lovers remains to the end a start, an attempt, an attempt to find a way to each other, but only as each allows the other his own freedom. Woe to the lover who, by whatever means, seeks to tear from his loved one his final secret! Not only is such an attempt impossible, but also by it he destroys the life of love. Only that which is given by the unsearchable freedom of love has power to reveal. And so analogously (the similarity is overruled by the greater dissimilarity!) the free self-disclosure of the divine heart sheds over all our existence, thought, loving, and action an incomparable light; and yet it comes from the God "who dwells in unapproachable light, whom no man has ever seen or can see" (1 Tim 6:16). And yet we are to draw near to the inaccessible one "in boldness and confidence through our faith in Jesus Christ" (Eph 3:12), who has "expounded" to us the inaccessible God "whom no man has seen" (Jn 1:18).

Christians today must be capable of withstanding the tension which is contained within these statements. On the one hand, they must abandon every attempt to penetrate into the hidden and free being of God with unbaptized reason, and on the other, they may reject no path which God himself offers men into the mystery of his eternal love. They may neither, on the one hand, push God away into a realm of inaccessible transcendence which then ultimately becomes a matter of indifference for men nor, on the other hand, so draw him into the historicity of the world that he forfeits his freedom over the world and falls victim to human *gnosis*.

The Personal God

I

Can we dare to apply the concept of person, personality, to the unutterable hidden ground of being from which has proceeded and continuously proceeds the mysterious multiplicity of the world in all its evolving and declining forms? These forms, of which we are one, stand out unprotected in the cold wind of existence. Perhaps from time to time we lean against each other in order to find a measure of support, perhaps from time to time another man's house seems to offer us something like home and security. But how precarious such dwellings are, hurriedly erected huts in the icy wind of fate which whistles around us on all sides and which from time to time tears away our or another's roof under which we had thought we might for a while find shelter. And if indeed we are so exposed to fate and if all our insurances against accidents, against old age, against illness are simply powerless attempts to protect ourselves against an overwhelming power, against the ultimately destructive blizzard of death, if our abandonment is indeed as extreme as this, no human fellowship can protect us against our loneliness, no hope for the future can alleviate the frightening situation of the world *now*. If, finally, no historical past provides us with the consolation which we fail to find in the present—because men have always lived in the same exposure—if that is all true, where shall we find the confidence to feel ourselves truly sheltered and protected in that deeply concealed womb and ground of being from which we have been cast out without our asking and into which we will at the end fall back at the will of fate? If it is true that (according to Nietzsche) everything which is mature wants to die, then that is not to say that it wants to return to the primal ground into which, dying, it falls.

Paul in his speech at the Areopagus offered the Greeks an unusual definition of our existence. God, he said, has scattered men over the surface of the earth and has given them particular and limited dwelling places; that is to say, he has set them in the midst of the finitude of space and time with all its questionableness, with all its painful edges and corners. They were, he says, to "seek God, in the hope that they might feel their way toward him and find him". Searching is the basic characteristic of man. It is a continual leaving behind of past results which have proved unsatisfactory. Now, of course, one would not keep on feeling one's way forward—after all the disappointments—if one did not know that there was a gap which must be filled at all costs. But what follows— "that they might feel their way toward him"—betrays a strange sense of helplessness. To feel their way toward him: that is the manner in which blind men behave. "In the hope that perhaps" makes it appear questionable whether such feeling will meet with success. It will apparently be a matter of pure luck, a mere chance hit, if those who are feeling after the truth should happen on anything of decisive importance. And what do they then find?

What is it that the Greeks to whom Paul turns have found? What is the concept of God to which they have fought their way through? At the beginning of the Greek culture stands Homer. For him there are many gods who wear a personal face. Above them stands the father of all, Zeus, who governs the fortunes both of Hellas and of Troy. But behind Zeus and the personal gods stands as a final authority the impersonal, unsearchable, inscrutable abyss of being: fate. It is the question mark of fate which concludes the beautiful, sunny poetry of the Greeks. It is in this fate that the great heroes of Greek tragedy stand, and to this fate and not to the friendly or inimical personal gods that they address their questions. And then follows philosophy: Plato, Aristotle, the Stoics; and what does it do? It takes over from the personal gods of mythology their anthropomorphic, good, and comforting characteristics: goodness, their readiness to care and provide for others, faithfulness, the love which is without envy. It lifts these characteristics like a cape from the shoulders of the personal gods and drapes them around the impersonal absolute. This was an enormously bold step. It required an unheard of courage to be, the courage to affirm existence. Now the ultimate principle which bears all things is the "*idea*" of the good or "*providence*". The question is, however, whether such a view of things can in the long run be upheld. As soon as philosophy arises, two ideas come into prominence. The first is the thought of Heraclitus: "The world is no more than a heap of sweepings scattered at random", and it is precisely these sweepings, precisely this terrible chaos and lack of order, this juxtaposition of extremes, precisely this which, according to him, is providence. The other idea comes from Parmenides: the sweepings, the contradictions and opposites in reality do not exist. In truth there is only one thing and that is being, that is God. The first says: The world as it in fact exists is God, or at least God takes responsibility for it; he is the sense which mediates between all this lack of sense. The second says: The world, conceived of as distinct from God, does not in reality exist and is consequently meaningless. Meaning can only be found beyond all distinctions in the very ground of things. Either God is absorbed in the world, or the world is absorbed or resolved in God. The sphere of being is round, and what could fall outside its compass? Only nothingness. And so consequently for philosophy which, as such, always wishes to reduce its subject matter to an explanation in terms of some one ultimate concept, God and the world are finally united and one in the sphere of being. And this philosophical tradition stretches via Plotinus and the Arab philosophers of the Middle Ages right down to Hegel, who was the last philosopher to make the attempt once again to embrace everything within absolute knowledge. The man Hegel, who thinks this all-embracing knowledge is a person, a professor in Berlin. The all-embracing knowledge which he thinks is not a person. All finite beings are sacrificed to the one whom he names the world spirit. Personal immortality, even the resurrection of the flesh, are for Hegel a laughable presumption on the part of the tiny individual in all his questionable mortality. What remains? Karl Marx replies: that which was there at the beginning before philosophy began: the questioning man standing out in the icy wind of fate. He must attempt on the basis of his own strength alone to build himself a house which is protection against the storms of fate. To tame and domesticate the terrifying strangeness of the world. To humanize inhumanity. Where theory could provide no answer, practice takes over. Practice at least does what it can: it attempts to provide for the man of tomorrow a house in which he may live. To the questions which the man of yesterday and today put to it, shouting them out in terror, practice can and will give no answer. Is there nowhere a unity of these fragments of theory and practice? Is there not anywhere beside all the false trails a road which will take us through the forest of being? If so, then there is only one. Something would have to happen which the blind man in his fumbling cannot take into account in his search: namely, that suddenly another hand would seize his and take over the lead. This other hand would not be the hand of his fellow man, promising us for a moment such shelter and refreshment in his hut as he can give; for tomorrow we will both be again confronted by the same fate and death. The hand of one's fellow man could offer us great promise and hope, but only if it was empowered to seize the hand of the searching man with the power of unconditional love.

What conditions must be satisfied if a hand—the hand of God, of the living, free, personal God—is suddenly to reach out and seize the fumbling hand of man? Above all, that the terrible suffering of man, his exposure to the night and wind, should lose nothing of its weight. Fine words do not bring comfort, even if they are divine. Existence is not only *maya*, a bad dream, from which one can awake, a veil or a net which one can tear asunder: it is reality. A true living God will have to recognize this terrible reality; indeed, if he is to help and to provide strength, he will have to take it more seriously than a man can. The one who embraces humanity will have to stand up to the force of reality, not by virtue of an omnipotence which from the outset unmans the power of reality, but from a position in which he could experience the terribleness of the power of the world. For only then would he be credible. The Cross of Christ on which God takes upon himself the burden of the whole suffering of the world is the authentication of the living God. It does not matter whether or not it resembles the myths of dying gods; for why should not the myths be a feeling after, as it were, an empty form of that which must occur in true history and yet which cannot be imagined in historical terms? Sayings, teaching, wisdom of all kinds would not have sufficed. There is much penetrating thought which one cannot piece together. It was necessary that there should be a word of a kind quite different from all the sayings of human wisdom, a word which is no word but a silent deed, a non-word, which Paul calls the folly of God. Such a word was necessary if the first condition was to be fulfilled.

II

Now, if this condition were fulfilled—and for the Christian it is indeed fulfilled in the event of the incarnate word and Son of God—may it not be that in that event he who wishes to be *sought* may stretch out his hand in order to let himself be *found*. The Bible bears witness to such a God; he gives proof of his life and personality most clearly in the fact that he again and again leads the people of Israel along paths which they do not want to follow, which they resist with all their instincts, obstinately, stubbornly, with their hackles raised. For "my thoughts are not your thoughts and my ways are not your ways. As the heavens are high above the earth, so are my ways above your ways and my thoughts above your thoughts" (Is 55:8f.). Will clashes with will, plan with plan. Whoever the God of Israel may be who redeems them from the house of bondage, who drags the unwilling people through the desert, imposes on them a law, gives them his promises; whoever this mysterious one may be who never yields up his name— "I am who I am, who I will be for you", whom you will always know from my dealings with you, even if you do not know my proper name, my hidden nature—whoever this free and living one, hidden and forcing himself on them, may be, one thing is certain for Israel: he *is*. He is the *other*, even if he is "all things" (Sir 43:27). He acts and speaks, he guides, promises, and fulfils. "He leads men down into the underworld and leads them up again."

Philosophers attempt to find out and express something of the nature of God. Israel does not philosophize. It does not seek to grasp God, for God has already grasped it, already has seized it by the scruff of its neck. With its mother's milk it learns the reality of the divine thou. An "I", a people, can only exist in relation to this thou. Pascal's alternative is vindicated: not the God of philosophers and of the learned, but the God of Abraham, Isaac, and Jacob, the God of Jesus Christ. The God of the philosophers is a mild, timeless, diffuse light,

Plato's sun of justice, the light of the Enlightenment. But the God of Israel is, to use Pascal's words, "fire!" Or in Jeremiah's words: "Does my word not burn like fire? Is it not like a hammer which smashes the rocks?" (23:29).

Other people too have had their gods and have addressed them as thou in prayer. But none of them has had anything remotely like the bitter experiences of its God that Israel underwent. No god has so relentlessly pressed its people on toward its goal, through thick and thin, through defeats, exiles, abandonment, till it reached the goal to which he wished to bring it through this history, till he had brought it to the place where in the deepest hiddenness he could unveil to them his face on which no man had ever set eyes—or rather not unveil it but make it discernible as absolute love. "No one has ever seen God", but "we have seen and bear witness that the Father has sent his son as savior of the world ... beloved, if God has shown us such great love ..." (1 Jn 4:12, 14, 11) and "God who has said: Out of darkness shall light shine! he it is who has made it to shine in our hearts, so that we were enlightened by the knowledge of the glory on the face of Jesus Christ" (2 Cor 4:6). These are paradoxical sayings which speak of not seeing and yet seeing, without cancelling each other out; sayings which transcend the laws of human language, because they are the self-interpretation of a deed which has been achieved; incarnate words in which the flesh more and more receives the primacy over the word; practice before theory. They break the sound barrier of that which for man is unutterable, they outstrip every hermeneutical problem, for they confront man with something done, so self-evident that it "stops the mouths" of many who would question it. And that which is done—"the fact"—is not simply cast before mankind, before the people of Israel at the end of God's ways, as a unilateral action on the part of God, but in the word becoming man the personal God creates for himself as it were in advance a personal answer. Out of the catastrophes of the disobedience of the Old Testament he has elicited for himself so much obedience that, as the fruit of the history of the people since Abraham, he can produce one woman who can say: "I am the handmaid of the Lord, let it be unto me according to thy word." And even her word is more deed than word: permitting the active word of God to occur. And the fruit of this fruit is Jesus, who is obedient to death on the Cross, but who at the same time knows that in this obedience to the other, to the Father, he has finally brought to light that God's hidden, always concealed name is love. Out of his love God the Father gives that which is most precious to him, his Son, for us. Out of his love the Son goes into the darkest places of the world, of death and hell, in order to bear the guilt of all his human brothers. And this love is given to us as the fruit poured into our hearts: God's Holy Spirit of love.

III

Man in his search for truth can never arrive by philosophizing—in however simple or academic a way—at the statement "God is love." For against this statement the world, as it appears, raises a categorical objection. At best man can push his way forward to the statement that God is the reconciliation of the contradictions internal to the world. A place of peace, where one no longer suffers, where one can forget life, where the painful boundaries between individuals finally fall away, where we are taken up into the realm of that which is without distinction. Unless, that is, man should prefer to dispense with such a peace *beyond* this earthly realm and to attempt to rise by his own heroic efforts to an affirmation of the world as it is in the *midst* of existence with all its divisiveness, as did Nietzsche; to say yes and amen in all eternity to this ruminating monster, this will to power. But such an affirmation may not exclude a single one of the concentration camps. Let him attempt it and see whether he can retain his sanity.

There was only one way by which men might approach the statement "God is love." God first had to reveal himself as the one who is all things in himself, who in his freedom disposes over all things, who predestines and promises, in brief, to show himself as the absolute person; as the one who takes our fumbling hand firmly, only too firmly, in his. The result is Jesus Christ. For him there is only the personal God, whom he addresses as Abba, tenderly loved Father. One can perhaps argue that Jesus was not objectively the unique Son of God. But one cannot dispute historically that he was conscious of his unique status as the one who in his origins stood in an incomparable relationship to a thoroughly personal God, and that all his efforts were directed toward bringing us into relationship with this his Father as his children. When you pray then say, "Thou, our Father ..." If one reflects for a while on this, keeping in mind the whole fate of Jesus up to his Cross, then perhaps the realization might begin to dawn that here occurred God's final, never to be exceeded self-revelation. That in this existence and in this dying abandonment by God, God has proclaimed his final "word", which from that point rings out undiminished down the centuries. What more then could be said than this? And yet has anyone ever penetrated so far into this final revelation that it does not always stand before him as his future?

But what is Christian does not oscillate uncertainly between past and future; by virtue of its unique form and figure, it lends support to the present at every stage. For what distinguishes and sets Christian faith above all other religious beliefs of mankind is this: the hand of the loving Father, who grasps the fumbling child, is the hand of a *human* thou. The hand of our neighbor. "Who is neighbor to him who fell among robbers? He answered, He who showed mercy on him. And Jesus said to him, go and do likewise" (Lk 10:36ff. RSV). The fact that God's hand is the hand of *one particular* fellow human being makes of the hand of every fellow human being something quite new. We may sense through its uncertainty the firmness, the trustworthiness of the divine hand. We can within a Christian marriage join hand in hand in the faith that weak human love will be strengthened by the love of God with an eternal power. Reliability and faithfulness from person to person bear fruit in the fact that we are together borne up by a personal God who shows us his faithfulness in human form. Only where God is person is man taken seriously as a person. Every man is addressed personally as thou by God and experiences here his irreplaceable value. It is with this insight that biblical religion, and in particular Christianity, has entered history. But this insight is in danger of being submerged and lost wherever God is no longer understood personally as freely loving. Moreover, he is only credible as a person where he does not stand over against the suffering of the world, teaching and pouring comfort on it with words, but where he acts by going to the Cross. The personhood of God, the Cross of Christ, the dignity of man, and human love are indissolubly interrelated. One may imagine that one could advocate the dignity of man without believing in God's person, indeed precisely by denying it. But the logic of history will again level out, either existentially or collectivistically, the persons who have thus been absolutized. It will turn them into cannon fodder and the objects of experiments, into manure for evolution. Only the personal God himself whose love is truth and whose truth is love can give to the I and thou between men a truly personal value, so that in the exchange in trust between the two something unique, something irreducible occurs, not an erotic illusion, not a trick of nature, not something which psychoanalysis can reveal as egoism, but pure truth.

The Incarnation of God

The statement "God became man" is without question central to the Christian witness. For any other religion—quite apart from other "world views"—it is an intolerable, basically self-contradictory statement. It isolates Christianity from all other philosophies and confessions. For the point is not simply that God who has all names and yet is without name, who is wholly other and (beyond this indeed) not other, because without opposites, that such a God at particular points and in particular people in the world and its history becomes "transparent". That is indeed an all too fashionable word today, and, with its help, it may appear possible to reduce to a common denominator with the basic Christian message Indian avatars and prophetic or mystical personalities—for example, in Judaism or Islam, or even in other religions. Rather, what sets Christianity apart from other religions is the offensive claim that the one who bears all names and yet is without name, who as the Scripture says "is everything" (Sir 43:27), has once and for all declared himself identical with a tiny something or someone in the vast cosmos and among the countless millions of swarming humanity—identical with someone who then can make such monstrously exclusive statements about himself as "I am the door ... all who have come before me are thieves and robbers" (Jn 10:7f.) and "No one knows the Father but the Son and him to whom the Son will reveal it" (Mt 11:27). Of course, once one has admitted that the "all" can become identical with the tiny "someone", then one has little choice but to accept such intolerably intolerant claims on the part of this "someone". But does not the very absurdity of claiming that all the broad rivers which link men of all cultures and religions with the unutterable ground of all things flow through this—his!—narrow gorge show that the very presuppositions of such a claim must be absurd and consequently undermine those claims? Moreover, quite apart from the logical nonsense of attempting to identify the whole with a part of itself (being with individual existents), is it not apparent that such an act would run directly contrary to those broadening, liberating effects which a religion ought indeed to have, namely, of gathering up into an all-embracing peace that which within the world is rent asunder in opposing camps, in a perpetual struggle, and so might it not seem that it is in effect designed "not to bring peace but the sword" and "to divide" men even in their households and families (Mt 10:34f.)? May not Christianity, with its intolerant history of men burned at the stake and religious wars, be a terrible step backward from a religious and political universalism which was beginning to show itself in the Hellenistic-Roman world, and which Christianity at its outset cripples? And may not Christianity, in its post-Christian, secularized form, have to be made responsible for the spirit of impatience and division which today—against the general direction of technical progress—delays and indeed demonically questions the unification of the world?

This indeed is how it appears if we approach the basic Christian claims from outside, in the abstract, unmediated, independently of the forms by which they are mediated to Christians, without making the effort to view them in their whole context, which context is indispensable for their understanding. The tender shoots at the top of a pine tree presuppose the whole powerful tree down to its deepest roots. But precisely this effort to think through the whole anew and more deeply in the light of the highest claims is what is demanded by Christianity; or rather, it is the fact that from its highest point it sheds over the whole a light which makes possible such a new and deeper appreciation. This light does not simply show up the weakness and frailty of all religious and nonreligious philosophies of mankind, of all attempts to find one's way through to an understanding of the mystery of the existence of the world: on the contrary, it brings such attempts and efforts to a fulfilment which far outreaches anything which might be expected, by setting the truths contained in such philosophies in their proper place and integrating them with the whole. What we shall attempt in the three following sections is to move from an abstract pair of opposites ("all"— "something", "God"— "man") into the realm of the concrete.

I

The mysterious ground of being from which finite things arose—things which require an explanation not only for the way they are but for their very existence—was addressed by Plato with the name of "the good". For even assuming that our experience of worldly existence would lead us to hesitate before declaring as "good" the existence of a world which is not identical with the ground of being, in particular the existence of a world full of incomprehensible suffering, and would further lead us to experience our distance from the ground of being, our falling away from it into a "region of dissimilarity" (*regio dissimilitudinis*), as a disaster; even assuming, that is, that what we regard as our worldly being, in its strangeness, inexplicableness, estrangement, was to be experienced rather as something to be overcome than as something for which we should be grateful (as for example in Buddhism); even so, the ground of being which one would then have to speak of (by contrast with worldly existents) as the "not-existing" would, in spite of all, be the good and that which was to be striven for by stripping oneself of the estranging illusion of finitude. It is impossible to conceive of the ground of being itself as evil, demonic, as that which is to be cursed. The "guilt" for the estrangement which attaches to finite existence (not, that is, simply for its mere otherness from the ground of being) is attributed therefore by the religions always to a secondary factor; for example, to the freedom of the pre-existent souls (Plato, Buddhism), or to a "demi-god" (gnosticism), or in radical modern utopianism to a principle of the past which stands in opposition to the absolute which is to come. Setting aside this utopianism, which cannot be thought through without contradiction, primal goodness still remains a justification of everything which in this mixed world can be called truly existent and positive; in this sense it is a diffusion of itself beyond the bounds of its fundamental being, communicating itself to its effects (*bonum diffusivum sui*). This principle which unites the religions is taken up in the biblical revelation of the Old and New Covenants and integrated into the supreme notion that the causing of a finite world by the good did not occur because the (infinite) good *needed* this (finite) world in order to be the good. In other words, God does not produce the world naturally because he is God, which would then mean that the world would be in the same measure divine and necessary as God himself; rather it is an absolute *freedom* which is the ground of the self-effusion of the ultimate good. This in turn has two consequences: that God in himself and independently of his relationship to the world is the good, or in Christian terms is love, and that the ultimate cause of the creation of a world can only be the free, loving communication of divine goodness to created beings. If one thinks this through, then one will have to say, over and above this, that precisely in the freedom of the love of the divine ground of being lies the possibility of there being such a thing as a world (which is not God, not the infinite and the all) at all. Indeed the final point may emerge dimly as a kind of limiting concept which will find its confirmation in the central assertions of the Christian faith: The ground of being can be called the good as free love only if it possesses *in itself* a spiritual *life* of love; that is to say, if there is within it a self-giving, a communing, a communality that does not impugn the identity of the absolute but indeed is the necessary condition of its truly being the absolute good.

II

If we consider creatures, which find their highest form in man, from this point of view, then it appears that man also, precisely as an individual, is not only a tiny something (as opposed to the all-embracing "all") but is something whose being and nature are fashioned and determined by the good which communicates *itself* to him. Man is "in the image" of God. As spirit—that is to say, in so far as he knows and thinks spiritually and wills freely—he is open to everything and to every existent, which is possible only if he is open to the perspective of being itself (he is *quodammodo omnia*). As he knows that he is not God, so too he knows that his being is from God, a knowledge grounded in a basic experience which may perhaps use other concepts, ideas, and words but which envisages the same matter as we have attempted to express here. His concern is with the question of the meaning of the world and existence as a whole. It is a secondary matter whether he seeks this meaning in a mysterious peace within the riddle of the world (a peace which, however, must lie beyond the pain which he experiences and can be found in an ascetic, mystical, perhaps technical overcoming of the painful states), or whether he denies the being of the world in the form in which he finds it, in order to find peace beyond it (for example, in the "idea" of the world as it is in God), or whether finally he despairs of his ability to find a solution and, while trying to make the best of his mortal life, sets the riddle aside. But if he encounters the idea that he, as this particular man (as indeed every man is a "particular" man), is the image of the freely loving God who consequently also wills him of his freedom, then a strange and remarkable light will be shed on his existence. On the one hand, it will become clear to him that the free divine good has intended him to be this particular person, this unmistakable person, and has consequently freely given to him his freedom and insight and responsibility; but that this, on the other hand, cannot be simply a matter of dismissing him, of sending him off without further interest into an estrangement from God. Rather he must realize his being as a man with free, rational responsibility precisely by relating the image to the original, not by turning away, but by turning to God. Here a realm of intimate inwardness is opened up which may take many forms and names: contact with the primal image, cherishing and contemplating memories and recollections, prayer, the attempt to make human insight and freedom in every situation transparent to absolute insight and freedom. It is an openness, ready to be formed and fulfilled; it is a making room for the one who may come to dwell, a readiness to be the womb which shall bear fruit each in one's own particular human worldly activity and efforts.

III

What we have been trying to do in these first two sections is to show how that which is ambiguous, dark, and impure in the many religious attempts of mankind to understand his world and its reality can be clarified and simplified in the light of the Christian answer, clarified moreover in such a way that the path from the universal, human understanding of the world to the Christian understanding could be shown here as a possible, internally consistent one. Does this mean to say that such an exercise as such has already led us to the Christian faith, perhaps indeed has postulated it a priori, constructed it, shown it to be necessary? No. Two elements must be added if we are to get it clearly in view. First, the extent and scale of the negative decisions of human freedom when measured by the standard of the absolute goodness of God—a standard which remains decisive where man's behavior toward God and toward the world in which he lives is to be measured. These negative decisions are both individual ("sin") and social ("common guilt", previously known as "original sin") in character; the historical world is consequently in a state of such deep confusion that it is totally beyond the power of any individual to outweigh the consequences of personal as well as of social guilt by his own decisions and enterprises. The concrete, unnatural figure of death sets on existence the seal of futility and makes the history of the world internally imperfectible —because the bloody way which may lead to a relatively final happy state can never be justified by this state itself—and remains for ever a warning and a reminder of this insuperable guilt. It thus constantly points up the perilous and indeed imperilling character of every program that would seek to lead men toward a greater freedom. For this always remains a freedom of choice, for better or for worse, so that every form of inner-worldly optimism vis-à-vis the future is not only naïve but pernicious. If, however, these are the consequences of the risk which God has taken in entrusting his creatures with genuine freedom (freedom ultimately to deny and to destroy themselves), then ultimately God could only take such a risk if he himself threw himself into the balance, assumed the risk himself, and of himself opened up a way where there were no ways. It is here that the biblical message interposes and proclaims, "God with us", God on our side! It proclaims not only "covenant", which assures us of God's faithfulness, even in spite of our breaches of that covenant and in spite of his just judgments ("if we are faithless, he remains faithful—for he cannot deny himself", 2 Tim 2:13 RSV), but a coming over to our side in order to open up a way for us from within our helplessness and hopelessness—yet without in any way overplaying that situation with his omnipotence; without, that is, impugning our freedom in any manner. A way which leads through death into life. Dying freely and obediently, he turns death, the sign of our guilt, into a monument of love.

Here, of course, our thoughts begin to stumble; the mystery begins. And how could it be otherwise if it is God who comes over to our side? In order that this one life and death might become significant for all, the divine gracious freedom had to coincide with human obedient freedom; only the self-exposition of Jesus' existence allows us to sense how this occurs: God's word of promise, his wisdom, his law, his faithfulness, are "sent" bodily to our side (so that consequently the mission of all other earlier mediators, wise men, and prophets is taken up and superseded by this mission). At first one sees the man, Jesus of Nazareth, who, like the prophets and yet more radically than they, obeys the spirit which has been given him from above and commits himself to the task given him by God to the point where he identifies his life (and death) with that task, until it becomes clear that he in his whole being has become the statement of God. But he could only become this if, regardless of the process of becoming, he had been so from the start. God's "word" carries out God's purposes for the world in the form of a man: the salvation of man by his own total self-commitment to him. We cannot here unfold the meaning of this statement, we can only point to it. For the "incarnation of God" to be possible in a Christian sense, God must be *able* to come over to our side without leaving his own "side"; but this opposition presupposes essentially that eternal opposition of which we spoke when considering the life of love within the Godhead. The world with its freedom finds a resting place in the final plan of God between God the Father and God the Son and is allowed to participate in that highest freedom which, Christianly speaking, is the Divine Spirit, the shared spirit proceeding from the Father and the Son which gives expression to their unity of love. Because the opposition within the Godhead is overcome in him and (in faith) becomes visible as a presupposition of eternal love, the opposition between God and man, which is an offense to reason, can (in faith) be understood as a presupposition of the one, free, self-giving of God to his world in his Holy Spirit.

And so the isolated position of Christianity, which at the beginning appeared only as a sign of its intolerance, finds its explanation. Such a position rests simply on the fact that Christianity makes the claim, which should now be intelligible, to be the ultimate expression of God and consequently his final self-giving and self-revelation. This cannot be transcended because God, who is "all things", here out of his free love goes not only into that which is "other" than himself, into the creature, which is a "something" and "nearly nothing", but also into that which is contrary to himself as he gathers up into himself the sin and the lostness and so the abandonment by God of his creature, gathers it up and transforms it. He does not thereby cease to be himself; indeed he shows precisely through this what he is in himself, what he is and what he can do. God can be dead without ceasing to be eternal life and he can, acting in this manner, prove finally that he is life and love and the goodness and grace which pours itself out in selfless self-giving. That is definitive, "eschatological", and it would be a self-contradiction if it, relativizing itself, should set other views alongside itself (which perhaps contain pointers toward this ultimate truth) as of equal importance. The heart is pierced, its spring uncovered, water and blood pour forth, there is nothing more than this.

What is the consequence of this death for the world? If it is what Christians believe, then the answer is that it gives meaning to the futility both of our individual existences and of the history of the world, that it gives hope to those who live under the rule of death, hope in a life with God which overcomes death. The way forward is for the individual and for humanity as a whole a way toward a final meaning. A way to a "peace" as the world cannot give (Jn 14:27), even if it made progress in pacifism, because it is first and foremost peace between heaven and earth, between God and men (Lk 2:14; Eph 2:14; Col 1:20). It is from this peace that we are sent out to work with all our power for the pacification of the world. There are Christian existences which radiate such peace, which are blessed for it and who are called "children of God" (Mt 5:9).

Our Love of Jesus Christ

Present-day discussion about the nature of a modern Christian spirituality centers round the relationship between love of God and love of one's neighbor. Is not the single yet sufficient criterion of our love of God that we love our neighbor? "For he who does not love his brother whom he has seen, cannot love God whom he has not seen" (1 Jn 4:20). Is it not such love of neighbor which provides the summary of the law and the prophets, since Yahweh did not wish to be honored by the lips of hypocrites (Is 29:13 LXX; Mt 15:8), who at the same time "sell the needy for a pair of sandals and trample the head of the poor into the dust of the earth" (Amos 2:6f.)? "Learn first to do good, seek justice, correct oppression; defend the fatherless, plead for the widow" (Is 1:17). Thus the disciple of love makes short work of the falsely pious man: "If anyone says, 'I love God', and hates his brother, he is a liar" (1 Jn 4:20 RSV). And he can draw the conclusion which not only makes the love of one's neighbor the criterion for something else, namely, the love of God, but seems to insist that love of neighbor is indeed the proper manner in which the love of God is to be exercised: "Beloved, let us love one another; for love is of God, and he who loves is born of God and knows God. He who does not love does not know God; for God is love" (1 Jn 4:7 RSV). In the outpouring of love from the I to the thou, the lover knows that he himself is not the source of love, that it comes from far away, from an external source, and—because it is only as a lover that he has become fully identified with his own actions—that he himself, thus liquefied, does not have his origins in himself, but equally comes from far away, "is born of God". It is as he himself "flows" and is conscious of owing himself entirely to the source of all flowing that the lover knows what God is. Now at last he knows God. No longer is such love based on painful human speculation about the absolute. No longer does it consist in an ascetic turning away from the values and non-values of the finite, transitory world, not even in the passionate affirmation of one's readiness to set the highest good above all other goods; all this now is seen to be like swimming against the stream of love: violently setting oneself against it, in an attempt to fight one's way up to the source, instead of allowing oneself to be carried along in the direction of the stream, from God to men and to things, in the direction of God's purposes and intentions, in which God himself flows, which is God himself, in which one experiences God himself. To reverse the direction is to do violence not only to man, who is dependent on his fellow man as thou and for whom God as he is in himself remains hidden; it means also to do violence to God himself, who is not knowable in any other way and who does not wish to be known except as man allows himself to be carried along with him in the stream of his love. To quote John again, "And no man has ever seen God; if we love one another, God abides in us and his love achieves in us its point of saturation" (1 Jn

4:12). "Transcendental" love is realized and effected in "categorical" love.

All this appears convincing in its consistency and coherence and can as such commend itself to our contemporaries as the dominant notion in a spirituality for today and tomorrow. Nor can one overlook the fact that this idea has Christian origins, even if it generously opens out onto a universal human realm that transcends the Christian realm. And so the decisive question remains whether and to what extent Christ is the never to be abandoned principle and ground of such a thought or merely its accidental discoverer and initiator. To put it another way, is what John refers to as "love" in the sentences we have quoted what it would generally be taken to be on the basis of human experience, or is it something completely particular and special? Is there a general overall concept of "love" which can be applied equally to God and to men? But God is the wholly other; no human concept can be applied to him without alteration. Consequently, in the intention of the Christian statement about love, the unique love of the unique God must remain the determinative model (*analogatum princeps)* for every love which is determined by him. As John says emphatically: "Herein is love: not that *we* have loved God, but that *he* has loved us" (by proving his unique love which man could not have even suspected by an equally inconceivable deed, "and has sent his son to be the expiation for our sins", 1 Jn 4:10). Here love between men is judged totally by the standard of the unique love of God toward us, which is not only the motive (though it is this also) but the necessary condition of its very existence: "By this we know love, that he laid down his life for us; and we ought to lay down our lives for the brethren" (1 Jn 3:16 RSV). The one who is not specifically named is Jesus Christ, but he is set over against the "we" in such a way that we sense behind the uniqueness of his common humanity the uniqueness of God, who gives his life, that which is most dear to him, his child, for us. Thus for the Bible the general human consequences of such love can never at any place be cut free from their unique grounding in God.

The way for this synthesis between that which occurs uniquely and that which occurs universally, between the love of God for the world and our love for one another, was already prepared in the Old Testament as a free work of God: *he* chooses, *he* frees, *he* pardons, *he* makes the covenant, *he* promises. Consequently, he is the prime and absolute content of Israel's faith, hope, and love, and the logical consequence of that for Israel is an attitude and behavior toward one's fellow men which is "worthy of God". Ethics is an echo and a thanksgiving for theology. "You shall not pervert the justice due to the sojourner or to the fatherless, or take a widow's garment in pledge; but you shall remember that you were a slave in Egypt and the Lord your God redeemed you from there; therefore I command you to do this" (Dt 24:17f. RSV). But within the old covenant the synthesis is only prepared: God acts "theologically" from his heaven; man acts in answer "ethically" on earth. The synthesis which finally and indissolubly knits theology and ethics together is achieved by God in Jesus Christ, the true God (Jn 1:1) and true man (Jn 1:14) in whom God brings a proof "which stops every mouth", a proof that he is "love".

One has continually to remind oneself of the infinite isolation, from all other theologies—and ethics—derived from the world, which the first Christians imposed on themselves by entertaining such ideas. Only the unique proof, which is Christ, can embolden a religion to the point where it gives God, in spite of the truly frightening countenance of the world, the name of "love". In the absence of such a proof, the best one can do is to refer to him as "the sun of the good", which cannot be held accountable for the fading of its light on the edges of "the material world" and of nothingness, or even as a smilingly relaxed indifference within or above the contradictions of the world as they fight out their destructive war. Man's ethical response will then be to attempt himself to achieve an equal indifference and lack of passion; in any case it will be something quite different from the "offering of one's life for the brethren". (It is only under the influence of Christianity that Buddhism has assumed social and ethical dimensions.) If, however, one abandons every attempt to seek God and without more ado turns away from fruitless philosophizing to action as the only practical, earthly way of changing the world, then one has again put the spiritual synthesis behind one (for in that case in what sense has the death of Christ changed the world? Nothing has been achieved!), and theology is reduced to ethics. It is important, however, to be clear that in the latter case one can no longer claim the Johannine love for one's own, for it is the stream which has its source beyond man. Here man must himself be the origin, progenitor, and source of love. He must achieve it and give it without having received it. If God in Jesus Christ has performed his work of love by becoming the representative of our sins, now in a post-Christian age we must see this work of representation as the fundamental ethical act itself. And if the relationship of one's fellow man to God is discarded as of no importance, then the burden of what has to be shouldered will at first no longer be so intolerably heavy. If everyone only did what was half possible, then perhaps the world would become half bearable. To say more, to hope for more, would here certainly be irresponsible utopianism.

If, however, we remain true to the principle under which Christianity first appeared, to the unity of theology and ethics on the basis of the deed performed by God in Christ Jesus, then within this indissoluble union God receives unconditional precedence: It is *his* love which has achieved the synthesis. In the first place, what is Christian will consist in recognizing this precedence: "This is love, not that we ..., but that he ..." Such a recognition of the priority of God's love over ours is called *faith*. And faith means a readiness to receive the love of God as a gift, as one acknowledges God's deed of love, as one permits it to occur to oneself. Such acceptance, such recognition then becomes the innermost ground of the human responding love and becomes indeed the initiator of such love. How impossible it would then be if, in the exercise of love, one were to forget its origin, were to want to love on one's own, without thanks for having received love! This would again be to water down the love of God into an abstract principle at one's disposal, a principle from which the element of uniqueness and divineness, of sovereignty and freedom, of sheer irreducibility would have disappeared. And so the gospel, which has at its center the figure and faith of Jesus Christ, would again have become a mere teaching, that is to say, a *gnosis*, from which one can extract a lasting moral kernel by discarding the historical husk.

Thus from a Christian point of view faith cannot be simply a springboard for love (of one's neighbor) but only its inner form. To have seen this is to have discovered that faith (as a recognition and acceptance of love) originally is itself love, indeed is "love in its originating". Thus one can only grasp the Christian meaning of the statement "God is love" when one has seen its proof. That is to say: "God so loved the world that he gave his only-begotten son [to represent us in our lostness]" (Jn 3:16) and: "He who did not spare his own son but gave him up for us all [to represent us in our lostness], will he not also give us all things with him?" (Rom 8:32 RSV). In this proof we see not only that God has loved the world and men *divinely*, but that *he* (and not in the first place we!) in the same act has loved the world and men also *humanly*. The original synthesis of love of God and of neighbor lies in *his* love; it is not first brought into being by the fact that his love is conjoined with our love (as it is turned toward God or toward man). But because his love is human, our love is from the very start already contained in it; that is the unheard of act of confidence or of "faith" on God's part to us-ward. The fact that *he* loves us humanly means that he has to count on our participation.

By the very fact that he loves us as his neighbor, he has established and given us the standard, the initiative, and the possibility of loving our neighbor. This presupposition made by God, which we called his "faith", is an element which can only be interpreted and almost, as it were, excused in terms of the defenselessness, of the folly of love; and only in this atmosphere is the human recognition of this divine risk and anticipation intelligible: the element of faith on the basis of our love.

It is therefore clear that the Old Testament primacy of the love of God as the greatest commandment (Dt 6:5) remains unchallenged within the New Testament synthesis of the love of God and neighbor. But this is not the point which we wish to make in this train of reflection, but rather that the synthesis achieved by God, which carries the name of Jesus Christ, remains the proper focus of Christian love. For only in him has the transcendental, unapproachable God become love for us in a manner which we can understand, has become, that is, both our neighbor whom we can love humanly and also the eternal vision of love springing from the primal source in the Father through whom we are enabled to love as Christians. In Jesus Christ love of God and love of man, transcendental and categorical love, can no longer be separated. Any attempt to do so would have to deny him any knowledge of the fact that he stands in a unique relationship to the Father, that his mission and task are eschatological ones, perfecting the Father's creation of the world in his suffering and Resurrection, would have to reduce his claim to that of a normal prophet or wise man and would thus, by such criticism, declare the whole understanding of Christ of the primitive Church and the New Testament writings to be a groundless illusion.

The understanding of Christ which we find in the New Testament leaves us no alternative but to see Jesus Christ as the content of Christian love always present to us, never to be superseded. We cannot, that is, see him merely as the presupposition of Christian love, as that which enabled us to love but which now lies behind us in the past, as that which "mediated" love to us. The love of the believers for their Lord which can everywhere be sensed in the Synoptic Gospels and in Paul as something accepted as a matter of course, but which is there not treated as a subject on its own, is given full expression in the Fourth Gospel. The Johannine Jesus demands for himself—as the personal expression of the Father's self-giving—a love appropriate to his nature as the revealer of love. "If God were your Father, then you would love *me*, for I have gone forth from the Father and have come from him" (Jn 8:42). "The Father loves you, because you have loved *me* and because you have believed that I went forth from God" (Jn 16:27). "If you loved *me*, then you would rejoice that I go to the Father" (Jn 21:15). "Simon, son of John, do you love *me* more than these?" (Jn 21:15). "Whoever loves the Father, loves his child" (1 Jn 5:1). And the corresponding negative expressions: "Whoever hates me, hates my Father too" (Jn 15:23). "Whoever denies the Son, has not the Father" (1 Jn 2:23), and so on. Only after such sayings can we list those which speak of the criterion of the love of Christ (and therein of our love of the Father): "If you love me, then keep my commandments" (Jn 14:15); "Whoever loves me, will keep my word" (14:23); "Remain in my love: if you keep my commandments, then you remain in my love, as I remain in the love of my Father, since I have kept his commandments" (15:10). Love begins with the Son, who traces it back at once to the source of love, the Father, and thus shows his own love as an obedient active love, which demands in believers the obedience of sharing in his active love of neighbor. The focus of love then opens up both dimensions: that which leads to its origin for which one must in faith give thanks, that which leads to its goal of so walking with our neighbor that he finds his way back with us to the origin. If Jesus after the Cross and Resurrection returns to the Father, then this is because he has fulfilled the total task which the Father has given him, the representation of all men, the eschatological deed of the triune God. And if he sends his own out into the world charging them to love their neighbor, then he sets them on the way which he has already gone, at whose end he therefore himself "returns". It is in this sense, then, that as the focus of our love he is both our past and our present and our future.

One could, of course, here raise a rather weak objection for which one might attempt to find some support in a rationalized Christology: Whoever claims to love Jesus Christ, it might be said, either loves God in him—but God is not objectifiable—or he loves a human person in him—but then he errs, for Christ according to dogmatics is not a human but a divine person; or if he does not err then Christ is indeed not God. This objection declares the synthesis achieved by God to be impossible and destroys it by reducing it to its historical components.

Nor does it pay attention to the evangelical claim of this "I"—"Do not worry, it is I", "it was said to you, but I say to you", and so on—which, long before any conceptually formulated Christology, contains the mystery of the synthesis and pours scorn on any attempt to give final definition to it. But one thing must be conceded: love of Jesus Christ demands internally the affirmation of the trinitarian character of love. Trinity, Christology, and Church form an indissoluble unity both theoretically and practically, theologically and ethically.

Trinity and Future

I

Religious thinkers have always known that one cannot conceive of God as the "other" who sovereignly and sublimely stands over against the world. For God is "everything" (Sir 43:27), and therefore he is also "all in all" (1 Cor 15:28) or—because things are as such not God—"above all, through all and in all" (Eph 4:6). But in order that it should be possible for him to be "in" something finite, without himself becoming finite, there must be attributed to him an incomparable sublimity, in biblical terms an incomparable, powerful freedom, to allow existents to exist of themselves. To credit the great religious thinkers of mankind with something other and more naïve, namely, a God distinct from this world, is unjust and only bears witness to the lack of religious sense prevalent in our modern age. It is true that no thinker whether ancient or modern has ever known how to derive the multiplicity of things from the uniqueness of God; only biblical or, more precisely, only Christian thought has been able to overcome the dilemma, which was always necessarily associated with the relationship of unity and multiplicity, of God and world; why the multiplicity, if the one God who is "everything" is self-sufficient? If he needs the many in order to be everything, is he in himself then not everything and consequently not God? As soon as we begin to speak of the free power of the creative God, then we have already begun to enter the world of the Bible. But the contours of this world come into focus only when it has been traversed to the end, when God, who at the beginning created heaven and earth and who could (as wisdom speculation saw more and more clearly) have created it only in himself, in his wisdom, his power, his essence—as a world of free creatures whose freedom stems from his own and precisely for this reason is not an illusory freedom, but a genuine, creative freedom endowing men with freedom of choice—when this God can gather back into himself the whole freedom of his creatures, including all the consequences of such freedom, including, that is, rebellion and self-damnation, can gather it in and bear it up. And still remain God: God who is not limited or conquered by the freedom of his creatures; who does not see that which was at the beginning good end in tragedy. That God can undertake such unforeseeable risks is not yet fully seen in the Old Testament; the "hell" into which the dying sink remains a dark, godless place; God's covenant is for the while valid only for the living, who are nevertheless mortal. The terrifying question is: How can God bear in himself that which is godless and which is yet a possible final consequence of human freedom?

The only valid answer, which no man could have arrived at of himself, is given when the man Jesus, who is the Son of the living God, descends into the God-forsakenness of hell and when consequently, from within the absolute freedom of the Creator God, is revealed the mystery of the triune love. If it is true that this Son of God as man takes upon himself out of the love of God the sickness unto death of the creature who has strayed away from God and so goes to the place from which no man can rescue himself (*lasciate ogni speranza*...), then this opens a view onto an opposition within the divine freedom and love itself which finally points to the reason why God at the beginning could seriously take responsibility for the opposition between divine and human freedom and could refer to it as "very good". This opposition between God, the creative origin (the "Father"), and the man who, faithful to the mission of the origin, ventures on into ultimate perdition (the "Son"), this bond stretched to the breaking point does not break because the same Spirit of absolute love (the "Spirit") informs both the one who sends and the one sent. God causes God to go into abandonment by God while accompanying him on the way with his Spirit. The Son can go into the estrangement from God of hell, because he understands his way as an expression of his love for the Father, and he can give to his love the character of obedience to such a degree that in it he experiences the complete godlessness of lost man. That seems like mythology but when thought out more deeply is the only acceptable (because not humanly discoverable) solution of the riddle of the world.

Let me make the point again. The world as a multiplicity (which, as such, cannot be God) only becomes intelligible in terms of a free creation; free creation gives creatures genuine freedom and implies necessarily the risk of their going astray; such a risk can only be assumed responsibly if the God of love is able to gather in such lostness into himself. This is possible in no other way than by God's going in powerlessness to share in man's lostness, but out of obedience to God; and so God must be triune. For the divine omnipotence cannot deal with the rebellious powerlessness of creaturely freedom from above and from outside; this truth has been lived through and lived out once and for all in the Book of Job. The terrible senseless suffering of the creature shouts down the "very good" which the Creator spoke at the beginning. Only if we presuppose a (possible) incarnation of God—to the point of death, abandonment, hell—can we continue, after the discovery that existence derives from the free creative act of God, to uphold the universal religious principle that God must be all in all (even in the godlessness of rebellious freedom). For only if an obedient love, out of its pure compliance to love itself, allows itself to be sent into lostness can the creature in his freedom be saved, and that not by being overwhelmed from outside but by being gathered up into the abyss of absolute love which embraces all abysses.

The ultimate laws of the world which correspond to the biblical revelation are not cosmological laws proper to the world itself but the laws of the mysterious dialogue between human freedom, which is allowed to speak its own last word, and divine freedom, whose final world is no longer a "word" but a deed which sinks down into total darkness. In this silence beyond all human posturing God reveals who and what God is. Our all too easy talk of the incomprehensibility of God will, if we catch sight at all of this deed of God, be brought up sharp and reduced to silence in front of this irrefutable proof which God himself offers. There is absolutely no reply which we can make. Simultaneously all things become clear: what sin and lostness are. Why God allowed them to become reality. How he can bear them in himself and overcome them in his patience: by the pain of God in which the eternal love pours out its blood from wounds which transcend all inner worldly hurts. God proves at the same time his Trinity and his Eucharist. Every pain can, as such, without being denied its quality as pain, participate in the blessedness of the triune love.

II

Viewed in this light, human freedom as the power of self-determination is unconditionally open and has a *future* which is determinable by no one but itself. This future and consequently freedom itself would be threatened if it were conceived in relation to a providence of the sort which infallibly controlled the process of human decisions from within or from above. One would then still not have broken out of a religious, philosophical, cosmological (*Stoa*), or Old Testament scheme. Creaturely freedom and its future can be gathered up into the sphere of God without loss and prejudice only if they are allowed their full range of open possibilities within the sphere of the world and if this sphere is nevertheless understood as a sphere *in God*, which God can enter, can determine, in which he can work his purposes. He does enter it, determine it, and achieve his purposes in it in the death, descent into hell, and Resurrection of the Son of God; that is—according to the self-understanding of the New Testament—the all-embracing event which establishes the possibility of human freedom and history. But it is all-embracing not as a boundary imposed upon it from without but as an opening up from within, as God shares in the exercise of human freedom, of new horizons which outstrip the possibilities of such freedom. This openness, which never hems in human and world historical freedom, is established and made possible in the event to which we have just referred, once and for all, finally, eschatologically, and that as the event within history which a priori transcends the farthest attainable boundaries of historical future, for it is fundamentally a trinitarian event.

This state of affairs molds the Christian understanding of historical time and future and distinguishes it from all other attempts to map out the horizon of time. The Christian understanding of the future can only be explained—for it is God who is involved—indirectly as the reef on which all attempts to set up a time scheme conceivable in human terms must founder.

In so far as the total history of human freedom arises from the empowering event of the death, descent into hell, and Resurrection of Christ, this event stands in a certain sense as a vertical to the horizontal of the time of the world with its true and undetermined future. One could compare this vertical position with that of a Platonic idea in relation to all its worldly realizations. Here it is significant that the New Testament speaks more than once of Christ as *the* mystery which, although "kept secret from all ages, has now been revealed" (Rom 16:25f.; cf. 1 Cor 2:7; Eph 3:9; Titus 1:2;

2 Tim 1:9), which existed as such—and not simply, for example, as an "element within the thought" of the divine providential plan for the world—an idea, moreover, which is also known to apocalyptic thought. We should not think here either of simply a divine *logos* who "subsequently" became flesh or of a gnostic Primal Man who before his descent has indeed a kind of heavenly corporality and can therefore only undergo an apparent incarnation. Rather we have to engage seriously with the decisive Christian claim that the history of Christ which occurs at a particular point on the horizontal level of time also at the same time stands in a vertical relationship to the whole course of time, is itself the very ground of the whole process and anchors it at the same time in the embracing freedom of the triune God.

Having said this, we can see that the Christian understanding of time approximates not only to the *Greek* and in a measure to the *apocalyptic*, but also that it is at the same time related to the *prophetic*. The event of Christ lies fully within an extension of that understanding of time: nor is it that event which first opens up the history of man's freedom to the possibility of future—for it had already possessed this, particularly in the prophetic view—but, rather, what the event of Christ does is to guarantee this open future an ultimate meaning and purpose. Not that this meaning lies in the hope of an earthly happy end (this is expressly averted by the New Testament with its perspective of judgment), but it is because God himself enters into his creature's open perspective of hope and shows it to be one worthy of

God, in accordance with God, in no sense a despairing view of things leading ultimately to nothing. God's humanity in Christ must establish an affinity between such a perspective of hope and the openness of God; and more: the unique event of Christ, who in his earthly existence lives in anticipation of an end of time (for he bears the sin of the world, also of future generations), is in his call to discipleship opened up to other men. They receive a share in his anticipation of and in his responsibility for the future (the first disciples' chronological expectation of an early end was a misunderstanding); they no longer confront this future merely as the abyss of empty possibility or as something utopian and impossible. Their prayer for the coming of the kingdom and the doing of his will is by the event of Christ joined inwardly to a practical sharing of responsibility, to the necessity of engaging actively in the pursuit of that for which one has prayed. Such responsibility for the future would be quite intolerable for mere men if they had to make their way to the end alongside and on a par with the Son of God and not (like the disciples on the road to Emmaus) accompanied and taught by the one who journeys with them, who as such has already both reached the end and also fulfilled the prophetic vision in all its aspects.

There can be no question of giving an exhaustive account of the interrelationship between these dimensions of time. Their intersection places the Christian in a form of time which remains incomprehensible even to himself, because it makes the human form of time, without in any way devaluing it, transparent to the trinitarian supratemporal time. The "exodus" of the Christian community, its character as a stranger in the world, is of a different nature from that of the Jewish people (and the extension of that into modern utopianism), of a different nature too from that of the Platonists, who long to find their way back from the region of their exile into the realm of supramundane ideas, or indeed from that of the Buddhists, for whom the course of time itself becomes unreal because non-temporal truth shines dimly through all things. This Christian understanding of time which we can never precisely pin down is always in danger of slipping off into one or other of these positions: now into a pure longing for that which is above (because "you have died, your life is hid with Christ in God and if Christ our life shall appear you too will appear with him in glory", Col 3:3f.), now into a pure longing for that which is to come ("I forget what lies behind me", Phil 3:13; "a hope which one can see, is no hope", Rom 8:24). The Christian understanding of time (but does it indeed understand itself?) is open to the point of the most extreme possibilities of Buddhism and can indeed enter into conversation with it, and equally it is open to the most extreme possibilities of Jewish utopianism and has no need to shy away from it. But against both views it must raise the objection that they both stand in danger of impugning the reality of the here and now, and must make this objection in the name of that vertical axis of the incarnation of God which now forever remains presently effective (in the Church, word, sacrament, faith) and which forbids every flight from time (whether to the realm above or to the realm of the future). By virtue of this axis the Christian remains firmly nailed to the harsh reality of the present moment, and it is this which gives him his calm, his realism, but also the pain which he must endure, in which and by which he is conformed to the Crucified. It is from within his situation in the present moment (Thérèse of Lisieux's "Little Way") that he allows himself without illusion, without evasion, but in faith, to be committed into that which is to be done. He no more has an overall picture of his form of time than did the Son of God who undertook what is humanly impossible, and only trinitarianly possible: namely, to gather the whole of the future into his finite existence. Such future was laid upon him, and he allowed it to occur. Whoever attempts to live seriously as a Christian lives in a time under the sway of the Trinity. He is molded by the event of Christ, his death on the Cross and his raising from the dead to God, by the mediation of his Spirit; this content presses him into service in such a way that his givenness (past), his being (present), and his ought (future) allow the Christian no time to give reflective and conceptual expression to his form of time.

All that is certain is that death has lost its sting. A sting which is retained in Jewish utopianism, where the prophetic, historical "time to come" may perhaps be achieved by a future generation, but where I as a mortal or as already dead can have no share in this earthly paradise; and which also remains in Platonism and Buddhism, where the ideal "above" behind death can justify its absurdity no more than it can justify the whole course of mortal life leading up to it. Only the Christian can look death and its terribleness in the face—no death will ever be as terrible as the death of Christ—and in so doing not abandon hope for mankind (and for himself in mankind), because the whole disaster of death is upheld and overcome by the trinitarian event in which God gave his Son into lostness in order not to allow man to remain alone in the lostness of his being.

The Communion of Saints

I

The term "communion of saints" is found in the Apostles' Creed between "I believe in the Holy Ghost, the Holy Catholic Church" and "the forgiveness of sins, the resurrection of the body, and the life everlasting", like a necessary link in the chain. The Holy Spirit is the foundation of all this: there would be no Holy Catholic Church without him. Jesus has entrusted the building up and extension of the Church to the Spirit, just as he has entrusted himself eucharistically to the Spirit who develops the "body" as the fulness of Christ from him who is the "head". If "communion of saints" is a closer, more intimate and secret description of the Catholic Church, then this means that, in the first place, the communion of those who have been sanctified with the sanctity of Jesus by the Holy Spirit—they are the "saints"—is a communion of those who have received a gift, who all communally share in something which of themselves they are not and could indeed never be. They do not become a communion of saints, if grace sanctifies them individually, on the basis of a universal human nature in which they already form a community; rather they became such a communion expressly through the community established by the Spirit (2 Cor 13:13), naturally on the basis of their call by the Father into the communion of his Son Jesus Christ (1 Cor 1:9), as it is realized particularly in the eucharistic community (1 Cor 10:16ff.). But the very fact that they have all received such a gift from above, a gift which itself creates community, produces of itself a horizontal community among them; the Holy Spirit, which founds the community, also fosters it among its members. The talk of "the encouragement of love, the community of the spirit, the deep sympathy and pity ... the same love, being in full accord and of one mind" (Phil 2:1f.) points in the same direction. More and more over the centuries, as the Church has reflected on her own nature, she has thought out and deepened this second horizontal element, without however detaching it from the first, in which it has its lasting foundations, and it is indeed that which deserves particular thought, because in other descriptions and definitions of the Church it is almost always given short measure.

The extent to which the "saints"—those who attempt to take seriously their sanctification by the holy triune God and to respond to it—are able in their community to be, to live, to work, and to suffer for one another can only begin to be realized when one has grasped the principle which welds them together into the unity of the community of the Church: the unity of the triune God manifested in the self-giving of Christ and poured out in the Holy Spirit. For this unity is nothing other than pure being-for-one-another. If there were a definition of God, then one would have to put it in the form: unity as being-for-one-another. That which we refer to, for want of a better word, as divine "persons" is the necessary condition of there being such a pure being-for-another in God. These "persons" do not have a primary being for themselves which is then only secondarily open to others; that which we might speak of as their "being-for-themselves", their self-consciousness, they have in common as the one, indivisible God; but this is integrated always from the beginning (and not subsequently) by the being-for-one-another. One cannot understand the Father except in his giving of himself in the begetting of his begotten Son, nor can one understand the Son except in his being for the Father. The self-giving of both to each other is further a "being-for-one-another" which in the writings of the New Covenant is clearly distinguished as "Holy Spirit" both from the Father and from the Son; it is personified "being-for-one-another" itself and the total self-giving of God to men.

If one now reflects that this gift of God which gives to the believers the form of the divine being for one another, gives it and impresses it on their very being and establishes the essence of the Church and so of the decisively Christian form of community, then one can see clearly what a total reversal of human relationships and structures has taken place here. It is true that men form among themselves a physical whole whose mysterious ramifications run back from the material realm into the spiritual (as, for example, C. G. Jung would claim to have described them in his theory of the collective unconscious) in a manner difficult to trace and to pin down. However that may be, what is essential is that the bright spiritual apexes of consciousness, where every man takes personal responsibility for his free decisions, are distinct and opposed to each other, in such a way that it is only on the basis of this distinction that they can open up to each other in dialogue. That this element of dialogue has a share in constituting the individual person and enables him to come into full possession and exercise of his personal freedom is not denied by this fact. But the form of the dialogue can indeed be very differently filled: with edifying, neutral, and destructive content.

The being-for-one-another which is given in the communion of saints by contrast opens up the individual to the other precisely from the apex of his personality. And this still occurs with increasing intensity, the more deeply the believing person allows himself to be determined, to be taken up into and, as it were, dispossessed by this divine form of being-for-one-another. Whoever gives his consent to this divine form of life, to a life in which from the outset one abandons all claim to possession in favor of the other, whoever holds out for the other's disposal everything which belongs to him, including that which is most private and apparently most incommunicable, of such a man the God of love disposes in all truth and effectiveness for the benefit of his brothers. It is here that the biblical concept of fruitfulness is introduced. This supersedes (but without destroying their limited meaning) the concepts of works and rewards, which at first, as images taken from the world of human labor, presuppose a system of individuals distinct from one another in order to be able to stress the effective "being-for" of the "saint" (that is to say, of the truly believing, hoping, loving man). The more "deserving" the being and behavior of a man are—and he is not to be deprived of his reward—the more profitable he is for the community. And this by no means exclusively or above all as a result of particular acts, like prayers or acts of renunciation, but because of his total bearing, his basic attitude, his will to understand himself as an expropriated being, as a being which may be given away. Of course, such an attitude has its roots, in so far as it can by virtue of its divine origins take root in the world of men, in the Eucharist of the Son: it is as the one imbued with the spirit of the Eucharist that he is the vine whose whole fruitfulness flows out of himself into the branches. The closest approximation of all to such an attitude is to be found in the saying of Mary offering herself as the handmaid, by which she consents to her total dispossession in order to become the receptacle of the Holy Spirit. From Origen down to the Middle Ages one spoke of such a dispossessed soul as an *anima ecclesiastica*, as a soul bearing the form of the Church: the soul is ready and willing to assume the form of being-for-one-another, and this without imposing any conditions, without, for instance, demanding to receive back again as much as it itself gives.

II

This final point makes it clear that the communion of saints cannot be a closed circle of those who exchange their merits and rewards among themselves, in much the same manner in which firms amalgamate, in order to get a higher yield on their capital. The communion of saints can only be an open circle of those who "give without counting the cost", who let their light shine into the world without looking for its reflection. Only that is truly *agape, caritas*, only so did Christ pour himself out on the Cross and in the Eucharist. And consequently, it is not possible to draw any dividing line around this open circle marking off its extent and the extent of its effectiveness. Only the man who is prepared to lose can become a member. "A power went forth from him" (Mk 5:30; Lk 6:19; 8:46) is what is said of the miracles of Jesus. And he behaves as if he did not know into whom it has passed. It is of course true if one equates the communion of saints with the "Holy Catholic Church", then there will indeed be many profiteers whom one has to count among its number. And the transition from the "losers" to the "winners" is such a gradual one that it will not in practice be possible to draw any sharp dividing lines. Who, even among the true saints, does not profit from Mary's word of assent? She is the archetype of those who bear fruit, the Virgin Mother herself. We all take shelter under her cloak. But there are others within this cloak who themselves have smaller cloaks, and they do not know who it is that finds shelter under them, for, at least on earth, only God knows what the extent and effect of the fruitfulness of the saints may be. Then by stages we come to those in whom sin grows and takes the upper hand but who nevertheless contribute a few drops of blood to the general circulation. Perhaps they take more than they give, but all the same they do give something. The serious sinner is the one who absorbs all grace for himself without giving anything at all away. Here also there is a counter-movement, but one cannot say that it simply outweighs the first. A rotten member in the body of the Church can poison a great deal in his vicinity. Evil is infectious. And yet it would not be proper to say that it has a kind of counter-fruitfulness. It only has the possibility of impeding true fruitfulness. It is only what is good and selfless that bears fruit; evil itself is unfruitfulness. And yet one knows that evil causes the good to suffer and that the suffering of the good is deepened fruitfulness. In his Eucharist Jesus gained victory by anticipation over his enemies, even over his final enemy, death. And consequently the goal of the communion of saints is not properly the communal struggle against evil—as a corporation or club might set itself a common goal—but nothing other than the dissemination of the good; indeed, not even that, for the good disseminates itself; the aim is quite simply to hold oneself ready; the aim is the abandonment of all aims of one's own, in order that God's aims may be fulfilled through his own people.

III

In the last section we touched briefly on the image of the circulation of blood. It is the old image used by Paul of the body of Christ in which the many members live and grow together in unity of purpose and in mutual care. In this picture the "Holy Catholic Church" and "the communion of saints" inter-penetrate each other and are woven seamlessly together. For here the principle of the structure in its external, visible arrangement is linked with the principle of the inner, organic life by being set in relationship to an invisible, active center: "all made to drink of *one* spirit" (1 Cor 12:13). And this spirit which circulates through the organism causes the members not only to care "horizontally" for one another but also (as Thomas Aquinas emphasized again and again) to love the whole more than themselves, the parts. And in the Church or in the communion of saints the whole is Christ, in whom the fulness of the Godhead dwells and who unfolds this fulness in his mystical body (Col 1:19; Eph 1:23). And so every member receives its fulness, the principle of its fruitfulness from him—"from his fulness have we all received" (Jn 1:16)—and no one can pour forth such fulness (horizontally) without having received it, without owing it to the real source (vertically). Fruitfulness is always eucharist, and eucharist means thanksgiving to the source, to the "Father of lights from whom every good endowment and every perfect gift comes down" (James 1:17). The life which flows through the organism—as Holy Spirit or as eucharist blood, for both belong indivisibly together—is that which gives every member its form and function and consequently at the same time relates it internally to the whole. No member of the human body lives its own separate life. It receives its vitality from the whole which transcends it, in order that it may in its turn serve the whole. And so Paul can move immediately from the organic level—leaving out the natural sociological level in which analogous and yet different laws obtain—to the level of the Church, where the vital principle repeats itself, yet in a surprisingly new way, in the realm of the Spirit. Only now the all-embracing vital principle is no longer natural but supernatural. We must not overwork the image and attempt to get more from it than an image can give. The supernatural correspondence runs out into something for which we can provide no metaphors, precisely at the point where the visible, functional, and charismatically ordered Catholic Church can no longer be equated without remainder with the invisibly functioning laws of the communion of saints. It is possible to observe and record a charism fairly extensively; but never the effects of spiritual fruitfulness.

There is perhaps no more comforting truth about the Church than that in her there is a community, a communion of saints. For, on the one hand, this means that there is a continually overflowing richness on which all the poor may draw; it is also called the treasure of the Church. It is precisely the same as the incalculable fruitfulness of those who offer themselves and all that they have to God to dispose of for the sake of the brotherhood. Real power goes forth from them; they are not spared by love (Rom 8:32) but are remorselessly shared out; who knows to whom I owe which grace in my life. This excess which comes to us makes us poor and humble, for we sense precisely that we can only draw on such richness in the same spirit in which it has been given. We feel in this that we have already received much more that is not our own than we have ourselves given of our own, that perhaps, in so far as we have regarded and handled that which was not our own as our own, we have misappropriated other men's goods. The idea of the communion of saints inspires no little caution in us. On the other hand, it also exhorts us not to underestimate the fruitfulness which has been given us by God. There are many who in old age or in sickness or in imprisonment or in any of the other cul-de-sacs of existence imagine that they have nothing more to give. They seem to themselves to be useless and may be tempted to end their life. Such people should remember that only the man who is poor and precisely the man who is poor, who is conscious of having lost all that he owned, has been put in a position to give. The widow at the treasury gave more than all the rest, "she gave of her poverty." Those who are poor in spirit not only gain the kingdom of heaven, they open it up to the others. Poor peoples have known of this mystery best.

> Misunderstood, abandoned even by her own husband she had buried six children but had not lost her natural readiness to help; regarded as strange by her sisters and sisters-in-law, a laughable person, who was stupid enough to work for others without reward, she had at the end of her life saved no possessions. A dirty white goat, a lame cat, rubber plants ...

> We all lived alongside her and none of us understood that she was that righteous person without whom, as the proverb says, no village can live.
>
> And no city.
>
> And not our whole country.
>
> (A. Solzhenitsyn: *Matriona's Farm*)

The Marian Principle

I

Karl Barth, who in his later years was a regular listener to the Roman Catholic sermons on a Sunday on the radio, once pointed out with satisfaction that he had never yet heard a sermon on Mary. "So you see, you can get on without her after all", he said with a certain jovial maliciousness. And what could one reply without disowning one's own people: ecumenical tactics? (But certainly not very good ones.) The return to the Scriptures? (But these in the eyes of the Church are full of pointers to the role of woman in creation and redemption.) The influence of the last Council? (But this brings its doctrine of the Church to a point in mariology.) Or perhaps the fear of men and the desire under no circumstances to gain the reputation of lagging behind the latest fashion of theological progressiveness?

However that may be, the slogan of the "evolution of dogma" (for which the evolution of mariology used to be cited as a prime example) has today become questionable from many points of view; we have long since abandoned the attempt to work out from the divine revelation entrusted to the Church as many "propositions of faith" as possible. Rather now we attempt to go back in our reflection to the basic structures, to the immutable "primal form" of this revelation in order to come at each attempt as close as possible to the divine event which is the origin of that primal form. For that form neither can grow old nor can it in a true sense develop, because as eternal truth and love it accompanies all temporal becoming. But the fact is that an important part of that basic form of the revelation is the role of woman in God's saving action, which starts with the creation, unfolds its definitive sense in the Old and New Covenants, is finally established in the history of the Church and the world, and in the visions of the Apocalypse points mysteriously forward to its final conclusion.

Before beginning to reflect on the principle, a preliminary note. The Church today has to pay the bitter price for the many mistakes which she has made in her long history, for the foreshortenings and one-sidednesses which have often crept in unnoticed but which then have had considerable consequences. In the sector of mariology everyone is conscious of the very questionable shifts in emphasis, not only in the realm of so-called "popular piety", which often regarded Mary more than her Son as its mediator to the Father—as is shown by a thorough examination both of iconography and also of the topography of places of pilgrimages and of the market in devotional objects—but also within academic theology, which at least in a very active branch has concerned itself and continues to do so extensively—in countless books, journals especially devoted to this subject, in frequent meetings and congresses, particularly in Latin countries—with the privileges of the Mother of God. We feel uncomfortable when we are confronted with this theological activity and notice that such an activity has its roots not so much in the universal tradition of the Church as in a predominantly modern undertaking.

Where the theology of Mary is concerned as a whole, one thing must be made perfectly clear from the start: such a theology existed from the very beginnings of theological reflection as an indispensable part of the objective Christian doctrine of salvation for more than a millennium before (particularly in the West) it became associated with an isolated, subjective form of devotion. The statement that Mary is *theotokos*, the one who gives birth to God, is in the first place a statement which has its rightful setting in Christology. The statement that her conception was immaculate is in the first place a statement whose setting is the doctrine of grace and redemption. The statement that she is a virgin, in order that she may become the Mother of Christ—in itself a simple repetition of the witness of Scripture—is in the reflection of the Church a statement taken from the theology of the Covenant and consequently from the doctrine of the people of the Church. And the dogma of the assumption of her body into heaven is, properly understood, a part of the universal Christian doctrine of the Last Things. We shall have more to say about that subsequently. What is essential for our purpose is to see that within dogmatics mariology existed in the Western Church for over a millennium—from Irenaeus via Augustine to Anselm and Bernard—without any widespread subjective excrescences, the one-sidedness of which one must regret and which one must certainly cut back. On the other side, there is nothing surprising about the fact, indeed it is rather to be expected, that a person who occupies such an extraordinary position within the divine plan of redemption as does Mary was not in the long run denied a devotion corresponding to her objective function, if only for the reason that thereby, by means of such honor given to her, the one who endowed her with such dignity, the God of grace, was himself properly honored. And so the second period of marian theology, which approximately begins with Bernard and is marked by an increased attention to the person of Mary, remains on the whole legitimate and only becomes questionable at the point where her person is isolated from the context of the theology of salvation and so is set up in competition with the saving function of the Son of God. This danger has been sufficiently countered by the Second Vatican Council's Constitution on the Church, which makes mariology the final chapter of the section on the doctrine of the Church and so reintegrates it back into the whole truth of salvation.

We can take a further step in these preliminary reflections and ask—and indeed here we shall also be asking our Protestant brothers—whether in these two millennia we have always accorded to Christology its proper value and position, namely, the one which Jesus gave to himself: as the way to the Father along which we are empowered to travel by the Holy Spirit. And if some have pursued an isolated mariology, then have not some also pursued an isolated cult of Christ and failed to get farther than the notion of the man Jesus as the supreme example of our common humanity, as the "great brother", as the "friend of souls", as the eucharistic food, and so on, instead of thinking of him as he always wished to be thought of: as the concrete proof of the love of the Father, as the active word of the Father's reconciliation with us, of the Father who is to become our ultimate thou and to whom the Son as our way will lead us? If it is true that all mariology must be embedded in the doctrine of the Church and of the person of Christ, then it is also true that all Christology must be rooted in the doctrine of the Trinity. And we have today to pay the cost of our neglect of the latter just as much as of our neglect of the former: the living unity of Christ is breaking apart into the mere man Jesus and a word of reconciliation proclaimed by him (*kerygma*), with which he is no longer identical.

II

Perhaps we may for a moment set aside our reservations about an isolated, subjective devotion to Mary and put the question about the proper objective element of mariology which is integral to the history of salvation.

It begins on the first page of Genesis, where God creates man in his image, and this as male and female. Man only exists in the opposition of the sexes, in the dependence of both forms of humanity the one on the other; their union is specified immediately after the designation of man as being in the image of God, which distinguishes him from all creatures which have to this point been created. The more clearly the element of opposition between the sexes is developed, the more strongly is expressed the interdependence, the relationship, the bracket of love. And the same is true indeed in God himself: the irreducible opposition in the paternal, filial, spiritual relationship and behavior is the basis of the unity of nature and the equality of the "personal" relationships. When Paul (Eph 5) later refers to the greatness of the mystery between male and female because of its reference to the bridal relationship and the "union in the flesh" between Christ and the Church, he reveals the underlying unity of God's ways: the way for the final form of relationship between God and man is prepared from the very start in the created form of man. That final relationship will not be possible without woman, neither in God's "becoming man" (for "man" exists only as male and female) nor in the final relationship between the triune God and man in which the relationship of male and female must also be perfected. According to the second imaginative account of creation, with its deep symbolism, Eve is created from Adam's rib and is his helpmate but for whom he would remain imperfect within the kingdom of the animals. Only in her can he be what he is, creating, procreating man. And so too, according to Paul, the woman is the *doxa*, the "glory" of man whose own creative glory, on the other hand, does not come from him but from God. There is for all the equality of persons and of their sexual functions (Eve is as unambiguously created by God as Adam!) an "order" in the realm of the sexual, a prefiguration of the quite other and yet analogous order between the new Adam and the new Eve. The link between the prefiguration and its fulfilment is provided by the people of Israel: the chosen "spouse" of the divine Lord of the Covenant, who, however, because she is a creature, must always remain conscious of her position as handmaid in relationship to God. Israel must be completely faithful to God and must remain unsullied and virginal for him alone; but she is unfaithful to him and all too often is denigrated as a whore. The Song of Songs stands alone in the Old Testament: an ideal which nowhere is realized in the history of salvation and which must wait for the New Testament before it can become the inner kernel of all thought about the history of salvation: when for once in all historical seriousness there would be found a sinless bride to correspond to the idyllic Shulamite.

III

In order that God's word (in the Old Testament) may become man, the "helpmate" must give evidence not only of a vague faith but of one which itself is fully incarnate: which embraces body, soul, spirit, and which she puts at God's disposal as a receptacle for his word. The fact that even a body can "believe" is the new truth at the threshold of the definitive covenant. Man does not achieve this by his own strength and efforts, but God's grace gives it to him (in the "pre-redemption" of the Mother), in order to mark out the totally new beginning which occurs within the course of the generations from Adam. And so Joseph *must* stand to one side and the divine spouse of Israel must take his place in the event of the incarnation. The word of God which had, as it were, for a long time been on its way from God and which takes bodily form in the man Jesus would be completely confused in its nature and in the message it announces if this man had had two fathers and if he had owed his existence to two, one in heaven and one on earth. He would no longer be *the* Son who *as such* is identical with *the* word. In order to arrive at the notion of Mary's virginity, one does not need to look beyond the bounds of the Bible toward Hellenistic myths of the gods. Everything in the Old Testament has been preparing the way for this final transcending step. From Sarah to Elizabeth, God miraculously makes fruitful (through, in some cases, physically impotent men) barren wombs; the final perfecting step he retains for himself, for his Holy Spirit. This is no isolated magical act but lies precisely along the axis of Old Testament covenant theology and leads over into the theology of the Church, as a physical, visible bride of God, in whose virgin womb the Son of God (in the sacraments and in proclamation) always wills again and again to become man. This accounts for the parallels between Mary and the Church, which are increasingly elaborated in the Fathers; at the beginning Mary is thought of more as a symbol of the Church, and then more strongly as her deepest origin and unsullied kernel: as that point in the center of the community where, by God's grace, that was truly achieved which as sinners we are all quite incapable of achieving and which yet had once really to be achieved, if the Church was to be more than a second synagogue. And it must be more if incarnation really occurred.

Every son receives from his mother. Mary the Mother wanted to be the pure "handmaid of the Lord". The Son, although he was our Lord and Master, wanted only to be among us as one who serves. He comes over from the Father to the side of men and in consequence to the side of the servants. And in addition to this he allows all the guilt of the world to be laden upon him as the "servant of God". How, then, could it be otherwise than that the "helpmate", the Mother and bride, the archetype of the Church, pierced by the sword, should take her place under the Cross? Indeed what else could she, the definitive Eve, do but take upon herself in her feminine role the birthpangs of the first Eve to the end of the world and so become a supratemporal feminine principle, which the apocalyptic seer sees crying out in her pains: Mary-Church, who to the very end brings forth the children of God in pain?

We can only hint at all this here; we cannot develop it in any way. But one thing may be added by way of testing the contrary of our thesis. Where the mystery of the marian character of the Church is obscured or abandoned, there Christianity must become unisexual (homo-sexual), that is to say, all male. Now it is true that from the beginning the leadership of the Church was restricted to men, nor can one say that such a decision was uninfluenced by contemporary views and attitudes both in Judaism and Hellenism. But at the same time one will not be able to deny that precisely in this decision expression was given to that permanent sexual "order", which in no way runs contrary to the personal equality of rights of man and woman or to the equality of status of their oppositional sexual functions. That this equality of rights could be established historically in the Christian consciousness only after a long period (what prejudices had to be overcome in this field!) need cause us no surprise; it comes sharply to expression in the fact that it is precisely on the basis of an ecclesiology determined by a marian point of view that a salutary relativization can be given to the hierarchical element within the Church. If today, however, this fruitful tension is slackened because mariology is deprived of its position, and if women as a consequence of the democratization of the Church begin to invest the hierarchical offices, then they will merely have jumped out of the frying pan into the fire. The

Church since the Council has to a large extent put off her mystical characteristics; she has become a Church of permanent conversations, organizations, advisory commissions, congresses, synods, commissions, academies, parties, pressure groups, functions, structures and restructurings, sociological experiments, statistics: that is to say, more than ever a male Church, if perhaps one should not say a sexless entity, in which woman may gain for herself a place to the extent that she is ready herself to become such an entity. The idea of the Church developed in evolutionary theology was the first step toward the view that what was of ultimate importance was to make use of the erotic forces for the development of the world; if anything is a male need, then it is this desire to subject everything to a purpose. The flow of love between the sexes has *meaning*, but this meaning transcends any purpose; the play of children has meaning, but it is not intended to fulfil any purpose. Great art has meaning, but no purpose. The power of Amor cannot be made to drive turbines any more than can the power of the *caritas* between Christ and the Church. What can one say of "political theology" and of "critical Catholicism"? They are outlines for discussion for professors of theology and anti-repressive students, but scarcely for a congregation which still consists of children, women, old men, and the sick—and not simply of vigorous young men—whose most important tasks are certainly other than that of giving expression to "eschatological reservations" over against the forms of the state. May not the reason for the domination of such typically male and abstract notions be because of the abandonment of the deep femininity of the marian character of the Church?

IV

The marian element holds sway in the Church in a hidden manner, just as a woman does in a household. But woman is not an abstract principle; on the contrary, she is a concrete person, and it is from her as a person that the female atmosphere emanates. Consequently the second period of marian theology, which emphasized and cast light on the personal in the theological principle, was not simply wrong. Only it is essential that it should be the true spirit of Mary which comes into the light: the spirit of the handmaid, of service, of inconspicuousness, the spirit which lives only to pass on what it has received, which lives only for others. No one demands personal "privileges" less than the Mother of Christ; she can rejoice in such only in so far as they are shared by all her children in the Church.

It is consequently in this marian spirit that all Mary's privileges must be thought out and expounded anew. Why is Mary "conceived immaculately"? Precisely because someone "representing the whole human race" (as Thomas Aquinas says) had to utter the full, unadulterated word of assent from Israel to God in order that his word might find a place where he could in his incarnation descend to earth. Mary uttered that word in its purity for us all, so that we too as disciples might become brothers, sisters, and mothers of Jesus who do the will of the Father. And why did Mary have to be a virgin in order to give birth to the Son of the Father, and this in a real and historical sense and not only theologically and symbolically, a distinction which today many exegetes and theologians attempt to draw but which would ultimately be destructive? Certainly, apart from anything else, it was for the reason, as we have said, that a totally new beginning had to be marked in God's saving activity, corresponding to the beginning in Adam; but also it was because every man who receives faith, that is to say, who receives the living word of God in his soul, must without reserve put his whole existence, body and soul, at God's disposal, must bear witness to the word of God with his whole physical life and must ultimately be prepared to die for it. And why was Mary taken up into heaven physically after her death in order in this manner to anticipate the resurrection of the dead? Because in this, too, she points us, in anticipation, to the real place for which we strive, where our whole spiritual and material existence is saved; because it is fitting that not only the bridegroom but also his bride, the heavenly Jerusalem, should really (and not only "ideally") partake of the ultimate salvation gained on the Cross, and that the eschatological marriage feast, of which the Book of Revelation speaks, should not be put off till some far distant future but should now already in a mysterious present be beginning. The "heavenly city" toward which we strive exists not only utopianly in the spirit but physically, and not only "masculinely" (in Christ) but in a universal human way in God—that is to say, both masculinely and femininely.

Without mariology Christianity threatens imperceptibly to become inhuman. The Church becomes functionalistic, soulless, a hectic enterprise without any point of rest, estranged from her true nature by the planners. And because, in this manly–masculine world, all that we have is one ideology replacing another, everything becomes polemical, critical, bitter, humorless, and ultimately boring, and people in their masses run away from such a Church.

From the Cross the Son hands his Mother over into the Church of the apostles; from now on her place is there. In a hidden manner her virginal motherhood holds sway throughout the whole sphere of the Church, gives it light, warmth, protection; her cloak makes the Church into a protective cloak. It requires no special gesture from her to show that we should look at the Son and not at her. Her very nature as handmaid reveals him. So, too, she can show the apostles and their successors how one can be both wholly effective presence and wholly extinguished service. For the Church was already present in her before men were set in office.

Tradition

I

The dying man who takes leave of his children and divides his goods among them, giving them his last words of advice and admonition, thereby sets the boundary to his own sphere of activity and at the same time gathers up his existence and throws it over the boundary to his survivors. It is not only objects which are to serve later to remind people of him; in his testament his living spirit will remain among them. His *ultima verba* carry all the weight and gravity of the finality of death, and it is that which gives them their lasting and surviving claim. Throughout folk literature this most solemn of all situations has always been exploited. Such has been the case in the Old Testament (Jacob, Moses, Joshua, Samuel, David, Mattathias; the whole of Deuteronomy is set in the form of a farewell speech of the Law Giver, whose center is "the greatest commandment"); in later Judaism frequently, and above all in the Testament of the Twelve Patriarchs (in which each one as he dies passes on to his tribe his original charisma), and in the New Testament, which shows Paul (in the speech at Miletus and in the Pastoral Epistles) and Peter (in the Second Epistle) in the situation of the one who passes on the tradition. But the supreme, both comparable and incomparable, case is Jesus' farewell discourse in its shorter form in Luke (before the passion and again before the ascension) and in its more extensive treatment in John, where in the introductory section the situation of the farewell and of Jesus' giving himself even beyond death is given the greatest possible emphasis:

> On the day before the Passover, when Jesus knew that his hour had come to depart out of this world to the Father, since he loved his own who were [to remain] in the world, he loved them to the end. And during supper when the devil had already put it into the heart of Judas Iscariot, Simon's son, to betray him Jesus, knowing that the Father had given all things into his hands and that he had come from the Father and was going to the Father, stood up from the meal ... (Jn 13:1–4).

Then follows the foot-washing and its double explanation: it is both Jesus' inimitable humiliation as the humiliation of the Lord and Master and the demand to the disciples to do the same to each other. Then the eucharistic offering (precisely to Judas), the great speech which is, as it were, the expression in words of that offering, and finally the farewell prayer, which squeezes out the total meaning of Jesus' existence like a final distillation and bequeaths it to men in the bowl of the trinitarian dialogue between the community of the disciples and the world. Here the literary form of the testament has become a form for that which is unique; it has become the self-abandonment of the eternal Son—given up by the Father out of his love for the world, handed over by the archetype of sinners, Judas, in his betrayal—in a definitive death which as such in the Eucharist and in the pouring out of the eternal word mediates definitive life to the world. This situation is one of such extremity that it cannot be in any way superseded; the Church can in her celebration of the Eucharist only again and again enter this situation "in remembrance of me" (and thereby "proclaim the death of the Lord, until he returns", 1 Cor 11:26) in order to begin anew as she returns to her origins in the spirit of the testamental tradition. She receives the body which has been given, the blood which has been shed, always firsthand, and at the same time she receives with these gifts the express interpretation of Jesus' self-giving. At each occasion we receive now that which was given once and for all; the tasks with which we are charged stem from him but are to be carried out in subsequent generations; only then will they be understood.

It is appropriate and proper that this event which was qualitatively unsurpassable—for what greater gift could God give to us than his Son given for the life of the world?—should subsequently, for the sake of us men, have been set down in a definitive literary form. But it is the unsurpassability of the content of the will in its utterance which is the decisive norm, and not the written document which bears witness to it. Christianity does not stand or fall on a book but on the ultimately decisive act of God in handing himself down for all men in Jesus Christ.

History, as it flows on its course through the world, moves farther and farther away from its sources; significant origins must, lest they be forgotten, be sought out anew by swimming back against the stream. The time of the Church, however, is of a different kind from that of worldly history; it is made possible and dominated by the presence of her origin which accompanies her in living form: "Lo, I am with you every day to the end of the world." The one who says this utters God's final decision, in that he himself is that decision: a definitive decision passed on the whole of history, never to be surpassed. It is a presence, which accompanies the Church not only from above, as it were from out of the timeless world, but which submerges itself eucharistically in every moment of time. And that the eucharistic self-offering of the one who dies is truly the source of the outpouring of his body through the ages is shown by the gift of the Holy Spirit of the Father and the Son, given by the risen Lord in the Church and poured into all her living members. This source is neither simply an historical beginning nor simply timelessly "above", but it also flows along truly accompanying the course of history, sharing in time, universally present in time: in the ever-occurring event of the Eucharist, of God's living word in human form (1 Thes 3:13ff.), in the ever-recurring participation of the Church which, as she partakes of Christ's corporality, becomes Christ's body, in the fate of her head, in her filling up of his sufferings out of that which can and should be suffered by the members (Col 1:24). And consequently the Scriptures too are in no sense what they appear to earthly eyes to be—that is to say, a document which is hopelessly located and tied down to a particular stage in history, but rather a witness given to the Church (as she believes, hopes, and suffers with her Lord) to accompany her on her way through history to his real and spiritual presence, a document which consequently possesses unconditionally the properties of a persistent actuality and accessibility, a document which instructs and illumines, which gives powerful comfort. In it the spirit has the upper hand over the letter, the immediate intelligibility has precendence over the need for interpretation; the Bible remains a word for the poor in spirit. One can see its spiritual character already in the fact that the picture of Jesus which is given to us (by means of the four Gospels) is given in such three-dimensional clarity that no attempt to reduce it to the level of the two-dimensional (of a photograph) will ever succeed.

There is no avoiding the work which must be done on this document, and which today is pursued more fiercely than ever, because it is indeed an historical and highly complex configuration which makes its claim to bear witness to that which is unique, unsurpassable. And such work is also very fruitful because the uncovering of its interrelationships with contemporary history and literature, of the successive phases of its redaction and of the utterances which thereby have been introduced at successive stages, each of them seeing things in a different and new way, has allowed the text to speak to us, to reveal itself to us, in a manner not previously known. This work must be pursued and made fruitful for the belief of the Church. The belief of the primitive Church—which is substantially the same as our own—has formed the document, and it would therefore be uncritical to attempt to put brackets round it in our research on the documents or to attempt to get behind it; it is the adequate eschatological answer to the eschatological will of God; both appear simultaneously or not at all; both either are of equally pressing importance today as they were then, or else they never possessed the importance at all which they once claimed. And so one cannot possibly insist on the validity of the original literary witness (viewing all subsequent developments as a decline from that) without affirming at the same time the validity for all time of that to which witness is borne, of which the living witness of faith is itself a part, for otherwise everything slips away into the realm of unreality: then only the written document itself retains the full gravity of the eschatological reality; historical reality is measured against the original witness preserved in the sacred shrine, by its verbal correspondence to it, and is found wanting. But, equally, we should not simply assume the authenticity of the faith as we have it today, no more than we should abandon, as of no importance, the orientation of such faith toward the reality witnessed to in this document. Such faith would be necessarily abstract, that is to say, drawn away, removed from the concrete eschatological saving deed of God, which can only have meaning for us in the present, as a deed incarnated and sealed by Jesus' death on the Cross and his Resurrection. Consequently, if one scrapes away layer after layer of the witness—like onion skins—rejecting them as conditioned by their own particular times, in order to get back to a "supratemporal", enduring (demythologized) kernel, then one has quite certainly understood the witness in a manner in which it itself did not intend to be understood. By analysis one has unmasked the central synthesis, which stands at the center of all the New Testament witnesses, as a derived, hybrid product in which unmixables have been mixed and which has then been overlaid in such a manner as to have been fundamentally obscured, whose historical truth for critical reason can only lie in the elements which precede the synthesis. Both positions—the effective identification of the eschatological event which the historical document witnesses and which bears witness to it, and the effective identification of present-day faith with the eschatological event, thereby bypassing the document itself—tend mutually to promote each other; but both fail to recognize that everything hangs on the actual gift from time to time (tradition) of the highest that God has and is to us who through all ages must always wait on receiving in the same manner the same gift. And in the tradition of the Church we pass on this faith which, if it is to remain intact, concrete, and undiminished in accordance with its origin, must continually take its bearings by the original witness. In the chain of tradition all receivers and answerers must check among themselves and for themselves whether they have received and answered with understanding the gift of God at its eschatological maximum, whether when they eat and drink, they "discern the body of the Lord", for otherwise—as they step out of line and isolate themselves because of their superior knowledge—they could eat and drink to themselves judgment instead of salvation; "that is why so many of you are weak and ill, and why so many have died" (1 Cor 11:30).

History for the Church is also a process of living change, but this is not change in the sense of a growing apart from her origin. Within the world all historical development brings with it a loss of intensity, a process of ageing. In so far as the Church truly travels the course of history, she is also familiar with this law: no stage which she reaches is absolute, that which has fallen below standard must be reformed in accordance with her origin, and the continual efforts to be true to her origin belong, like change itself, positively to the phenomenon of her living tradition. Change means to become different, to alter, but believing change is a change within the context of an alteration which has taken place once and for all, which is the deed of God: in the transformation from life to death as it is hidden and always present in the transformation of the Eucharist.

This should make it clear why "Scripture and tradition" are not two principles which can be set up against each other but aspects of a larger occurrence which is exhausted by neither of them, which in its very nature is historically unique and (as a consequence) of universal historical significance. It is unique because in the event of Christ the whole fulness of God's self-giving is contained. There is no development beyond it and away from it. It is of universal significance because the continual re-presentation of this fulness in the Church, in her faith, prayer, suffering, and hidden victory, belongs internally to the being and activity of Christ. There is no head without a body, no child without a mother, no bridegroom without a bride. The Church and her history are the "fulness of him who fills all in all" (Eph 1:23 RSV), and but for this fulfilled fulness he would not be the fulfiller.

II

A first sketch of what the actual course of Church history is like is offered by the Acts of the Apostles, which is a beginning; it is also offered by the letters of the apostles which—in the midst of all the problems which engross the individual congregations which stand in need of much correction and reformation—make visible the principle of the living unity of Christ and the Church in the common, shared Holy Spirit. We will pick out three main points.

1. The mystery of the incarnation of God in Christ, of his suffering for the world as a whole, of his victory in his return to the Father, is so inexhaustible that it calls for ever-renewed contemplation and will have constantly to be rethought, re-examined, and more richly and if possible more precisely formulated. Where such attempts clearly err, either to the right or to the left, then formulae must be found which signpost the way to the center, which allows the mystery to remain unimpugned. That is the intention of the "directions for use" which are offered by the first ecumenical council. It is furthermore appropriate that, against the background of the Old Testament action of God in history, which travels swiftly up toward Jesus Christ, concentrating upon him as center, an attempt should be made to think out, to open up in theological and dogmatic work the divine truth which is concentrated, as it were, on its apex in the New Testament. Such attempts at unfolding the truth will, it is true, remain children of their age, conditioned by their time, but where they hold fast to that which is essential, they will also bring into being in their time that which is essential, which cannot be lost, and which must be taken along with one on one's way. The theology of the Fathers and of the Schoolmen cannot simply be measured by the explicit statements of Scripture, nor is the unfolding simply to be set aside as a dispensable, indeed positively damaging addition. For that would be to measure

the youth by the child, the growing plant by the seed. Only those who do not know the great tradition or who know it only superficially (which comes to the same thing), who judge it by catch-phrases and slogans, who have never been overwhelmed by the wealth of its theological insights, can play off Scripture against tradition. Admittedly, one must always keep the whole course of history in view: one must see Origen alongside Irenaeus, and Irenaeus alongside Augustine, while not committing oneself to the view that Augustine is the "Father of the West", but recognizing how in Thomas Aquinas there are the beginnings of a new openness to the "secular world"; without again committing oneself to seeing Thomas as the unsurpassable climax of theology but, rather, seeing him in his relationships both to the past and to the future. Nor should we presume, because in Thomas' theology certain biblical dimensions are missing (who reads his biblical commentaries anyway?) and because in Augustine's work the remains of late antiquity are still here and there to be found, that we can today (as dwarfs alongside the giants) despise their massive achievements and begin again from the beginning. The giants were humble; we dwarfs are presumptuous.

2. Christianity is not merely theory, but practice. God acts, and it is only in acting that man can reply; and consequently there is here an experience and certainty which can only be won through acting. Whoever does the will of the Father who sends him "will realize whether my doctrine comes from God or whether I speak from myself" (Jn 7:17). Whoever does not do it is merely confronted by his own face in the mirror, a face which as

soon as he turns away he forgets again (so much for its importance; see James 1:24). Since Abraham, God himself has not ceased to "test" the faith of his own; how will they perform, how will they behave when it comes to the test? There the truth will come to light. The tradition of the Church is a chain of Christian experience handed on from one generation to the other, and so a chain of distinctions and divisions which have been made in test cases as men have proved themselves, shown their worth, or been unmasked. Such testing occurs in the hidden life of every day as much as in public confession and ultimately in the witness of blood: The hidden test is for the living tradition not less important than the spectacular martyrdom; it occurs daily wherever parents live out for their children their Christian experience and hand it on to them with or without words, wherever a Christian example is consciously or unconsciously ignited and sends out a spark of faith, of hope, of love, wherever, as Christianity is lived out (and not only at the conference table of the pastoral sociologists!), Christian imagination thinks out creatively new ways by which the Church may come to men. Such ways are discovered not principally as a result of disappointments with the old ways which have now become unpassable, but as a result of mysterious, lived experiences of the reality of Jesus Christ. And, because you either do or do not have experiences, there is scarcely room here for debate; one does not argue about experiences, one can at the most invite other men to share them. The man who does not care to accept such an invitation has a fairly easy time of it: he only needs to insist "on the basis of his experience" that "God is dead", that at least he has never had a living encounter with him; and even if Christians in earlier ages were encountered by God on a massive scale, that is of no concern to him (as a psychologist anyway he suspects that this must have been a matter of mass suggestion); and if experience is to be made a criterion of Christian truth, then any popular opinion poll will prove conclusively that the time of this truth has now passed, and so on. The tone of such statements betrays that the speaker will not take the trouble to enter into the circle of the gift and its reception. One cannot deny that the Catholic universal religion was in its whole tradition ultimately esoteric. The experience of total self-giving between man and woman (we are not referring to merely occasional intercourse) is always unique; it sets its seal on life. The covenant between God and man, which in Jesus Christ penetrates into the very heart of men and is there sealed, is compared in Scripture on many occasions with the marriage covenant. Christians pass on to one another this "sacred public mystery"; they know the value of the pearl of great price and the reason why one does not cast it before swine.

3. Those who above all have undergone and enjoyed such experience have in every age been the saints. Church history is above all, perhaps, the history of the saints, known and unknown. Those who have staked everything on one card and, by their daring, become pure mirrors have in a rich spectrum cast the light from within onto our dark outside. They are the great history of the interpretation of the gospel, more genuine and with more power of conviction than all exegesis. They are the proof both of the fulness and of the presence. One should be careful not to discard as outmoded

things which from century to century they have experienced again and again (for example, their encounters with the angels of God and with the demon right down to the Curé d'Ars and Don Bosco), nor to de- spise the pure mirror of Bernadette and what it reflects of the truth of Mary by comparison with our little exegetical discoveries. Much is said and written today about the temporally conditioned character of the saints' view of the world, and much of it is right. But that does not relieve us of the task of measuring up to their central concern, their unconditional desire to take seriously their love toward God in Christ, and—on the basis of this dispossession, of thus being taken out of themselves into the absolute love—their allowing themselves to be given over to their fellow men (in this order and not the opposite). Love of neighbor was for them never a substitute for love of God and of Christ. Their love is kindled by the fact that they know themselves to be loved absolutely and desire to answer that absolute love with their whole existence. In order to gain a picture of what it is to be a saint, one only needs to look at Paul, who sets himself up as an "example" only in so far as he himself is totally dispossessed, and so far as he has been taken up into Christ, who is his model. Perhaps even better by looking at "the disciple whom Jesus loved" and for whom love of Christ and love of one's neighbor are inseparable from faith in the absolute priority of the love of the triune God toward us (1 Jn 3:16; 4:10). But let us not despair of there being in our time men and women who love and bear witness in this way. The tradition is not broken.

The tradition is fully as necessary as Scripture. For the latter (or rather its content: Christ) expounds itself again and again as it takes form in Christian existence. The latter does not move away from its origin but allows that origin (as it looks toward Scripture) to be present in each moment in the power of the Holy Spirit which has been given to it. The Church grows as a body, even if she does not grow in accordance with the determinable laws which govern the evolution of the world. But if Mary had not lived through thirty-three years, she would scarcely have been able to *stand* under the Cross. If the Church had not gone on her way steadfastly for these two thousand years, she would not have the experience to enable her to *withstand* a situation like the present. We Christians are in no sense individuals who, without parents or in revolt against parents who re- fuse to make concessions to us, make our way alone in the present. We are and remain members of the Church, branches of her tree, nourished by the sap of her total experience, which ultimately rise up out of the unfathomable experiences of Jesus Christ. It is in these powers which work in us that we should trust, for they too mediate to us, indispensably, the way to him who is himself true immediacy.

Authority

I

The Worldly Spheres

The indispensability of the concept of authority, despite the radical questioning to which it has recently been subjected, is shown precisely by the dialectic of the alternatives which our society develops in its place in the name of a freedom which, it is admitted, has yet to be developed or indeed brought into being. On the one side, there is anarchy which destroys all culture; on the other, despotism which tramples down all human dignity. In the magnetic fields of these antagonisms an edifying authority—*auctoritas* means in its original sense "promoting", "increasing" power—can no longer hold its own because it can only develop and flower in an interplay with that which is to be "increased" in a fundamental relationship of trust. Such interplay can assume various yet analogous forms in the different areas of worldly existence, forms which are built up on basic principles.

1. Every existent possesses a certain degree of powerfulness of being (*Seinsmächtigkeit*) in such a way that he poses a demand to the world around him to allow the validity of his own being and of the claims to existence, to self-development and recognition which are connected with it. This powerfulness of being is revealed most

clearly on the level of personal spirits, for each one of them puts forward this fundamental claim to all the others, but equally must allow it to all others so that in this authority of being (or alternatively in these personal values) brotherhood and mutual service are also given. If on top of this one considers the physical duality of man as male and female, then each sex contains an authority appropriate to its essential structure (*Wesensstruktur*) over the other, which would have to be examined separately. This powerfulness of being is a sharing in the absolute powerfulness of being of the Creator (in Hebrew, *kabod*, the personal power, the dignity, the awesomeness, and the glory; in Latin, *maiestas* and *gloria*), in the dependence which self-evidently belongs to the creature. All this belongs to the original sinless order of being (*Seinsordnung*).

2. Our world is a "fallen" world, infected on all sides by weakness, powerlessness, and guilt, but nevertheless not in such a manner that the original order has, as a consequence, been simply destroyed; but nowhere is it any longer completely intact. In our real world authority occurs fundamentally in a double form: as an authority which has gradually to make itself superfluous by the education of natures (*Wesen*) which temporarily only share to a very small degree in being, for instance the authority of parents over their children, of teachers at all levels over their pupils. This gradual transition can occur, even in a family, without serious disruption only where there is an understanding and accompanying love. But there is also an authority which, because of the sinfulness and weakness of men, cannot simply be outgrown but

remains as a permanent feature: the authority of social order with the right to "bear the sword" and to "punish evil-doers" (Rom 13) for the sake of the common good (for whose sake such an institution must be constituted and in the service of which it must constantly remain). Both in his function as an educationalist and in his function as one who is to create order, the man who exercises authority must be a pointer to an authority which is superior to himself, that is to say, to God. Earthly duties are not something which are at the discretion of the one who has to obey, but must be categorically followed; consequently the one who represents such demands must make it clear in all forms of the exercise of his authority that he represents a final authority which he as creature must obey himself and must thereby himself provide an example of obedience if he is to be able credibly to exercise his role as a servant in representing that highest authority to his fellow men.

II

Christ and His Authority

In the revelation of the Old Testament, God no longer allowed himself to be represented in the power of his being (*kabod*, glory) simply by the power of created being (*Seinsmacht*) (cf. Ps 8:6: "Thou hast set him [man] only a little under the heavenly beings, and hast crowned him with glory and awesome splendor"), but emerges himself personally as the electing, loving, and law-giving Lord of the covenant of Israel. This "multiform" order of salvation he crowned in the incarnation of his "Word which bears all things and has authority over all things", which he has "ordained as his Son to be the universal heir over all things" (Heb 1:2–3). In him God reveals his personal innermost being: his most humble love in the world to the point of his putting off of all his own power (Phil 2:6–7), to the point of obedience on the Cross of shame (Phil 2:8), and precisely in all this the breaking forth of the light of his absolute superiority over every power opposed to himself which is not love: "All power in heaven and earth has been given to me" (Mt 28:18). The two-sidedness of this final representation of God the Father by the Son in the world cannot for us be abolished. Christ has come and remains as the one who realizes (by his Cross) God's decision of absolute love for the world (Jn 3:16; Rom 8:3, and so on) and as its "sacrament". As such he "illumines" (as he judges) every man (Jn 1:9), because the Father has given over to him all judgment (Jn 6:22): in an open or hidden process man's fate is decided by the authority of divine love which judges him, which man must recognize as the absolute authority (that is to say, as the absolute power of being [*Seinsmacht*] beyond which there can be no further court of appeal), but which he can also reject.

III

Christ's Solidarity with Supernatural Authority and with the Authority of the Old and New Testament

After the cleansing of the temple the scribes and elders put to Jesus the question of his authority (*Vollmacht*). "Who has given you the right?" He answers with a counter-question, saying that he will only tell them if they first answer his question. "Whence came John's baptism? From heaven or from men?" This poses a dilemma for his questioners: "If we say from heaven then he will reply, why did you then not believe him? But if we say from men, then we must fear the people for they all believe John to be a prophet. So they replied to Jesus, We do not know. Then he replied to them, Then no more shall I tell you in whose authority I act" (Mt 21:23–7).

That means in the first place that Jesus declares his solidarity with the authority of the forerunner, which most evidently came from heaven; and since the Baptist is the last and greatest of the prophets, he thus declares his solidarity with all the figures of the Old Covenant, in whom God has allowed his authority to take concrete form: Moses, David, the prophets, and so on. All these men found God's authority to be a heavy burden. The prophet is existentially dispossessed by the word of God, he must serve him with his whole existence and on occasion in the face of the opposition of all his hearers (Jeremiah). But in this sense, too, Jesus declares his solidarity with his forerunners, "for it cannot be that a prophet should perish except in Jerusalem", which, as it were, professionally "stones" the messengers of God (Lk 13:33–4; for the Baptist: Mk 1:14). By giving divine authority to his Church, to Peter, to the twelve and to those to whom they would subsequently delegate, Jesus again declares his solidarity with their authority: "As the Father sends me, so send I you" (Jn 20:21); "He who hears you, hears me; he who rejects you, rejects me, and he who rejects me, rejects him who sent me" (Lk 10:16).

Three things should be noticed about Jesus' delegation of his authority to the Church: (1) All the important texts are concerned primarily with the authority ("the power of the keys") of forgiving sins, which was the primary office of the Redeemer (Mt 16:19; 18:21ff.; Jn 20:22f.). (2) Peter can only assume the "burden of Christ" by himself, like the good shepherd, laying down his life for his sheep (Jn 21:18f.), just as it is said of all the other bearers of office within the Church that they will meet with persecution, rejection, and death (Mt 10; Jn 15–16); Paul is himself the supreme example of Christ's suffering and of the humiliations of the bearers of authority within the Church. (3) Because, however, all Christ's disciples are directly baptized into his death and Resurrection and in the Eucharist receive a direct share in his total existence, becoming one body with him, they also all receive a share in his authority by which he represents God the Father in the Holy Spirit to the world: they all receive the Holy Spirit who sanctifies them and sends them out into the world (Acts 2:17); from all is demanded the witness of their life (to the point of martyrdom); all must expressly or at least in their disposition preach Christ; all have not only the right but, as Christians, a strict duty with God in Christ to forgive their neighbor his sins ("Our Father", Mt 5:24; 18:23ff.); all can in principle baptize, husbands and wives can give to each other the sacramental blessing of marriage, all are authorized to share in the celebration of the Eucharist, and so on. Thus the presence in the Church of Christ's authority can again only be understood in an analogous sense, a sense which in the Catholic realm can never be turned into a matter of strict identity: an analogy between the authority of the people of the Church in their totality (*all* are laymen, belong to the *laos hagios*, to the holy people!) and the authority of those who by Christ are endowed with particular authority among the people (in the historical handing over of authority to the college of the apostles united in the primacy of Peter), an analogy in which the presence of the authority of God in Christ is made concrete (incarnate) for the people in their differentiation.

This analogy to which Scripture so clearly bears witness, and which in its uniqueness always threatens to elude our grasp (is priestly authority really "from heavven", or is it not "from men", that is to say, merely delegation by a democratically conceived Church?), causes confusion today among a large part of the younger clergy who give to the urgent question about the ultimate origin of their own authority the answer of despair, "we do not know." And thus the clear view of the authority of Christ in all its concreteness is lost to the Church of today; we no longer hear Christ's answer, because we cast doubt on his solidarity with the authority of the Church; by relativizing the second, we spiritualize the first.

The difficulty in relation to the authority of the

Church is that, on the one hand, it must at the very least be an image and continuation of Christ's office, and, on the other hand, it can under no circumstances measure up to that office. For only Christ can be priest and sacrifice in identity for the sins of the world as a whole. But Peter received the promise (and Christ prayed for him in this respect: Lk 22:32) that he, at least substantially, could bring into unity his office and his loving offering of his life (Jn 21:15f., 18f.). Consequently, the first letter ascribed to Peter strictly forbids all his "fellow elders" to feed their flocks from a sense of "compulsion", out of "a seeking for gain" or as "despotic rulers"; only when it is exercised in humble love is Christian authority (in the discipleship of Christ) credible at all and bearable to the people. Here the old Catholic axiom is found in its most perfect form: *Gratia supponit naturam*. The law which is found in one way on a natural level becomes supremely true on a higher, supernatural level; supremely so because here it is no longer a matter simply of the servant's representation of the majesty of God but of the representation of crucified love in which all divine majesty finds in the New Testament its definitive form of appearance. The authority of the Church must again and again submit to humiliation, as indeed Christ repeatedly humiliated Peter; it must also understand that it can function only within the analogy of the total authority of the people of the Church, or, to put it in modern and concrete terms, in a continual dialogue between the whole Church and the Church leadership (the bishops in collegiality and their head, the Pope); the "infallibility", or rather "the right sense of direction", lies both in the "sense of the believers" of the generality of the Church (to which individual groups may not lay claim for themselves) and in the general college of the bishops and in the head which, as it were, sums up and epitomizes them, but which none the less is only "head" *of* and *for* and *with* something.

IV

A Model: "The Exercises"

The Ignatian *Exercises* are a means of introducing a Christian by way of evangelical "repentance" (First Week) into a life of personal discipleship of Christ and of rehearsing him in that life (Second to Fourth Week), and this essentially within the Catholic Church. This then leads to his choice of a place (or of a state of life) within this Church and his training in conforming with the "mind of the Church" (nos. 352ff.). In accordance with the New Testament, however, it is only the Church herself which can introduce men into the discipleship of Christ and into her own mind, just as also the Bible is a book of the Church (composed in her, put together by her in the formation of the Canon, by her alone authentically understood and expounded). And consequently someone has to be appointed to lead men along this way into the innermost heart of Christ's mind and of the mind of the Church—someone appointed by the Church to represent her, who has "to give" the Exercises. His task is not only and principally to present the "points for meditation", but he must possess experience and authority in the "discernment of spirits" (nos. 6–10; 313–36), of the spirits which will unfailingly be aroused on this way into the heart of the divine revelation. Such spirits are by nature opposed to each other: the spirit of Christ and the spirit of Anti-Christ (nos. 136–48), the spirit, on the one hand, of "humble service", on the other hand, of "worldly honor" and of "overweening pride", and the man who wishes to find entry into the heart of the Christian mystery will not succeed in finding his way between these spirits without the help of the Church. The introductory authority of the one who gives the exercises is intended however—because it is an educational one—from the very start to tend to make itself transparent, superfluous, to mediate the immediacy between God and the soul, is intended "to remain in the middle like the pivot of a pair of scales and so to allow the creator to act immediately on his creature and the creature on his creator" (no. 15). But from a Christian point of view this immediacy is never something which could dispense with Christ and the Church (for Ignatius, the Church is always very close to Mary): for precisely the Church (Mary) is a permanent mediator to Christ, and Christ permanently mediates to the Father. Thus, theologically speaking, on the basis of the Exercises, one can distinguish three levels of authority.

1. The one who is being introduced learns, under the guidance of the authority of the one giving the Exercises, who represents concretely the authority of the Church, "at the knees of mother Church" (Claudel), what it means in reality to be a Christian. He must in the first

place "believe" the Church, that things are as she says, in a manner analogous to the way every child "believes" his mother, every pupil "believes" his teacher, before he learns insight itself.

2. But this obedience to the Church gives place in the Christian realm not to a more or less autonomous knowledge but to the belief of the Church herself; as he learns the "mind of the Church", the believer identifies more and more deeply with the act of faith in the revelation of God in Christ which as such constitutes the Church. Christ is the authority in the Church which can never be surpassed. But he does not exercise his authority one-sidedly as the exalted, law-giving, judging Christ, but as *the* appearance of God who is exalted only in humiliation, legislates only in love, and judges only as he forgives.

3. It is for this reason that discipleship of Christ is possible for the Church (for otherwise all that would be achieved would be "subjection to Christ"): because Christ himself as man is always both the humiliated and the exalted one, who can be both in the unity of his obedient love for the Father, for "the Father is greater than I." God the Father has acted in Jesus Christ so definitively toward the world that he has at the same time laid open in him the inmost parts of his heart, his trinitarian love, and has given him an obedience to authority (which reveals this love in the event of his bearing the sin of the world) which enables him, as he abandons and transcends all the desires of his own will, all his own insights, to give himself in death

totally into the hands of God (who "abandons" him, who disappears, who "dies"). It is the task of the conductor of the Exercises to lead men into this mystery at the heart of the Christian faith (in the Third Week, which remains decisive, cf. nos. 196, 98, 147, 167,), a task he shares with the Church herself, which knows no higher object of adoration than this self-representation of eternal love (compare the introductory prayer: *Anima Christi*).

Paul and John, the concluding interpreters of the Christian mystery, see the freedom and adulthood of Christians in the fact that they have been grasped by this mystery and that they live out of it: that they have died and are risen with Christ, that they allow themselves to be led by his Spirit. External Church authority, rightly exercised, can properly only *recall* the individual to that which he from the very depths of his heart has always "known" (1 Jn 2:27f.) in so far as he himself *is* the internal Church—the Church of the saints and of Mary, the Church of faith, love, and hope.

Our Shared Responsibility

Everyone who is familiar with the founding documents of Christianity knows that in the churches (which together are the one Church of Jesus Christ) all are called actively to share responsibility with one another and that the serving officers of the Church with their authority are instituted with the purpose of arousing this shared responsibility of all and not, for example, with the intention of substituting themselves for it. The offices are there in order to train the saints (this means all the baptized) for the execution of their service, for building up the body of Christ.

> For we are no longer to be immature children, tossed to and fro and carried about with every wind of doctrine by the deceitful ways of men ... no, we are to give expression to the truth by our loving and to allow everything to grow up to him who is the head, to Christ. By him the whole body is joined together and held firmly together by each individual member which has to perform a particular service according to the role which is appropriate to every individual part and in this manner the growth of the body occurs until the point when it has built itself up in love (Eph 4:14–16).

It would not be possible to give stronger expression to the element of shared responsibility in the Church, to its indispensability. Ultimately the serving offices of the Church with their authority are only prompters to ensure that this self-building-up of the whole Church occurs as a result of the proper functioning of all her members: in a growth "from below" and "from without" which presupposes a single "from above", namely, of the head who is Christ, who is the only reason why there is a body of the Church at all, who however makes use of each individual member and his particular task and mission in the ordering and growth of the body.

It should be noticed that neither here nor anywhere else have we equated "shared responsibility" with "authority". The authority which Christ institutes in his Church belongs to individuals and comes indeed from him and not from the total complex of the Church; this authority is exercised as a service in order to activate the shared responsibility of all. It cannot relieve men of the burden of such responsibility, but it must heap it on them and maintain it. But, equally, it has in no sense taken out a lease on Christian truth with the consequence that the others would simply have to buy truth from it (and would in such a case rather refrain from such transactions), for the dogmatic and theoretical truth which is put forward with authority in the Church and "held up to men to believe" is only the one-half of Christian truth which appears in its totality only when it is done in love by all her members. The dogmatic, theoretical form of Christian truth certainly belongs in a special way to the serving offices (the list here gives "apostles", "prophets", "evangelists", "shepherds", "teachers"; Eph 4:11); but, equally, such a form of truth exists to serve the members of the Church whose task is to give living and existential expression to it—that is to say, Christian expression—in the exercise of love. It is only in this realization that dogmatic truth becomes Christian in the full sense, namely, conformed to Christ, for Christ referred to himself as "truth" for the very reason that he in his "life" did the truth and in so doing became for us the "way".

Once one has understood this structure it becomes impossible to play off orthodoxy and orthopraxis the one against the other. For, if it is certain that no dogmatic theology produced by the theologians and no catechizing by pastors and catechists, no orthodoxy of any Christian can properly be called Christian unless it achieves the aim of its service, namely, practice, it is equally certain that the body of the Church in the shared responsibility of all her members simply cannot build itself up in accordance with right practice if it has no conception of the overall plan and direction of such growth. Since this goal transcends the purely human, the practical Christian cannot simply discover it in himself but must, particularly if he is to exercise his own judgment responsibly and correctly, always be able to take his bearings by the "right faith" as it is held up to him at any particular time. Right practice is certainly the normative form of Christian truth vis-à-vis the world—"if you love one another then all will know that you are my disciples" (Jn 13:35)—but right practice itself requires an inner norm which it accepts as a point from which it can take its bearings; otherwise it will very quickly equate itself with the truth, equate love of God with love of men, and allow God to be subsumed in man. And that would be the end of Christianity.

Nor is there any use appealing against such considerations to the Holy Spirit who dwells in all the members of the Church, who is powerful enough to guide the individual in his right action without any truth being proclaimed officially. Just as it is true that without such guidance of the members there could in no way be a Church animated from within, so too it is true that the Holy Spirit can nowhere be divided from Jesus Christ, can nowhere be relatively opposed to him; it is Christ who has promised and given to his Church the Spirit, and the Spirit leads us into all truth by expounding to us the truth of Christ (Jn 16:13f.). But it is also Christ who has given to his Church the ministerial office and endowed it with its authority: "Whoever hears you, hears me; whoever despises you, despises me; whoever despises me, despises him who sent me" (Lk 10:16). For our purposes we can disregard the question of whether these words were spoken only to the apostles or also to the bearers of office subsequently in the Church (the latter is evident); we could restrict the reference of the saying simply to the authority of Scripture (although it is spoken to men who are alive and speaking): in any case what is meant is some authority which points to the truth other than the internal voice of the Holy Spirit in the individually acting Christian. Both, the voice of proclamation and the internal spirit, must ring out together, must complement one another, must point to each other. Authority and the shared responsibility of all can only be two poles of the one Church of Christ, which further and mutually strengthen each other.

It is here that we encounter all the questions which today test the Church to the breaking point. The question of the "reception" by the people of the Church or, alternatively, of the non-reception or contestation of what is propounded by the teaching and pastoral office of the Church. The question of whether and to what extent the Holy Spirit speaks as *Vox Populi Dei* and the question of whether and to what extent the serving office of the Church must listen to this voice and obey it. The fundamental solution of these questions—and we cannot offer here any more than that—lies in what we have already said. What must be excluded is the claim to normativeness of a purely practical Christian truth, which despises any attempt to refer back to the content of faith formulated in Scripture, tradition, and the teaching office of the Church, and similarly we shall have to exclude the claim of a purely theoretical formulation of faith to represent the whole Christian truth, for such a claim would mean that the serving office of the Church had forgotten its serving function and was laying claim to dictatorial power with reference to Christian life. Both, theory and practice, are together dependent on their common higher origin: it is as together they look up toward this origin that they gain their true and proper function and at the same time their true interplay. This is a delicately balanced matter which never achieves true balance definitively, for that is something which has to be discovered anew in every age.

If we are to speak of the "reception" by the "base" of the "apex" in its exercise of its leadership, then such a reception can only be legitimate if the base which is the realm of shared responsibility does not for that reason also demand shared authority with the apex and, further, if this shared responsibility has its roots in an insight into things which is inspired by the same Holy Spirit which forms the whole Church as the spirit of Jesus Christ and of the gospel. If we accept that the "apex" leads the people of God according to certain aspects of the Christian revelation, which however are selected one-sidedly or which are not sufficiently adapted to the circumstances of the time, then it is incumbent on the base with its shared responsibility, the base which in the Holy Spirit, in its knowledge of gospel and tradition has its own immediate access to the sources, to point out that which is lacking or incongruous. It is this, and this alone, which justifies contestation within the Church. Under no circumstances can the base bypass the function of the serving office and design for itself a gospel and corresponding program of action which seems suitable to it and attempt to follow it. The Church cannot exist without the ministerial function which has been given and—even if one wanted to reduce its role and sphere of operation to a minimum—could not exist without the spiritual canon of a clearly defined and in no sense vague primitive Christian belief, such as the Early Church set down in her writings. If one simply chooses individual aspects of this formulated faith and leaves others aside, then one arrives at the state of pluralism which today is advocated by many who, though admitting its novelty, assert its inevitability. But such pluralism in fact negates and destroys the innermost nature of the Church. And this both theoretically and practically: the former, because in such a case shared responsibility is equated with instituted authority in such a way that the group or the individual can set himself up as an authentic interpreter of the revelation, setting forward an interpretation which no longer needs to harmonize with that of other groups or individuals; the latter, because the Church no longer consists in the common building up of the body in the love of all members, through which alone "everything can grow up into him who is the head", but rather this "everything", which now comprises both worldly and political circumstances, grows on toward some point in which, so we are led to believe, it will flourish by virtue of Christian impulses, in which, so we are again given to believe, the mentality of Jesus will reign, but in which the *Catholica* will no longer be encountered. This is to say that the problem of the base and its "reception" and "contestation" cannot be resolved except in a dialogue with an apex which is recognized as an authority, in a dialogue which can be difficult, because the apex appears not to wish to listen to what is spoken charismatically by the base, which however, if conducted properly, will produce the right results at the given time (as the life and work of the teacher of the Church, Catherine of Siena, can show in an exemplary manner). Such a dialogue, even if it is fierce, is conducted properly when it is pursued in the love of a common Lord. But if one side or the other sins against love (and that also includes love for the Church as she is structured by Christ, which is to say, therefore, love for the ministerial office), then such imperiousness will never establish its claim to be charismatic.

At this point we should say something about the so-called "sense of faith" of the whole Church (*sensus fidelium*) and its "infallibility", something which raises very considerable problems, because it can in no wise claim such infallibility in a democratic, numerical sense, but only in a qualitative, pneumatic sense, which is all the more easily forgotten, the more the mass of the faithful can be manipulated mechanically by the mass-media and mechanical statistics. It is laughable to take a vote about truths of faith. In a Church which is essentially the "little flock" it is not the majority which is right; it never has been, and today it is so less than ever. Those believers are right whose sense of belief is deep, living, comprehensive, close to the sources, those who pray and give themselves, whose inner ear is open to the Spirit. They are perhaps few and perhaps quite other people than one would assume. They are certainly not those who demagogically challenge the mass of the faithful to take up their stance against the serving office of the Church on the basis of their sense of faith. For the sense of faith is indeed really the sense of *faith* and not some "instinct" or other for things which are in the air and which according to the popular view ought to be happening now; the sense of *faith* does mean, however, that the world ought to be moved by the total, unwished for, offensive, if you like revolutionary initiative and engagement of Christians in a way which corresponds to the gospel of the love of the triune God toward men and toward mankind, the gospel of the solidarity of Jesus with sinners and with the poor which reaches its climax in the Cross and triumphs in the Resurrection. Even today, away from the bustle of the great theological fairground, there is an untold amount of true evangelical and Christian zeal for the cause of the poor, of the lowly, and of the offended. And yet this does not lead to an attack—supposedly inspired by the same zealous enthusiasm—on the serving offices of the Church which attempt as best they can to fulfil their task, nor to the attempt to isolate them from the community of the Church. It is precisely in view of such results that the true sense of faith becomes mistrustful and pricks up its ears. It knows that something is not quite right here.

On the other hand, we must say something about the situation of the "apex". Nobody can deny that the rejection of the base's exercise of its shared responsibility—a rejection the grounds for which often have hidden roots in a confusion between service and the exercise of power (understood in some measure in a worldly manner) where the office of the Church was concerned—has often, and perhaps to an increasing extent, obscured the nature of that office. The measure of such obscuring is to be read off from the way in which the dialogue between the office and the people of God with their shared responsibility has dried up, from the way in which theoretical theological definition has been over-valued and the verification of the Christian truth in practice has been misunderstood, from the way in which the circulation of the blood through all members of the body of Christ has been slowed down and can lead to highly dangerous thrombosis. And so the present state of the Church demands that the office of the Church should listen not only to what comes from "above", from the Lord of the Church who is the Spirit, but equally to what comes from "below", where the same Spirit of the same Lord is at work, with the purpose not only of getting the dialogue and the circulation going again but with the purpose within all this of distinguishing that which in the voices from "below" corresponds to that which is demanded from "above", a distinction which is in no sense easy to make. The history of the Church can provide examples of both extremes: cases where the true balance of faith was predominantly upheld by the sense of faith of the Christian people, in opposition to a wavering or disunited episcopacy (cf. Newman's Rambler affair and his exemplification of this in terms of fourth-century Arianism), or cases where the faith had to be saved against the weight of an oppressive majority by a few (Athanasius, Maximus the Confessor) who had to go to the point of martyrdom. Such a situation cannot be mastered either by a "soft line" or by a "hard front", for both approaches ultimately spring from diplomatic considerations and are, as programs of action, equally false. There is such a thing as a cowardly readiness to make concessions and also an unintelligent stubbornness; both spring from disobedience to the Holy Spirit. The cowardice takes refuge behind the principle of the shared responsibility of all in the Church and hands over the reins which it ought to keep in its own hands. The stubbornness misunderstands the blowing of the Spirit in the true members of the body and wishes to make all the decisions itself. To avoid the ditches on either side and keep to the middle of the road is an art which surpasses the strength of an individual and which can force him into a state of resignation. It is here that the shared responsibility of all who think in accordance with the mind of the Church has a great and delicate task, which can only be exercised in a spirit of respect and reticence. It means that, where the serving office of the Church is concerned, one must behave in such a manner that it neither is forced into either of the extremes nor loses the courage to hold to the middle path. Such action, however, is only possible when it is inspired by a loving faithfulness which is as far on the one side from a kind of condescending goodwill ("the poor Pope means so well, but ...") as it is on the other from an ultra-montane papolatry which sets up the serving office above the Church ("For Pope and Church"—what an incredible lack of thought is betrayed by that motto!). The Christian laity has today a fundamental responsibility for the possibility of the proper exercise of the serving office, alongside all its other responsibilities in parish and diocese, in the world of today and tomorrow. Such a wealth of responsibilities can only be borne and carried out on the basis of a calm and well-centered view of the Catholic faith as a whole, a view which can be given to the individual only in humility and in his inner openness in prayer. It is then that he discovers again and again that things which he had believed to be clear and indisputable have again to be thought through and to be placed within the greater overall complex of the gospel. If he had previously thought of himself as being like the Pauline "strong brother" over against the weaker brothers, now he is no longer sure if he himself does not perhaps (precisely because he thought himself so strong) belong to the weak. Yet if, as he becomes weak, he holds on to his shared responsibility, then that other saying of Paul will be true of him: "If I am weak, then I am strong."

The Pope Today

> If anyone says that the Roman Pontiff has only an office of inspection or direction and not full and sovereign power of jurisdiction over the whole Church, not only concerning matters of faith and morals, but also concerning matters of discipline and of the government of the Church, or that he only has the major part and not the plenitude of his supreme power both over all Churches without exception and over all pastors and faithful without exception, let him be anathema.

These words form the conclusion of the third chapter of the constitution adopted in the course of the fourth session of the twentieth ecumenical council, the First Vatican Council, which here expresses itself with the greatest solemnity. It is astonishing to reflect that for a century a man has been invested with such power and has yet not broken under his burden. One is less astonished at the tempest which has finally been unleashed against him. Quite evidently its cause is not to be sought in a personality which has been too convinced of his own inspiration or who has not given enough attention to the counselors who surround him; the storm has been building up for a long time, the whole edifice was mined. If one closely examines—not without the sensation of terror—this old text of a century ago, one can see the cracks in the supporting piers, cracks due to basic errors

The reader should Keep in mind that this book was first published in 1971.

in the design, and one is filled with a sense of fear for every vehicle which one can see during that century driving across this bridge of San Luis Rey. As if he had sensed the danger, Pope John the Good governed with as little reference as possible to the threatening text, never seeking a head-on confrontation, till the point where he saw himself no longer able to resist the pressures of those around him and called a new council. The Second Vatican Council did not annul the first; it confirmed it; but it brought in all the additions and modifications necessary to establish an overall equilibrium. One might be tempted to believe that this manner of proceeding proves that the preceding council had been profoundly mistaken, that it finished by refuting itself in its own consequences. Indeed, this seems so evident to some that for them it has become superfluous to ask whether councils may not be terribly mistaken even in their solemn proclamation. One then has to have recourse to historical and sociological explanations which go back more or less far along the course of history—taking as one's starting point the reform of Luther, of Cluny, or even indeed the Constantinian era—in order to find attenuating circumstances for this massive accident.

But those who offer such well-meaning excuses for the Church put themselves among the ranks of the *terribles simplificateurs*. The drama which is played out between Christ and his Church, which is also played out between the Church and this Peter to whom Jesus has entrusted his heavy keys and whom he has charged with the task of feeding an innumerable flock, seems more complex. Historical inevitabilities cannot get to the heart of the matter. Guilt also always plays its part. How could it be otherwise when a "sinful man" (Lk 5:8) who would much have preferred to have been allowed to go, conscious as he is of his unworthiness, sees himself obliged to remain, to take upon himself a burden even heavier than that which he has feared; when he is forced into contradiction, forced to admit that he, the only one who had three times denied Jesus, loves him "more than the others" (Jn 21:15)? Where Peter is concerned, everything turns out for the best: he succeeds in overcoming his betrayal (which was only the last of a series of embarrassing misunderstandings about the real significance of Christ's existence). In tears he finally replies as he should to the paradoxical question about the intensity of his love; and now we see him almost as in a fairytale, set on a gold throne from which he can govern the Church in an acceptable manner precisely because he is a man who knows his own weakness. But each of his "successors" will also have to go through the whole drama, starting at the beginning. And for them the contradictions will be redoubled, for if Peter only received his office after he had given the express assurance "Yes, Lord, you know that I love you", how might his successors succeed to the same charge and exercise the office without giving the same assurance? Let us not insist on the history of those contradictions which, as a result of human ambition, have darkened the figure of certain of them. Let us rather turn our attention to another point: it is always easy for those who exercise a particular function to delegate their ultimate responsibility to a higher power. One battery is charged up to such an extent that the other lamps need to give off less light and warmth. Whatever the complex and sometimes highly obscure motives may have been of those who in 1870 concentrated in the hands of the Roman Pontiff this plenitude of power—in spite of the warnings of many men more far-sighted and more concerned for the future—if one looks at the matter objectively, what happened was in any case that people exercising a ministerial function did not hesitate to discharge themselves with docility, and even with a certain haste, of a part of their responsibilities. It is to this defective attitude—adopted by the "successors" of the apostles toward the "successors" of Peter—to which attention must once and for all be drawn, for it is one of the causes of the internal crisis which today shakes the Church. I do not want to say by this that the function which was then attributed to the Pope does not belong to him "by right" (and consequently that the First Vatican Council was "mistaken"), although its formulation in such isolation totally lacks equilibrium; I would like simply to point out that this episode, where one sees men loading on another man such a burden, can *also* be the revelation of a culpable mistake. But who would feel capable of untangling such an intricate problem when all we can see is the confusion, without being able to perceive the line of the individual thread? Light comes from elsewhere. Having established Peter in his office ("Feed my sheep"), the Lord continues without break: "In truth, in very truth, I tell you when you were young you girded yourself and went where you would; but when you are old you will stretch out your hand and another will gird you and lead you where you would not." By this he indicated the manner of death by which Peter was to glorify God. Having said this, he said to him, "Follow me" (Jn 21:18ff.). This prophecy takes us beyond a double contradiction (that the one who strains to break away is compelled to become a fisher of men and that the threefold traitor is compelled to confess that he loves the one he has betrayed more than the rest), even takes us beyond the double abuse which his successors will make of his office (that they themselves will use the office of the good shepherd to concentrate power in their own hands and that other shepherds, successors of the apostles, will shift their own authority and power onto the shoulders of Peter). Over and above such contingencies, the prophecy proclaims a discipleship which will lead to the Cross. To the Cross which is seen expressly as discipleship of Christ. Such a cross means, above all, shame and derision ("let him come down now!" "let him save himself!") and abandonment by God; it means taking one's stand in, or rather hanging and being cast out into, the place of the outcasts. At this ultimate point, as he is nailed between heaven and earth, the question of who is responsible for the crime is quite simply no longer asked. Jesus on the Cross no longer distinguishes between the guilt of others and his own (lack of) guilt; he bears the guilt, exposing it publicly to men (the inscription on the Cross) and to the darkened heaven. He does not want to know who is guilty and who is not. For those who pass sentence of death, but also for God who conceived this plan of reconciliation, he simply gets his deserts according to divine and human law.

Peter is led where he does not wish to go (Jesus himself longed with his whole soul to go there and yet could not will it—that would have been inhuman—but gave himself up to the will of the Father), and even the papacy today is led where it does not want to go. But it is precisely this way which completes the promise made to Peter. It not only gives him the final blessing, but it also makes clear what "authority" really means in such an office; it makes clear what position one must occupy if one is to exercise such authority properly. The lowest place, which is where, by definition, the "servus servorum" must stand, the place of final contempt and insult, the rubbish-heap on which one is "a worm and no longer a man", this place which no man willingly occupies, is precisely the place where the office which he exercises may at last regain the greatest possible respect and credibility. For it is in this place that it becomes clear what Paul means when he says that "the weapons with which we fight are not of the flesh but are truly powerful", it becomes clear why he can claim with them "to tear down the bulwarks, destroy false arguments and raze to the ground every fortress set up against the knowledge of God" (2 Cor 10:4f.). He knows in what currency such spiritual power has to be paid for: "For this reason I am content with weaknesses, with insults, with hardships, with persecution and fears for Christ's sake, for if I am weak, then I am strong" (2 Cor 12:10). And finally, to make all things quite clear, "we rejoice when we are weak and you are strong" (2 Cor 13:9); for this is the meaning of the authority of the ministerial office, which is a spiritual, Christian power only to be exercised as one undergoes humiliation oneself, only to be exercised for the benefit of others who by it may become strong—which, however, ultimately means for them too that they must become weak, that they must be crucified with Christ, that they must share in bearing the guilt of all.

This image of the crucified Lord appears clearly and brightly in the Church behind the Iron Curtain, which is beaten and tortured, which perishes in the concentration camps, but it is equally visible in the man of the Vatican who finds himself the subject of so much scorn and derision. External acts of consolation ("For Pope and Church", and so on) may be as touching as Veronica's action in wiping our Lord's face with a cloth, but they are for the most part inspired by old messianic ideals; "O daughters of Jerusalem, weep for yourselves and for your children." In the process of humiliation it is necessary to distinguish between the burdensome responsibilities which are accepted for the wrong reasons (even if in good faith) and that pastoral load which the man who follows in Peter's tracks cannot pass on to other men. The formulations promulgated in such an inflated style by Vatican I will, in a quite different style, retain their truth, a very humble truth, without sparkle or strength, for as long at least as men do not seek spontaneously to take the lowest place.

On the other hand, the loud-mouthed, Christian, mostly clerical rogues who take such pleasure in attacking Rome can study their own physiognomies in the satirical pictures of Bosch and Breughel. They will never be truly in the right even if they themselves imagine that they are angels of truth sent by heaven or by the human race or by the future to the Church, and even if it appears that they again and again receive plausible confirmation of their views by the innumerable faux-pas of the central government of the Church. They have all the laughs on their side. But Peter must have seemed fairly laughable too when he was crucified upside down; it was simply a good joke, simply an allusion to the Rabbi Yod, reducing the tragic opera to the level of a review, turning Bach into jazz, his own juice running down unremittingly into his nostrils and, as a motto over his toes, the inscription in all languages of the world: *summus pontifex christianorum*. The hierarchical Church standing on her head, held firmly in place by nails as a precautionary measure lest she should bounce up again back onto her feet and continue her old ways of pontificating, promulgating, and excommunicating. For the time being at least an end has been put to all that sort of performance. Distinguished theologians have forbidden her ever to allow such ideas to enter her head again.

Such a crucifixion, upside-down, has its advantages; it avoids any confusion between the two, and yet we are given a mirror image by which we may be reminded of the pure, of that which is upright, in the muddied waters of Christian, all too Christian existence. Here penance is done for sins reaching back into time immemorial, which have heaped up guilt on the system to the point where it tipped over. And the penitent cannot, as it were, shed his solidarity with this guilt; it sticks to him, less because he himself has done it than because it has been handed out to him as a burden which he has as a matter of course to bear. As a part of his office, of his responsibility. Or rather as a weight which has already become heavier than any man even in an official position can bear, so that it is no longer the man who bears the cross but the cross which bears the man. The denigrators, with their all too plausible accusations, assume in this spectacle nameless and changing roles, for the whole story of their guilt is represented here in the guilty man whose fall is accomplished. Woe indeed to us if there is not a point where our common sins are concentrated and become visible, just as the poison circulating in an organism is concentrated at one point and breaks out as an abscess. And therefore blessed the office—whether it is the Pope or the bishops or simple priests who stand firm, or anyone else who feels responsible when people start saying "the Church should do this and that"—which offers itself to fulfil this function, to be the seat of the illness. There is no honor to be won in this role, but if the crowd is to have its fun, a face is needed which one can slap in order to try one's own strength: the oscillation of the needle tells one infallibly how strong one is.[1] And that, too, is a form of infallibility.

[1] An allusion to a game found in the Prater at Vienna—TRANS.

The Priest I Want

I

When one is ill, one goes to the doctor; when one wants to make one's will, one goes to a lawyer, to a specialist. But is there a specialist for God's relationship to me? God is governed by no law in his free condescension to a man—which is not to deny sociologists or psychologists any part of their subject, for what they study is at best the average religious behavior of the "species man" toward a so-called absolute. But nor am I in my uniqueness, as I turn to the unique God, governed by any general law. And so in my relationship with God, which must be determined by God's relationship to me, I am alone; no one can fully understand, can explain or mediate. Just as everyone must die alone, so ultimately everyone also prays alone, must enter into "his chamber" and stand before God in heaven, to understand and to follow God's will for him, precisely for him. "That is the point where no one can take his place."

God's word has become flesh and encounters man, the blind, the lame, the deaf in Jesus Christ. Always as the unique word. The command to follow him is given to the tax-gatherer Levi, not to the others who sit beside him. There is no socio-psychological law which governs Jesus' behavior or the behavior of those who are addressed by him when, freely and uniquely, he lays claim to them. If those who are thus addressed look to the normal laws of human behavior—taking one's farewell, burying one's father, and so on—this proves to be false; then they are "not worthy of him". I cannot force God's word to me and the famous "concrete situation" into a calculus in such a way as to make of them a parallelogram of forces.

Jesus, God's word for me, encounters me in the Church which preserves his word as a lively force, living and actual today. It encounters me in preaching and the sacraments—both a part of the same whole. For example, when I receive the assurance "ego te absolvo a peccatis tuis". It encounters me in the Church in whose fellowship I am to receive the assurance that God's word does not speak to me out of the distant past but speaks with an immediacy and an urgency and a clarity proportionate to the concreteness of my own existence here and now. But does that not mean to say that the Church again becomes a kind of general law which, in her exposition of God's unique will for me, places herself between me and God, claiming on the basis of her perhaps unique socio-psychological experience over the centuries to know better? "In this sort of situation God usually means this or that sort of thing." In that case both God and I would ultimately have been reduced to anonymous factors in a calculus, and if I wanted to discover my own personal destiny I would have to leave such a Church.

And yet, if the Church as the *ecclesia* is the community of those who have been called, if she has been entrusted with the word of God and the keys of the kingdom of heaven, if the Holy Spirit has been bestowed on her by God and by Jesus Christ, the Spirit which as God is in every way as unique as the Father and the Son and which can expound to us the Father's will in the Son with true originality: then why should I not be directed to the Church when I attempt to put my life under the truth of the living God? But which Church, who in the Church can help me? I too am a member of the Church, but I can neither claim for myself the Holy Spirit in all his fulness with which he inspires the Church, nor refer to myself wholeheartedly as a "good Christian" who lives close to the heart of the Church and who by osmosis communicates with her innermost mind. Rather I know, if I am honest, all too well how far I fall short of the demands of God and how ready I am to reduce these demands to my own: "That is just the way men are." "Taking a broad view, and taking into account my natural dispositions, one can scarcely demand any more from me."

II

What we have said so far seems to portray the position of the man looking for help as very difficult and indeed dismal. Can the demands which I make be satisfied by any man? He would have to help me to enter fully into that relationship with God which is mine alone without reducing that relationship to this-worldly generalities. He would consequently have to know, on the basis of his own unique relationship to God, the true nature of such uniqueness, and at the same time would have to have been given the special task and with it the necessary authority to enable him in the Holy Spirit to make it known to others, to give them the appropriate directions.

That is to say, he needs both the commission and authority from God and the experience in the Spirit: that would entitle him to demand of me, not for himself but for God and for me, things which I do not dare to demand for myself.

This is the first quality that the priest I am looking for would have to have; for he would have to be a priest, or at any rate he would have to have been commissioned and authorized from above, by Christ, to confront me with God's incarnate word in such a manner that I can be sure that it is not I who am making use of it; I have to know that I have not from the very outset emasculated it by psychologizing, interpreting, demythologizing it away to such an extent that it can no longer create in me what it wills. No, what I am looking for is the man who can confront me with it in such a way that I cannot escape its demands, because I meet them in the concrete form of the authority of the Church which, as a serving authority, actualizes the concrete form of the divine authority. It may perhaps be that I have reached the point of being confronted with this demand. But he must also help me to stand firm, not to run away, by sitting it out with me with an unrelenting love. With a terrible love which again and again says to me, "But that is what you really want." With a love for which in one's heart of hearts one gives thanks because it cannot be replaced by anything else. Such a man at certain times is comparable to the angel on the Mount of Olives who gives one strength to enter into the presence of God alone. The power with which this man does this comes indeed from his commission (which contains something of the strength and relentlessness of God), but at the same time from his own strength, which has grown from his own experience of being alone with God. On the basis both of his commission and of his experience he can embody both the relentlessness and the love which are to be found in God's will in such a way that one can no longer and will no longer run away.

If he did not have this experience, then he could not even proclaim God's word from the pulpit, but could at the most be a lifeless echo of what others (for example, Paul) have proclaimed of the word of God in their existence. Even less would he be able to accompany a believer existentially in his existential confrontation with the word of God and to hold him in that confrontation. "If he did not have this experience ...": it may sound then as if he is after all a "specialist", but that will not do. For in that which is in every case unique there can be no "special subjects", no classifications. Even the word "science" must be avoided. One can speak at the most of a certain "wisdom" which the Holy Spirit gives to those who are familiar with his "blowing where he wills". It is true that men have on occasion set out "rules for the discerning of spirits" and have spoken of a "science of the saints"; but such rules, if they are genuine and usable, can only be handed on, on the basis of personal experience within the Church, to those who themselves are looking for such experience, and such "science" is intended as one of the seven gifts of the Holy Spirit and can therefore only be handed on to and understood by those who are attempting in prayer and in the conduct of their lives to enter into the medium of the Spirit.

III

And so, for the man who undertakes the task in the Church of proclaiming officially the word of God which is Christ and of confronting the individual with it in its very particularity, there is no other way of doing this thoroughly and of remaining faithful to one's task than by giving up one's whole existence totally to it. He must identify himself with it; for that is what the apostles did at Jesus' command when they left everything to follow him, not only their possessions and their parental home, but also wife and children. Of course the abandonment of material possessions, in order to offer one's life to the word of God, is only the starting point; it only becomes a criterion for the "priest I want" if this first step becomes a sustained form of life. From a worldly point of view such a form of life is and must remain senseless, because it cannot be re-interpreted in terms of any sociological state of life; and all attempts to give ecclesiastical status to such a state of life by drawing on parallels in paganism or in Judaism always remained questionable. A priest must always be prepared for the possibility of again being excluded from the organization of society. Here, if anywhere, Augustine's saying is true that whoever builds his life on Christ does not stand but hangs or "stands above himself". And it is only through God in Christ that we receive the guarantee that whoever leaves everything "for my sake and for the sake of the gospel" does not fall into the void, does not fall between two stools, but (as he hangs) will be borne along in his impossible existence. That such a person can have no sort of "self-understanding" must be clear; he has given up interpreting himself, so that he may be interpreted by God alone. He does not judge himself but holds himself open to God's direction, who knows him and judges him aright. It is the fact that he has abandoned his self-understanding that makes him the priest I want, one who with his existence can become for me a word and a light of God. The abandonment of existence with its own light is the thing that alone provides the guarantee of the essential humility which makes a man transparent for a life other than his own, which shines forth with a light which does not interest the man who has abandoned himself, on which he does not reflect, which he does not cultivate. The fire which burns in the truly humble man is that of love for God and for his incarnate word; it does not have its focus in the man himself but in the object of his love and is fanned by the idea that love, God, is not loved in the world, that it is despised or that men take offense at its weakness. "When men take offense, must I not burn?" Humility and zeal grow together.

The humble priest will not be tempted to offer me anything other than the word of God for me; the zealous priest will not tolerate my attempts to slide away from this word. He will make me stick to my last, and I can easily accuse him of intruding and interfering; but what intrudes and interferes in truth is only the word of God itself. If I find the one I want, then I cannot reasonably object if he behaves toward me with a confidence which is not appropriate in a man. As if he ought only to offer suggestions about the general direction in which my way toward God might run, ought to leave it to me and to my personal conscience to test such suggestions, to accept them or to reject them. His commission leaves him no room for false modesty, once assuming that he has abandoned his own existence in accepting his authority. If this is not the case, then he will only represent authority in the Church partially and in a distorted manner. But where there is genuine transparency or self-giving stemming from prayer in union with God, from humility which is itself a readiness to pass on what it has received, then the miracle can occur that in the Holy Spirit within the Church I receive true instruction from God, in such a way that, however uncomfortable it may be, I cannot afford to neglect it. The grace of confidence is given only to the one who in his simplicity does not force *himself* upon men. He may rejoice with those who rejoice, mourn with those who mourn, but in no case is he allowed to falter with those who are faltering and uncertain simply on the grounds of solidarity with them. His experience with God has taught him what the darkness is like in which one can only find one's way by holding close to the walls, walls which sometimes in the darkness are no longer there, so that one fumbles around and finds no support; such experience is given to the priest in order that in humility he may lend strength to the brother with whom he watches.

IV

We have just spoken of a "miracle". A good priest is always a miracle of grace. More often it happens that the Churches have to suffer under those who have not fulfilled their vocation. There are too many who, as they stand at their lecture desks or in their pulpits, imagine that they are of the light; one must avoid them. Ostensibly they speak about God, but it is to themselves they refer; God does not appear. Whether they declare him to be dead or alive, whether they claim to know too little or too much about him, is almost irrelevant. There are the others who dream up methods of attracting people's attention to themselves; they have language problems; they think that, if only people could suddenly hear them speaking in their worldly language about God, that they would again listen and perhaps understand a little; as it were, a stage-managed Pentecost miracle. Among their own ranks they are much admired, but by those whom they would win over they are despised. For they have nothing to say to them. And there are the deserters who were called to the form of life of Jesus Christ but became afraid that they were no longer finding a response among men, who side-stepped the real issue and allowed love of God to be submerged in love of one's neighbor. And so they have nothing more to proclaim and have no commission or authority to demand of men anything else than that which is already contained in their self-understanding. They simply disappear in the anonymity of the human. And finally there are those fearful spirits who, as the old inherited forms crumble away, cling all the more desperately to those which remain. They know indeed that the Spirit becomes incarnate in historical forms, but they have not the freedom to allow him to blow where he will, and so they confuse him with the forms. Their very denials lend credence to the positions which are fast overtaking them.

The miracle for which one is looking would indeed be nothing other than sanctity: sanctity of a man who in God has become so unimportant to himself that for him only God still counts. Who he himself is, is no longer a matter of any concern to him. And in consequence he is as ordinary and as nourishing as a loaf of bread from which everyone can break off a piece. The manner in which he distributes himself merges into the manner in which God's word distributes itself in bread and wine. Such a man knows too how one breaks and expounds God's word. He will not, like the preacher of today, send me home from the desert with an indigestible ration of empty phrases about the openness of the Church to the world. And what am I to offer to the hungry around me if not bread? But where am I to find it, if it is not offered to me? How is the Church to go to the world outside herself, if there is no longer anything inside her to be externalized? Or does she merely give voice to her insecurity about her own identity because she has no longer any experience of what her true internal aspect is? This internal aspect is not herself—the Church cannot reflect upon herself—but Christ, her head and her soul through whom the triune God is present in her.

In earlier ages there were monks: in East and West, on Mount Athos, in Clairvaux and in Ranft, in Kiev and Optina. They experienced and knew. They gave instruction. Their light was bread. They came from the innermost parts of the Church to her door, where their experience crystallized into a given word. Perhaps it is not absolutely necessary to cut oneself off from the world in such an external manner in order to come to know the internal aspect of the Church; there is enough loneliness blowing through the empty spaces between men. Only, their emptiness is not filled automatically with this precious content. Even in the hopeless emptiness of the heart of fellow man I find the holy mystery of divine poverty only if I have already sought it, if I already bring it with me, if it has already been disclosed to me. Otherwise the only encounter which occurs is between one emptiness and another, and the word has no power to support but collapses, lifeless and helpless.

In common parlance one calls priests in German the "spiritual ones"—that is to say, in Greek, the *pneumatikoi*, a word which also used to refer to the monks. In Orthodoxy it has for many centuries always been the monastic orders who provided the candidates for the higher echelons of the hierarchy. Spiritual men are those who have experience of the Holy Spirit and who, on the basis of such experience, can recognize and fan the hidden, unrecognized, and trammelled spirit in us, in me. How scarce such spiritual men have become. Should one be satisfied with a spiritual substitute? It is, perhaps, above all psychology which offers some kind of spiritual substitute—which is not to say that a good, humble psychologist cannot be transparent to the Holy Spirit—but its object is the general laws of the human psyche. The spirit by contrast is always unique. The spiritual man must allow the unique Spirit to work through him, in order that he may meet the need of this unique man standing before him. It is not by the activation of medial powers that I may be helped but by the one who is open to the grace of the living God, who in freedom promises me his word of love, which is both benevolent and strict—by the priest whom I want.

We have not forgotten the sacramental grace of the priestly office. This helps him to dispossess himself, but it is not a substitute for such dispossession. The ordained man who does not open himself to such grace will be marked out negatively by it. There is a particular sort of lack of spirituality which only the "spiritual one", the priest who has failed, can exhibit. Stupid, crafty, busy, and imposing. He wants to be heard, he rushes to get on the media. He lies like mildew on the fields of the Church of today. Perhaps their own plight will teach the "spiritual ones" to pray again; meanwhile let us pray for them.

Unmodern Prayer

The Christian who no longer prays must try to find as best he can reasons which excuse him or indeed even justify him. For example: Prayer belongs to a past age of the world; it was principally magic. One asked for the things which one needed; today one sets to work oneself, and that is God's will. Or, prayer belongs at the very best to the Old Testament; in Christ God has become man, and man now should no longer send empty words up to heaven, but with God should descend to his fellow men: active love is not a substitute for prayer, but in a Christian setting is its proper form. Or, if prayer is to bear fruit, it presupposes a world of silence, of nature in which God is present; it presupposes leisure for contemplation; there God indeed may be alive and accessible; in the world of uninterrupted noise, of technology and enforced socialization, there is no room and no time for the luxury of prayer; where it is attempted the lack of success shows that the God of prayer is dead, that the inner well has dried up, and that one is well advised to desist from this exercise. To put the matter more tersely: It is dishonest for me to do what I cannot do.

The Christian stands and falls with prayer. The content of his faith is simply that God has loved him and all men—not only all men anonymously but each one individually, himself included—and that he continues to love them. Israel's election was the beginning: You and no other shall be my partner, said God to the people, and not because you are beautiful or great or powerful, but because I in my unsearchable freedom have chosen you to enter into love, into mutual love with me. A terrifying fate, thus to stand face to face before God. Israel might turn its head away, but its sideways glances were unmasked as the prostitute's leer. Israel is transfixed by a word which has its origins in a groundless freedom: the instruction and wisdom of the Lord. And God vows to himself that his word will not return to himself without bearing the fruit of Israel's answer from the earth (Is 55:10f.). And the people achieved the answer of the liturgical psalms: the song of praise, of thanksgiving, of supplication, of hiding oneself under God's wings. That is good and will and must remain. But in the man Christ the God who elects no longer comes globally to a whole people but—more pressingly than in the prophetic calls—to individuals. You, follow me. The weight of my hand is laid on you, choosing you out, challenging you, making you my servant. The one called leaves everything where it is and follows: he has nothing to fall back on, no reserve in case things turn out wrong. And if he is offered his freedom, then he can only reply, "Lord to whom shall we go, you have the words of eternal life." I have staked my life on your words, which ring out to me from eternity: How then can I deny you your reply? A reply not by deeds of great fecundity, appropriate as such to Christ's commission, performed for men and for the world, but a direct reply as the heart, which has heard itself addressed from eternity as thou, draws itself together and itself replies in formed or soundless words with a "thou!" to the eternal love which chooses it. All the work which the apostles carried out in the world was but the echo spreading out from this most original of "thous" in the heart of the one who was sent. Where is there more personal prayer than in the letters of Paul? Often he takes up the liturgical prayer of the community and blends it into a prayer of his own heart. This not because he has retained manners of prayer from his earlier life as a Pharisee. But the Lord whom he serves is the word of God the Father, the word which was not first spoken into the world at large by the Father's mouth, but the eternal subsisting word which was always from the beginning the praising, grateful answer to the Father, *eucharistia*. Notably in Luke, Jesus prays continually, withdraws to lonely places for personal prayer; his baptism, his transfiguration, the beginning of his passion occur during his prayer (3:21; 5:16; 6:12; 9:18–21; 11:1). In John, Jesus summarizes his whole mission in the "high-priestly prayer" (chap. 17), in which he commends all his work, from his going forth from the Father to his return to him, into his Father's hands. Even in his dying words he is still in dialogue with God.

The Christian of all ages, even of today, is placed into this prayer. He has no excuse, no evasions will be permitted. He may not seek refuge in mere action or simply in the liturgy, or in solidarity with all those who can no longer pray or who know nothing more of prayer.

Not in action. Of course it is true that in earlier ages many men sought relief from the efforts of action in the enjoyment of contemplation as a foretaste of heaven or simply as the easier way of buying off God. (Yet people like John of the Cross or de Foucauld can teach us what an enormous effort and overtaxing of the man's total existence the Christian, *true* way of contemplation is.) It is possible too that the apostles and many of their successors underestimated the active effort which was demanded of them, when they remained gathered in prayer in Jerusalem and only undertook minor apostolic excursions into the surrounding country; then it was Paul who had to show them what true, world-transforming apostolate really is. The fact that today young Christians demand above all a Christian witness through deeds, and indeed deeds which truly change and revolutionize the structures of society, is intelligible and justified when one sees the terrible state of affairs in the world and how, lifeless, crippled, and unimaginatively, we Christians gaze at all the horror and the anguish. Enough of saying "Lord, Lord", the time has come to do the will of God, to put one's hand to the plough. Enough of walking past the beaten and bleeding man, piously saying one's rosary and breviary; the time has come to get down from one's saddle like the Samaritan. To do for the least of the brothers in the underdeveloped countries that which Christ himself reckoned as being done to him. In spite of this—and this is said to conscious Christians—*Christian* action must, if it is to earn this name and be distinguished from this-worldly action, have its roots not simply in human sympathy but farther afield, namely, in the knowledge of and gratitude for God's sympathy on the Cross, and must equally be prepared to go to greater lengths: to the point of suffering, of participating in the Cross. Christian action is a mediating link between the offering of oneself in prayer and the giving of oneself as one abandons oneself completely to God to let him work his will.

Not in the liturgy. For good reasons the Middle Ages built their cathedrals so large that they could never be filled by liturgical acts. Only in an age when man gives up his personal prayer and contents himself with being simply a communal animal in the church can one design churches which are determined purely functionally by the services of the congregation. The restoration of the genuine liturgical congregation by radical reforms of language, text, homilies, by the introduction of dialogical forms as well as by the appropriate reorganization of old and new buildings to accommodate these new forms: all that was both right and important. But, alas, what a welcome alibi it provides for a new clerical *dirigisme,* for a busy clerical activity, which never stops moving the altar around, fumigating churches, buying new vestments for the servers and a thousand other oddments, while all the time it is putting its emphases in the wrong place. As if a break of two minutes after the sermon or after Communion could satisfy man's elementary need of silence in God, of communion from the heart with him! And who can, as he swallows the Host, "realize" what Holy Communion means? Does he not need for that the unfunctional, silent "adoration before the holy of holies" or silent, personal meditation on the holy Scriptures? The clergy, whether old or young, should make no mistake about it: no matter how far the sermon has been worked out by the standards of modern exegesis and of pastoral sociology (at least in those cases where they still find time for such work), if it has not been achieved in personal prayer, they are still offering to their congregation stones instead of bread. And the faithful have a very fine sense for judging whether or not the words of a preacher come from the depths of his personal prayer or ultimately are as flat and as vain as anything they might read in a newspaper. The clergy would do better, if what they want is a "new image" for priests, to ask themselves what the congregation asks of them as its ideal of a priest, by what ideal it measures them, rather than consider what is the most modern fare that they can set before the congregation.

Two things in the Old Testament were superseded by Christ: servitude to the law and the liturgy of the temple. The first was expounded by Paul, the second by the Epistle to the Hebrews. Today everyone welcomes the first, to the point of reaching a kind of Manichaean dualism between law and gospel, which comes however not from the Gospel itself but from Luther and was scorned by Kierkegaard:[1] there is so much "gospel" and "spirit" that there is nothing left of the fulfilling of the law by the gospel! But the second point, namely, that the liturgy of the temple has equally been outmoded, is hardly something you would notice in our present liturgical spring. The very action of hammering out new forms makes one both "pious" and modern at the same time. And yet how uncreative of word and gesture is our age. And consequently, no sooner are forms worked out than they are themselves outmoded, and on all sides people are in danger of becoming disillusioned with all this liturgical magic. And then one supposes there will remain no prayer of any sort, but only political action, as long as the regime allows it. Liturgical prayer must in the Christian sphere be grounded in personal prayer and find

[1] Cf. H. Roos, *Kierkegaard nachkonziliar* (1967), 55ff.

its way back into such prayer. At the core of the liturgical event it is Christ who prays; it is the communion of the true saints, who are always men of prayer, which prays.

Finally: *not a flight into solidarity* with those who do not pray. The latter have established far-reaching theories about why "Modern Man" (which is always written with capitals) can no longer pray, theories which are regarded with admiration by many Christians. Because God is dead. That is the simplest way of looking at it; there is no point in speaking to corpses. Because God is unobjectifiable, uncategorical, and because one should not think of him naïvely as a "thou" who stands over against us, as someone whom one addresses (and consequently it is no wonder if he remains silent). Or more mildly: Because God's will occurs no matter what (for he is absolute will, and it is childish to wish to interfere and to alter that will). Others maintain that they have honestly made the attempt to pray but have only prayed into a void, to a wall; they have not received the slightest trace of an answer, only the uncanny echo of their own voice. The eclipse of the sun; the absence and distance of God which mark out our age. That, so it is said, is the experience of the majority of our brothers: How then should we want to have it better than they do, to experience the "comforts of religion"?

But is it really a question of "comforts"? And not, rather, the assumption of responsibilities? Could any Christian want to pray merely for himself, without including his brothers who do not pray, in his prayer before God? Since Christ prayed and suffered for all, prayer can only be catholic, universal. Can only become a living mouthpiece for all those who are silent before God. Can only offer itself to bear the burdens of all those who are a burden to themselves and perhaps also to God; and if anyone takes it seriously, who knows how seriously he may then be taken by God. It is scarcely of much use to men who are fumbling in the dark if I choose to fumble with them rather than to turn on the flashlight which I am carrying with me. Instead of "shining like the stars in the universe" (Phil 2:15) from the tiny point which I occupy. If many, indeed if all Christians together would shine as best they could, then we would somehow find our way through this moonless night. The only one who shows true solidarity is the one who for the benefit of all contributes what he has (received as a gift).

Such a man will pray out of gratitude to God and out of responsibility for his fellow men. He will not pay a great deal of attention to his own feelings or lack of feelings, to the extent to which he experiences God's presence or absence. Perhaps he will be allowed to feel the absent God of those who do not pray, in order that the latter may catch an intimation of the God who is present. Such things are given within the *communio sanctorum*, which in the widest sense is the community of all those for whom God on the Cross has borne and suffered total abandonment. And that indeed is everyone.

The Veneration of the Holy of Holies

I

The name sounds as outmoded as the thing itself. What can possibly be the point of kneeling for hours in front of a piece of bread—however transubstantiated it may be—and "worshipping"? There are too many objections, quite apart from the emptiness of the minutes which pass by: Bread is for eating, not for looking at or for thinking about, and the presence of Christ is no more limited by church walls than it is by the tabernacle or the monstrance. You can neither imagine Jesus in the room where they celebrated the Last Supper offering the disciples a piece of bread to venerate rather than to eat, nor conceive how he may feel as an object exhibited on the altars of the church. One sees clearly where things—even if very gradually, over centuries—have got onto the wrong track, have moved away from the pneumatic more and more toward the material: the event became static, the process became a state, that which offered itself incomprehensibly became that which was offered in graspable form, that which transcended sight became that which was seen, the presence of the divine was turned into an earthly presence. All that sounds plausible. But perhaps, if we think it through more deeply, we shall not be able to bring it down to such simple formulae. And if we pause to take stock of the counter-movement, is not the impoverishment which it has brought only too evident? Are we not now moving along the arc in the opposite direction toward a pneumatic view of the divine without substance?

Let us begin by considering the expression "holy of holies". It is an expression wrapped in mystery and awe like the Latin *sanctissimum*. Perhaps there is an allusion to an Old Testament notion: the plan of the temple as the seat of the presence of God recognized degrees of sanctity. Only the high priest, once yearly at the feast of atonement, went into the innermost sanctuary, into the holy of holies. Since the incarnation the temple of God, in whom the fulness of the Godhead is pleased to dwell, has become the physical person of Jesus; in the saying "Tear this temple down and I will build it again in three days", Jesus shows himself conscious of this change. He becomes the place of God's presence and of the worship of God. "Woman, believe me, the hour is coming when you will worship the Father neither on this mountain nor in Jerusalem. You worship what you do not know; we worship what we know: for salvation comes from the Jews. But the hour is coming, and is already here, when those who truly worship the Father will worship him in spirit and in truth, for such the Father seeks to worship him" (Jn 4:21–3). And Jesus is not one worshipper among others; he is the supreme worshipper in whom all worship in spirit and truth is concentrated, is made perfect in truth as it is purified, is transformed in the Spirit; in him everything which strives toward the holiness of God, which desires to participate in it, is drawn into and set alight by the fire of the holy of holies.

But why not reserve the phrase "holy of holies" for God the Father in heaven; why use it to refer to the Eucharist of the Son of God? Because it is here that the two flames fall upon each other: the holiness of heaven falling down like fire on the earth, devouring the earthly prayers and sacrifices, and the holiness rising up to heaven of the man who obeys and offers himself and is devoured for the sake of all men, on whom God's pleasure rests and whom God transfigures on the mountain into his uncreated light. It is not possible to conceive of anything more intensive, more devouring, more compelling than this encounter of the two fires which fuse into one. For what is happening here to man? "This is my body which is given for you. This cup is the New Covenant in my blood, which is shed for you." This man is fanned into countless sparks by the fire of God (*non confractus, non divisus*), he is in the state of such abandonment to God that God can distribute him indefinitely, inexhaustibly through all time and space. For it is God the Father who distributes to us the eucharistic Son, and it is God the Spirit who again and again brings about the unutterable multiplication of the unique into that which is universal. But, above all, he who was once given, slain on the Cross, poured out, pierced, will never again take back his gift, his gift of himself. He will never gather into himself his eucharistic fragmentation in order to be at one with himself. Even as the risen Lord he lives as the one who has given himself and has poured himself out. One has here to purge oneself of all mythical pictures of the world which would pin him down to a cosmologically precise place from which he might, as it were, travel to those places, or at least relate himself to those places, where in the celebration of the Mass men commemorate his death and Resurrection. He lives on simply as the bodily Eucharist, as that thanksgiving which he has succeeded in achieving: the gathering in and bearing in himself of the ends of the world in his sacrifice for the glorification of the Father, the sacrifice in which he poured out the grace of the Father to the ends of the world. This is no reason for saying that he has therefore forfeited his true humanity, that he has become a nameless power flowing amorphously through the world. "I have power to lay down my life and to take it again": to be again myself, but from now on only in a permanent state of self-givenness. As the Risen One who shows his wounds to his disciples and who appears to Paul that he may transform him too into an almost eucharistic flame, he is in every way himself; speaking and disposing in every way as majestically, sovereignly, and lovingly as before his death. He is in every way as much as then the center from which men receive their mission and their instruction, grace and judgment. But this center now has both a centrifugal force of radiation and a centripetal force of attraction which draws everything into its spell.

The thought that the eucharistic Lord at the celebration of the Last Supper should, while we think of him, materialize among us from somewhere (but from where?) remains mythical and naïve. But we get into extreme difficulties if we try and speak less naïvely; for, in accordance with our Lord's promise, his Eucharist does indeed occur anew during our celebration. One must, however, attempt to grasp the mystery (which in this-worldly terms is unthinkable) that, although each new entry of this event has its beginnings, it nevertheless has no end. The Lord comes, that is his act; but this is not followed by the act of his going away. We could put it otherwise: the celebration of the Eucharist is a true event, as it were, an inbreaking of eternity into time; but this is not followed by a withdrawal of eternity from time. For eternity has finally met with time and is from now onward permanently in a state of transition into time; and time and place have found in Christ's self-giving "for us", "for all", the means of transcending their limits and thus achieving a universal temporality and spatiality by which we may know that this self-giving is one with the self-giving of the eternal Father and the eternal Spirit. And so the distinction between state and event must be abandoned: the eternal event of the triune love of God, which is at the same time his eternal state, has revealed itself to the world in an unmistakable, unique, historical event in the incarnation, living and dying and rising of Jesus Christ. It is this unique event which has allowed the divine event-state to become an event for the world, "once for all" (*ephapax*), so that every holy Mass proclaims anew this "once for all" of the death of Jesus Christ. Yet it proclaims it in such a way that, while affirming the permanent state of the eucharistic outpouring of the Lord, it again and again emphasizes the original element of his coming at this present moment, of his living, dying, and distributing himself for us men in our world of time and space. *Quoad nos*. For our sakes and toward us. We ourselves are the object of the proclamation when we are allowed to proclaim anew "the death of the Lord till he returns".

And consequently there is such a thing as "spiritual communion", which is not intended to replace sacramental communion but which, as it were, flows out from the latter onto all those who desire to share in the great banquet which the Father gives. And consequently there is, too, such a thing as the "veneration of the holy of holies" wherever bread and wine from the celebration of the Mass are reserved, whether visible to the faithful or not. Such veneration is the act of the heart as it meditates on and thinks itself toward that point where the eternal love breaks into time and where time is broken open to the approach of eternal love. No one can fully realize such meditation and thought during the celebration within the congregation. He goes up and receives the bread and perhaps the wine, he swallows and returns to his place, and after five minutes he leaves the church building. He does not know what has happened to him and how it has happened. He believes as best he can, but he knows that he has not realized it. He comforts himself with the thought that he will not realize it no matter how long he lives. He allows it to occur, and that is right. And yet nevertheless he has a bad conscience about it: he has received in himself God's self-offering and has thereby affirmed it, but does not such an affirmation mean that he should begin to conform his life to the character of this self-offering and to expand his life into its dimensions? But how is he to do that? He carries on his everyday life as best he can. With the best intention. But does such a so-called best intention stand in any relationship to this boundless outpouring of God's very self in Jesus Christ? Has he indeed any criterion by which to judge this relationship?

II

There is, however, in the life of faith of Christians a kind of correspondence to the duality of event and state of the Lord in the Eucharist. It is the duality of action and contemplation. The sacramental action points beyond itself, indeed it contains, because it is primarily the reception of God's love, an essentially contemplative element, which has an in-built tendency to unfold itself beyond the act of contemplation proper. I must and I will think over more deeply and more broadly "what great things the Lord has done to me". I must and will open up the dimensions of my spirit and of my existence to the impact of the material eating and drinking, for it is precisely those dimensions which are addressed by the Lord who gives himself to me. The act of reception must be an act which involves the whole range of my existence, which is then as a whole embraced and encompassed by the event-state of the eucharistic Lord who is the "holy of holies". It is the whole range of my profane existence which is illuminated and shot through with light by this most sacral of all things. I cannot, consciously at least, respond adequately to this effulgence of light in any other way than by contemplation. I should not say that the light will automatically spread in me (that the Communion will have its effect of itself in me), if only I get on doing my daily work honestly. With all due respect to such honesty, the idea of a sacramental automatism is unworthy of the Christian. But if he senses this unworthiness and yet still rejects the idea of contemplation, then he will go over to saying that the celebration of the Eucharist is a mere "memorial" of an historical event, or is nothing more than a spiritual and temporally limited encounter, and will attempt to allay his conscience by watering down the mystery in this and similar ways. Contemplation, on the other hand, is the attempt of the believer to be grateful. The attempt to realize spiritually what he has been given sacramentally. To absorb and to digest spiritually what he has swallowed materially. On man's part it will never be more than an attempt. But the eucharistic grace will come to meet this attempt and broaden it out into the dimensions of the eucharistic state. Whoever makes the attempt to perform the act of contemplation will with time be given something like the state of contemplation. The kind of sustained organ-stop which is held under the confused melody of his day-to-day business and which makes itself heard whenever there is a short pause in the activities. He then knows—for he has actively steeped himself in this knowledge—that the whole range of his profane existence is undergirded by a holy of holies and justified by that. Why? Because all this profane existence which shouts so loudly the importance and purposefulness of its own claims is ultimately meaningless, for it cannot find in its own realm any ultimate grounding; it retains something of a ghostly and despairing character, it flees from one meaningless present into an ostensibly more meaningful future, a future however whose deep perilousness, ambiguity, unredeemability, is an open secret for all. But is not this meaningless, this senselessness which undergirds our daily pursuit of meaning as relentlessly as death, taken up for the Christian into the most holy senselessness of the Eucharist: for what could be more pointless than the total self-giving of God in Christ in which he is emptied out, devoured, and thrown away, cast as pearls before swine? This ultimate senselessness is the only center of meaning by which we can take our bearings, if we will only for once put our calculating machines aside and reflect on our condition. For even a computer cannot provide easily a total meaning for the meaninglessness of our existence. But "God's folly is wiser than men, and God's weakness is stronger than men" (1 Cor 1:25). And if ever a meaning is to be found before God's judgment-seat for man's unceasing pursuit of meaning down the course of the world's history, then it will only be in so far as it is a whole undergirded and measured and justified by the folly and weakness of the love of God in Christ.

The veneration of the holy of holies is not one of the peripheral acts of worship in the Church. It can assume accidental forms: as it is displayed in richly bejewelled monstrances, to the accompaniment of incense, of certain hymns and prayers, or as it is given as a final blessing with the ciborium. Everything that is accidental can have its meaning, and where it is intended for many people it does not have to suit everyone in every respect. And it can, because it is accidental, also be altered again. The holy of holies can be accessible in a particular area marked out from, though linked to, the main body of the Church and set aside for silent worship. Old people, lonely people, can find in this silence a home. And the churches are still open for everyone who can and will find time to pause for reflection and meditation in front of the eucharistic Lord. To enter into this presence will help him to leave the noise and the peripheral aspects of existence outside and to approach the center to which he is drawn. But there is also, if there is no church on one's way, a spiritual act of entering in. In order to move from the profane to the holy of holies all that is needed is a single step. Then it surrounds us on all sides and we have, as Paul says, at all times free access to God. We are children of the house who do not need to stand in the antechamber and wait on our calling. "One beat of the wings—and behind us lie the ages." One act of attention, and we are in the heart of God. For what God is has been made known to us and given to us in his Eucharist.

An Apology for Contemplatives

I

Today's world seems to allow increasingly little room for contemplatives. Just as on earth there is no natural nature left but only artificially fenced-off "national parks", where nature is allowed to lead an existence similar to that of the Indians in their reservations, so too it seems that technical civilization with all its business and astringency must penetrate even into the places of contemplation: radio and television make themselves at home in the silence of Carmel; even where the strict observance of the closed orders is still upheld externally (even if in a milder form), it is becoming increasingly a formality whose true spirit has been lost. And, as often, what appears inevitable in the light of the general condition of our world is justified and furthered by theological reflection. Such reflection moves in three stages, which come progressively closer to the heart of the matter.

1. The history of Christian spirituality, taken as a whole, betrays unmistakably an irreversible movement from solitariness to communality, from "a flight from the world" to "a turning toward the world". Monasticism begins with Antony the Great and a widespread desire, which is to us almost incomprehensible, to flee from the cultivated world into the desert. And even if from the

beginning the strict life of the hermit was an exception, because scores of pupils quickly gathered around the spiritually experienced contemplatives and men of prayer, with the consequence that the life in monastic communities soon gained the upper hand, nevertheless the ideal of the hermit living in strict isolation remained as a peak of religious perfection down to the Middle Ages. The "perfect" monks on Athos lived wholly or for considerable periods in practically inaccessible hideouts in the rocks, and even Thomas Aquinas (*S. Th.* II/II, 188.8), if at the same time he gives serious warnings about the dangers of spiritual deceptions, still defends the fundamental superiority of the life of the solitary contemplative over that of the life in community. And yet the general trend is moving in the opposite direction: away from the contemplative, communal life toward the opening of the monasteries to the world. The monk becomes an apostle, the cup of his vision flows over into missionary action, in the mendicant orders the balance of concentration and action is tipping toward the latter; the more one nears the modern age, the stronger becomes the openness to the world, the loving engagement with it, until finally, in the secular institutes, this openness to the world becomes a complete submersion in it. The few traces of contemplative prayer in the rules of such communities must be wrested painfully from the rushing tide of the secular.

2. Such historical visual aids are now reinforced by theological reflection, which ousts contemplation from its original position within the mystery of faith and allocates it to a very different one. The Christian theory of con-

templation, so it is argued, departing from the theories of the ancient and oriental world, teaches us to see that even the most solitary contemplation, when it is exercised in a right spirit, has its function—perhaps a very important one—within the structure of the Church and hence of the salvation of the world: the idea is to be found as early as Origen and Augustine (*De Mor. Eccl.* 31); it holds sway among the Carmelites from the time of Teresa of Avila (where contemplation is seen as help given by prayer to the Church in her conflict with the Reformation) and reaches its peak in the theory of Thérèse of Lisieux that the contemplative and atoning life of Carmel is the innermost spring of all Church action. Was not the root of Jesus' own turning to men his perpetual turning to the Father, and is there not in the Church a division of labor among the "charisms" which are exercised in discipleship of Christ, in such a way that certain more central "charisms" may provide the foundation for and further other more special gifts?

3. But the decisive consideration starts at an altogether deeper level. We have all of us, even those of us who are Christians and theologians, learned from Hegel to see God and the world in an indissoluble interrelationship. Where does the Bible speak to us about a worldless God? Does it not always, when it speaks of God's word and wisdom, also have his creation in view? And even if Paul does speak of a "mystery" hidden from before all ages and now revealed to him, does he not evidently refer to the God-man Jesus Christ—and not to an inner trinitarian Logos before the creation of the world—that first and

ultimate primal thought of God with the world, which embraces and integrates in itself all things, and behind which we can ourselves perceive no "worldless" state of God? Indeed the biblical writers understood the "pre-existence of Christ" in a manner so realistic as to be scarcely comprehensible to us, but perhaps today we can approach it most easily by way of a Christian interpretation of Hegel. If taken seriously, that would give us a radically Christocentric picture of the world. God could then be known in no other way than in his eternal decision to reveal himself in Christ to the cosmos, while the cosmos could not be understood otherwise than in its self-transcendence toward God, as seen most clearly in Christ. Nor would this any longer be conceived within the (Neoplatonic) framework of God's going forth into that which is other than himself and returning from that which is other than himself (at the most bringing that other back with him) to himself, as it was conceived in high Scholasticism (*egressus-regressus*), but in such a way that it now appears that the God who gives himself to the world in Christ is only properly understood and imitated by the world when it joins in and identifies itself with the self-giving eucharistic movement of God, where being with God is seen as sharing in God's movement away from God. This also seems to be the heart of the Johannine *agape*: God is invisible; who lives the love of his neighbor, in him is God, and he knows and experiences what God is.

This indeed would provide the final justification for the historical development of the religious orders and also for the theological displacement which has occurred in the understanding of contemplation. In this way all the fruitless, indeed tragic, dualisms in the history of Christian spirituality would be overcome, dualisms which again and again in their different ways opposed turning to God and turning to the world and only allowed validity to the latter with a bad conscience because it seemed that it must lead to a loss of the former. But in Christ both acts of "turning" are identical. Are not both indissolubly one in his "self-consecration" for the world (Jn 17:19), united in a single movement: total self-giving to the Father in order that the loving will of the Father may be fully effected toward his creatures? Does not then this "consecration" finally bring us to a point beyond a merely "contemplative" disposition, namely, to the *unity of self-giving* which unites action and passivity, the act of giving oneself and the act of allowing oneself to be used? The time for "pure contemplation" would finally, both culturally and theologically, be past.

II

It is worth, however, taking the trouble to test this hastily fashioned synthesis to see how strong it is. The totality which Hegel sighted, and which is a product of God and the world, can certainly not be expounded by Christians in the sense that God becomes God only through his progression through the states of consciousness of the world. And even allowing that the Bible always presents us with God as already involved with the plan of the world and its execution, this can nevertheless never justify us in stepping over the line which asserts that God does not need the world in order to be God. It is not the creation of the fulness of the world which makes it true to say of God that "he is the all", and to continue: "for he is the great one, over and above all his works" (Sir 43:27–8). If the world exists, then it rests on the ground of an incomprehensible grace which holds it in suspense over the void of nothingness. Of itself the world can only receive itself and give thanks for itself as a continual gift. And no one has the right to say that God, because he is love, is compelled by himself to pour himself out unlimitedly. The supremely free love of the absolute cannot be comprehended by human logic, even if everything which owes its existence to it bears in itself the traces of the Logos and of Wisdom.

This becomes most clear in the case of the Logos in human form, Jesus Christ. He is indeed praised by the believers as the mediator and consequently as the apparent "mean"—to which both God and the world are then related—but, on the other hand, he himself would not see himself in this manner. He knows very clearly that he comes as the revealer who is to carry out the Father's commission, who, when he has fulfilled his mission in death, "exaltation", "return", "assumption", "ascension", "returns" to the Father, creates an immediacy between the world and the Father, sends the Father's Spirit into the world (Jn 16:26). That is certainly not to reduce the whole world and God's movement of incarnation to an identity of God with himself before all worlds, where the "multiplicity" of things, their "otherness" than God, their "relatedness" to him would be set aside as if it were no more than a temporary appearance. But rather, if even the firstborn Son of the Father forces himself back into the womb in this manner, then it points to the infinite superiority which God retains over against the world, which the origin retains over against that which has its origin in him. Christ knows no Christocentrism; Christocentrism is valid only in so far as one allows oneself to be led by the movement of the center back to its origin, like the virgins in the Song of Songs who hurry after the scent of the bridegroom.

How are we to account for the present upsurge, openly or under more or less recognizable disguises, of that desire for contact with the immediate-absolute, which Hegel believed he could leave behind him as merely the first dawning of man's consciousness and his freedom? A good deal of this longing is derived from and encouraged by the growing disappointment which men feel with the cheapness of what is offered by our mass consumer society, from which one tends anyway to choose those products which allow one a temporary evasion from precisely this society itself. Unions with the absolute can, according to the latest results, be achieved both by following the way of mystical training and, more simply, by the use of chemicals. But we are not concerned at the moment to distinguish between true and false ways of arriving at such a goal, nor to distinguish between the motives which underlie such a striving, but rather only to notice a tendency which, unexpectedly and, as it were, out of time, is again appearing on the scene. And to turn to something which is of central significance within the Christian faith: What has a figure like the figure of Charles de Foucauld lost in our century?

How are we to explain the fact that we take a saint of the desert—who unlike others not only began his life of sanctity in isolation but also ended it in solitariness, indeed buried it more and more deeply in such loneliness—with such seriousness? It would seem that something which had been lost, to which we attach permanent value, has here again been discovered. The three steps which we took so rationally forward, in company with the spirit of history as well as with the spirit of theological reason, may perhaps be able to be retraced again.

The first stage toward the recovery of our original position would be gained by putting a question mark against Christocentricism in so far as it is understood as a static center of Christianity: Christ goes to the Father in order to prepare a place for us there. He will lay the kingdom in which he was the mediator finally at the feet of the Father, in order that God may be all in all (1 Cor 15:28). "God" here means the Father as the source of all reality who groundlessly (for what ground could compel free love?) communicates himself and, when he has become all in all, saturates everything with the spirit of this groundlessly outpouring and self-giving reality. "The Father is greater than I", because that which pours itself out is prior to that which is poured out, that which groundlessly grounds is prior to that which is grounded. Consider, for instance, the expression of Christ in Rembrandt's *Ascension* in the Pinakothek in Munich.

But that then brings us strangely close to the point of taking the second step back. There is no denying that there is much truth in this step. It is true, as little St. Thérèse [of Lisieux] says, that all finite and deliberate "action" on the part of the Church is based on a "contemplation" which simply gives itself to God, is free and open for him and his will, and in such openness becomes a fruitful womb. It is the marian principle but for which everything in the Church is reduced to a short-lived business. There is something unintentional, undeliberate in the principle of contemplative "fruitfulness", whereas the principle of deliberate action always contains something utilitarian and is consequently limited and finite. There are those who have considered it a great achievement that the mystical element in the Church can be traced back to the charismatic element—that is to say, that in all experience of God which is made by individuals under grace there is always also a social dimension, a dimension which embraces a commission to the Church and to the world, that the dispossession which God brings to pass in a man makes him poor in order that he may make many others rich. But does not one here immediately think again of de Foucauld or of little St. Thérèse? In so far as this insight into the ecclesiastical, generally redemptive import of true experience of God was asserted over against a simply individual understanding of such experience, it must in no way be again questioned. But the greatest care must be taken lest, unnoticed, one should smuggle back into the principle of "fruitfulness" an element of "success". One prays, and makes one's sacrifices, and knows: prayer and sacrifice will "be of benefit" somewhere and sometime to "the soul". We may not know how this will happen, but we can rest in the knowledge that God will "use" all that is given. Those who suffer, and to whom their pain seems meaningless, must again and again be assured of this; how otherwise could they bear it? But what is meant here by "use"? Surely only that what is given is taken up into the great groundless giving of God as a wave is taken back into the sea. Or at least that one surrenders it and that God must do with it what he will. One should not, just because one has in one's own self-abandonment given up counting one's own success, assume that therefore God will pick up the calculations which one has put aside and will himself start counting. It is not without reason that God takes away from his saints the spirit of calculation for so long and so thoroughly that they neither any longer know whether in their suffering and their prayer they are producing anything of use nor ask whether God can do anything with their work, if indeed there is any longer such a thing. The charismatic and consequently "func- tionalizable" side of mysticism must not jeopardize its openness to the groundlessness of God. One must not reproach the great seekers after God with the fact that they wanted to give themselves groundlessly to the groundless one. John of the Cross and countless other men of prayer from the Christian West and East did no less than that. Does this mean that one should say that they forgot the needs of the world and of the Church, their duties as members of the mystical body? They preferred God with all the strength of their being; they recognized God's supremacy over and above everything which sprang from him. That is to say, they preferred love itself above all that is worthy of love. Even in Christ there is no balance between God and the world. God is all, and the world exists only by virtue of and in this all. Such an insight does not belong less to the Christian sphere than to the realm of abstract religious and philosophical thought.

But we must take care lest the Christian world which is so over-populated with images, concepts, and historical events does not cause us to lose sight of the "one thing necessary", of the mystery which holds sway over all and in all, the mystery of the unconditional, groundlessly self-giving love. Wherever a man is overwhelmed by this love, at that point a window is opened up from our hermetically sealed world onto the truth. He himself does not flee from the world; he is himself a part of the world which is open to the truth. Many on Athos will have understood this, even if they were not much given to speculation about the "fruitfulness" of their contemplation. There is certainly a balance in the narrow Christian existence, and even Eckhart, following John and James, spoke of the fact that love of God must always give proof of itself in its active turning toward its neighbor. But should this lead us to say, at a time when the needs of the world bear in so terribly upon us, that they appear to demand our whole existence (and more than that), that preferring God is an act which can without further ado be held over for the "life to come"? But is it not completely wrong to imagine the life of the other world as "contemplation" by contrast with the life of this world which is seen as "action"? Should we not rather contrast the two in terms of the revelation in the life to come of that which is here already present though concealed? If that were so, then one would have to concede that the preference of the love which is God above all that is worthy of love and in need of help must now already subconsciously accompany all earthly behavior.

And so one would venture, with all precautions taken against the errors which lie in wait for one at this point, to take the third step back which brings us back to our point of departure. This step could consist simply in stating that acts in men's lives which in truth have no other content than the pure love of God for its own sake, than pure praise and pure worship of God even beyond every intention of representing the society of the Church or of fulfilling a task within that society, are and remain even today fundamental Christian acts. Every Christian must implicitly know them as the foundation on which all his other acts rest. And there is nothing to prevent some individuals placing such acts in the center of their life and thus exposing to view for all to see the foundation on which everything else in Christology, in the Eucharist, in the life of the Church, properly rests. And this should prevent us from saying that all those who have, for instance, understood and translated into Christian terms Plotinus' quest of the spirit for the "One", or with Dionysius the Areopagite have sunk down in worship before the mystery of the bright darkness of God, or with Eckhart have searched in the multiplicity of the world for the unique oneness, or have longed for the abyss of the inconceivable Godhead behind a Trinity which was only conceivable and formulable in conceptual terms, or who with Gregory Palamas (and this is indeed open to considerable misunderstanding) have venerated God's unknowable "essence" behind all the "energies" which proceed from him, that all these have simply been walking along false tracks which we today thankfully no longer need to tread.

III

The desert settlements of the old monks will not return, nor should they. We do not need to go out from our world in order to find the desert, as the spiritual family of de Foucauld has realized. "The desert grows" around us and in us whether we like it or not; we can remain where we are. What we call our culture flees blindly from the meaninglessness which surrounds us on all sides, from the emptiness and the ever present death; it refuses to die the decisive death of abandoning itself to the unconditional and precisely for this reason pronounces dead the God into whom it should itself die. Humanity undergoes this "experience" (of refusing to give God supremacy) together, communally. Christians may not withdraw from this experience simply by ecclesiastical busy-ness, nor may they simply note it as a matter of statistics, without drawing the consequences for themselves; rather they must take up their position in this general purge at the point where they have to prove themselves: by giving preference to God, each in his own way. Anything that is not built on this foundation remains wood, hay, and straw. And that includes all attempts at reform of the Church from within and all turning to the world by Christians. The decision must be taken at the heart of the matter; either one secures for oneself one's place in the "system" (which, with Hegel, embraces God and the world), or one puts oneself in one's poverty and defenselessness at the source point from which everything springs, without reason or system, from the freedom of love. Either one holds on all the tighter, or one relaxes one's grip. It is not that one cuts all one's ties with the world but, rather, that one frees a bit of the world from its tenseness and tautness. Everything which is truly effective comes from this source; its distinctive mark is that it in no way wants to be "efficient", that it has no ambition for itself or for the Church or indeed for God. One is content to rest in God and even, like the children in Péguy's *Mysteries*, to sleep. It is almost always the case that the great messengers of God come to us from a long time spent in the desert. It is mistaken to think that this time is subsequently seen by them as a wasted time or perhaps merely a time which is past or which was taken too literally. But for Manresa there would be no Ignatius; but for Subiaco there would be no Benedict; but for the enclosure in her parental home there would be no Catherine; but for the desert beyond Jordan there would not be the "voice of one crying in the wilderness" which prepares the way of the Lord. One cannot say in advance how such a time in the desert will impinge on the life of a Christian, if indeed he does not flee from it. But it is right that he should count on such a time, that he should allow space for it. Perhaps it may stand at the very center of his vocation. But one can also find the desert and bare rock in prison, in the concentration camp, in life in the satellite states, in the first circle of hell, in the cancer ward. These are the great schools of God who rises up like an ancient range of mountains behind the ruined human landscape. But there is also no lack of small, unimposing schools, the gray monotony of life in an office or a factory, disappointment in a person, increasing loneliness in old age as life sheds its leaves, when little or nothing remains to be hoped for, when daily, hourly, a courage is demanded of one which is praised by no one: Where can one find strength for such things if not in abandoning oneself to the ground which bears all? The fading, dying light does not think of any "reward" in such a self-abandonment, and that is good. He feels in his shame his total unimportance, but in humiliation he is intended to feel himself near to the poverty of the ground itself which hides itself so deeply in its own self-giving.

The monks voluntarily placed themselves from the outset at that final point to which men in the world are gradually and remorselessly driven, to the point where they are exposed in all their nakedness before God. In so far as the final stripping at death is something in which man totally acquiesces, the point at which God receives all the supremacy due to him and also a moment which, if it is affirmed and appropriated by the one who is dying, can become an atonement for much that he has done on his own account without God, there is nothing which prevents this act of acquiescence, which we can call contemplation, being exercised by a free choice as the fundamental act of our life: and that in every epoch of Christianity.*

*This is to say nothing either about the duration or about the form of a "contemplative" existence. To have time for God without any ulterior thoughts about one's own gain, and to give this time precedence in one's daily work, is something that can be realized in many ways, by communal singing of the Hours, in the Benedictine *Ora* which demands as a counterweight the fellowship of the monastry and its *Labora*, by times of silent worship and meditation in an otherwise active life, etc. In communities for whom the act of "contemplation" belongs to the very heart of their vocation it will need considerable discretion to determine how the rest of their daily work in the world is to be ordered so that the act of contemplation should not suffer and may even perhaps shed its light onto the world around the community. One will have to exercise care in the application of psychological standards. Whoever has consciously and definitively given himself to absolute love as a "living burnt-offering" will not subsequently be concerned to preserve his human integrity by the necessary "dialogical" counter-balances. One can, as documents of the last council frequently did, maintain that the life of contemplation and indeed the evangelical counsels do not damage or destroy the "personality", but if they are properly understood and lived out, but, on the contrary, they lead to its development. But one must not make out of this "development of the personality" a fixed postulate by which the formation of the contemplative life is to be measured. The candle which is consumed as it burns has no right to expect to find itself again and again restored to its original unconsumed state. Whoever makes that a condition of the contemplative life has not understood the meaning of its central act. And yet, on the other hand, such acts of consuming can never be institutionalized; the rules of a religious order are not intended to make exceptions into standard cases and so to play off love of God against love of neighbor, but rather to make the latter the normal place where the former is tested and proved, as indeed all the great rules have done as they follow the Old and New Testaments. But precisely the selflessness which the disciple of genuine love of one's neighbor creates is intended, in the rules of contemplatives, expressly to lead to the unreflected selflessness of the loving self-giving to God, as it is intended to have its very origin and source in such surrender.

The Three Evangelical Counsels

The continuous bombardment from every conceivable side and with every conceivable sort of explosive shows that the position itself is good and is being held. It would fill a book simply to list the weapons which have been brought into action against them. Unevangelical: their introduction in a systematic form occurs late in the history of the Church: till then one had done very well without them. The arbitrariness of the selection from the many other pieces of advice given by Jesus. A double morality: one for the better Christians who are distinguished from the plebs of the normal observers of the commandments: Pharisaism. Platonism: as if this world were only an antechamber of heaven, a greedy or indolent anticipation in contemplation of other-worldly pleasures. Manichaeism: the condemnation of the body and of man's sexuality. A permanent state of tutelage which however, thank heaven, is contradicted by the development of spirituality itself: the always growing emigration from closed monasteries into apostolic orders and societies and from these to secular institutes which can exercise the counsels only in an extenuated, metaphorical sense and then from the institutes into the normal Christian life in the world, that is to say, the historical self-contradiction of the whole estate of those living under the evangelical counsels. The abolition of the whole notion of states of life within the Church. The present sociological situation of humanity makes obedience (adulthood! responsibility! competence!), poverty (life insurances! professional qualifications!), and ultimately even celibacy (with its unbelievable comic figure, without experience in one of the most important sectors of human existence) impossible.

If one is to make any reply to so many objections in a short space, then one must from the start get rid of a few misunderstandings. The three evangelical counsels, celibacy, poverty, obedience, outline as it were from without, negatively, a living faith and a form of life which internally, positively, appears as a discipleship of Christ directly demanded by him: "Sell all ... then come and follow me" (Mk 10:21). The individual "counsels" lie more or less hidden in essence in the unconditionality of this discipleship, and it is only gradually that they are developed subsequently by reflection. Thus one will seek in vain in the gospel for a fully formulated "counsel of obedience", and yet it is there under one's eyes, if one can only see that in the unconditionality of this "follow me" lies the demand to carry out the total will of the master and nothing but that will, although the disciples before the Resurrection are far removed from seeing in Jesus anything other than a man commissioned by God, accredited by him, and endowed with particular authority. And consequently the question of which century it was in which the "three counsels" were formulated as such and made the basis of a life of particular discipleship is of only secondary importance: they were lived out implicitly but quite clearly in the earlier forms of this life of discipleship, for example, in the whole of Benedictine monasticism. One further point: One must, instead of delivering oneself of broadside negative judgments without any sense for historical situations, be very careful to distinguish a terminology taken over from the cultural world of antiquity (and such incarnation within a different culture belongs to the very essence and task of Christianity) from the changed meaning which many words and concepts take on in the Christian sphere and, equally, one must take care to distinguish the traditional ideologies from the lives which were actually led, which latter (as J. Sudbrack has demonstrated on a number of occasions) again and again energetically contradicted the former throughout all the historical phases of that life of discipleship. It may well be that there are still odd pieces of eggshell sticking to the chicken long after it has ceased to need them and, indeed, has even ceased to notice them. And finally: in order to come to terms with the whole complex associated with the counsels and to ascribe to it its present-day importance and status, one will have to abandon attempts to think in terms of historical processes of evolution and to think, rather, directly from its Christian origin. Of course one can be of the opinion that its subsequent evolution makes the original situation of no importance for today; the whole phenomenon of Jesus of Nazareth is sinking irrevocably into the past, with the consequence that the life of discipleship in the context of the "three evangelical counsels" is also disappearing unsung into the grave. What we have to say in what follows can only be of importance for those for whom Jesus is still Lord and Son of God.

1. In the first place, the post-conciliar Christian will have to relearn certain things, or at least to add something to the all too popular statement that "the Church is the people of God": namely, that the Church is built up on the foundation of the apostles and of the New Testament prophets (Eph 2:20). The truth of this is shown by a look at Paul, who has not the least intention of abandoning the congregations which he has founded to their democratic fate or to a charismatic chaos, but who remains energetically and at times by no means pleasantly active as the foundation on which they rest and as the principle of order to which they owe their form. The initial structure of the congregation is so little conceived of as a provisional form that even the form of the heavenly Jerusalem, in which there is now no temple apart from the Lamb and no lamp apart from the glory of God and again the Lamb, nevertheless remains built up on the "twelve foundation stones on which are written the twelve names of the twelve apostles of the Lamb" (Rev 21:14). Even the number of the elect who form the final people of God, the hundred and forty-four thousand, is derived from the twelve and has its basis in them. The twelve, however, whatever their function vis-à-vis the people may be, are neither those who strive for perfection and offer themselves for discipleship (like the rich young man), nor are they in the first place pupils who receive a particular training as functionaries, but they are men who have been called ("he called to himself those whom he wanted himself", Mk 3:13). From now on that call is their be-all and end-all, they must leave everything behind, must even break the laws of elementary hallowed

piety (not taking leave of those at home, not burying their father), must stake all on Jesus, who himself has nowhere to lay his head, must stake their whole person on his person (and so Luke, after due reflection—but Jesus did not divide what he finds already linked by the heavenly Father—also mentions the wife as well as house, parents, children, goods, among the things which have to be left behind, and indeed puts her at the head of the list; Lk 18:29). Everything else comes later: the fact that many of the apostles seemed to have travelled around with their wives, that in the Pastoral Epistles there are married church elders, that Peter (in what has been demonstrated to be a redactional insertion) asks about his wages, that those who have left all behind are promised a hundredfold return even in this world, that Luke (rightly) draws a lesson for all from the literal command given to those who are called to leave everything, namely, in terms of cultivating the spirit of poverty, for the foundation naturally determines the style of the building, and so on. The water poured into the wine cannot prevent us from enjoying the original taste of the unmixed wine of Jesus, and the spiritual understanding of the "counsels" is derived from an understanding of them which is almost brutal, literal, material, or perhaps better, incarnational. Both Greek and Indian philosophers are acquainted with the "spirit of the counsels"; indeed they are also acquainted with many of its material forms, but the point of the Christian understanding is precisely not the external manifestations or exercise of that spirit, but the leaving everything "for my sake" (Mk 10:29), the "follow me" (Mk 2:14), the "follow along behind me" (Mk 1:17).

One does not stake oneself on a "path to the truth", or on the absolute, but one is taken by the "I" who himself stakes himself absolutely and is torn free of all one's earthly ties so that one stands and depends on him alone. The same thing will again, more spectacularly, happen to Paul, and he will not be sparing with his words in his attempts to bring it home to his congregation that they too are tailored to his model. There is no "Jesus and ...", but it is in Jesus and only in him that the Father gives himself, it is only as the Spirit of Jesus that the Father gives the divine Spirit. There is quite simply no talk of charisms in the calling of the twelve and their obedience. Charisms will be given later when the people of God is divided up into its different members by the Spirit. There would be no point in putting the question even to the rich young man whether he has or has not the charism of poverty or of chastity. It is the absolute claim with which he is confronted: *C'est à prendre ou à laisser.* And naturally that means "leave everything, follow me", for life. It is laughable to assert that a man is incapable of committing his whole existence and that, consequently, we can make our decisions only on a temporary basis, decisions about marriage, about the monastic life. Rather it is the whole person who is lifted up bodily and carried off (like the gates of Gaza on Samson's back). One can, if one is not averse to the somewhat unctuous tone, speak of "a consecration for life" (and there are many who are very keen to do so today); and indeed such talk expresses more clearly the simple totality of being taken and of allowing oneself to be taken than the language of the "three counsels" which we have chosen to follow, a language which is itself derived, reflected, and not a little mercantile in style, or the still more distant and obscure language of the "three vows", for one can only bind oneself seriously to someone with *one* (all-embracing) vow.

What is important here is, first, only that the whole city of God rests on the radicalism of these twelve called disciples—like Venice on its piles. The Church stands on her pillars (Gal 2:9), and there is a continuation of this function ("Whoever conquers him will I make a pillar in the temple of God", Rev 3:12) because Jesus' call to discipleship continues to ring out. Naturally in the Church. And somehow it runs contrary to all the Church's well-ordered structures, it cares little for the consequences (they will appear in their own time) and simply calls men back to the Church's origin. The Church which has now come into existence is shown what the Church is in her becoming. The Church which has been born is shown what the Church is in her conceiving. Call and unconditional discipleship are absolute fruitfulness, the act of begetting itself.

2. All this should have made clear the purpose and value of the so-called "counsel". It is right that the Church should have given her mind to the question of the kinds of thing that a man can abandon in order to exercise the act of discipleship; and he cannot give more than his external goods (poverty), his free disposition over his physical procreatory function (celibacy) and over his spiritual decisions (obedience). In this respect the inventory is exhaustive. But nothing has been said about the attitude of the man who gives himself, and it is here that

the weak point lies in our talk about the counsels. They mean discipleship, not only material but, above all, spiritual discipleship. They mean precisely and centrally our total offering of ourselves to be disposed of by the Lord, just as he puts himself totally at the disposition of the Father's will. This will of the Father can be borne in on him from several sources—by an internal intimation, by a mission represented to him in its complete outline, by the Old Testament tradition into which he was born with its laws and prophecies which Jesus must fulfil in accordance with the will of the Father—all that flows together into an indivisible unity; it is not merely a ragbag of injunctions, nor even a synthesis created skilfully by Jesus himself. With his whole being he listens for the unity of the Father's will which comes to him in the totality of his life situation. There can be no question of "ifs" and "buts". Nowhere is there any limit set: this and not that, so far and no farther. He draws sustenance through all his pores from the instructions which flow down upon him: "My food is to do the will of the Father". His abandonment of everything else sets him free to enjoy the simplicity which allows itself to be distracted by nothing, to enjoy this freshness with which the child looks in anticipation to the face of his father to see what he will venture, do, undertake. "As the eyes of a servant look to the hand of his master, as the eyes of a handmaid to the hand of her mistress" (Ps 123:2). Like Paul in Damascus: "Lord what will you have me to do?" (Acts 9:6 Vulg.). Like the boy Samuel: "Speak Lord, your servant hears" (1 Sam 3:10). Like, finally, the archetypal handmaid: "See, I am the handmaid of the Lord, may I be disposed of according to your word" (Lk 1:38).

It is this readiness to be disposed of which gives the "counsels" their inner life. Abstracted from this attitude they are nothing more than *means* to it, means of which one can make good and less good and bad use. But when they are enlivened by such an attitude, they become an *expression* of the Christian attitude, which consists in allowing oneself to be molded by nothing other than by Jesus' attitude. This attitude is the loving assumption of the will of the loved Father, and in an identical act the Father loves the Son and the world and allows the Son to bring back the world to the Father in his self-giving even to the point of death. Thus the willingness of the disciple who had been called to allow himself to be disposed of is taken up directly into the universal saving will of God. It is, in Jesus' call, the permission to offer one's existence to this saving will to be disposed of by it. Everything rests on the triune love of the Father: the one who offers himself turns to it as the origin of all love. And in the free obedience of the Son whom the disciple follows this love of the Father appears to him concretely. But it is always from the very beginning pure love of the world, pure mission to the brothers, pure representation of the world before God. It is of secondary importance whether this readiness to be disposed of finds expression subsequently in prayer and in contemplation or in the active offices of the Church and in service of the world, or in a life made up of both elements. Everyone who is called must ask himself in which kind of service God wishes to place him. But what is decisive is that it should be the pureness of his readiness to be disposed of in all free areas of self-giving which should leave its impress and be the true criterion of all that he does. This becomes particularly clear where poverty is concerned: Jesus' poverty was not one of crying need, for such poverty would not have allowed him to fulfil his mission. It was a question of not worrying about material things—his only concern and care was for the kingdom of God—expressed in his request for that which was sufficient for each day. It was a spirit of loving squandering of oneself with its final expression in the Eucharist: this is the proof that his poverty is perfect. Of course it is true that the poverty of those who have been called should be a witness for the Church and the world and should therefore have a credible visible form. But it will gain in credibility—even in the powerhouse of our present prosperous society—from its readiness to be disposed of: nothing of my possessions is reserved, out of reach. Celibacy, understood from the Christian point of view, is a readiness to put one's whole person, including, more particularly, its spiritual, physical fruitfulness, at the disposal of the kingdom. How God uses this fruitfulness which is offered to him, how he multiplies it and turns it to the advantage of his kingdom, remains mysterious and can be grasped only in the fruitfulness of the chaste and self-denying body of Jesus in the Eucharist. It is here that the celibate may find an understanding of the inner effectiveness of his witness. Jesus interpreted marriage anew from its origin and affirmed it (Mk 10:1–12), consecrated it by his presence at a wedding, and we are told that no one shall cast any suspicion on it (1 Tim 4:3f.). But we cannot interpret away the fact that, in the parable of the great supper, marriage is mentioned alongside the concern for material goods as an obstacle to such readiness to be disposed of (Lk 14:20), nor can we overlook the saying about those who have been made eunuchs for the sake of the kingdom of heaven ("He who is able to receive this, let him receive it", Mt 19:12 RSV), and St. Paul's crystal clear idea that the one who is unmarried is more wholly and undividedly at the disposal of the "affairs of the Lord": he "wants to be holy in body and soul" (1 Cor 7:32,34)—and "holy" in this context means nothing other than being again freely consecrated to God and his service alone, a service which will straightaway take concrete form in the Church and in the world. Again such readiness to be disposed of by God takes on the form of obedience; for I can never know once and for all privately what God wants of me; I can only ever fully discover his will in the context of the Church, I must also listen to her and to her instruction as the pillar and foundation of truth (1 Tim 4:15). And it is also true that within the great Church such readiness to be disposed of can again take more concrete form in communities whose rule presents the gospel in a more concentrated and existential manner and whose superiors are authorized to expound to me this rule in the name of God and of the Church. In the great Church, to whose attitude of service the Christian, and above all the one who is called, must as he is confronted by the Lord conform himself, the ways and means—sermon, catechizing, personal guidance—are often all too distant and ineffectual. In the communities to which we have been referring, however, something of the original event of the Church is kept alive. And just as Jesus' readiness to conform himself to the will of the Father is given concrete direction by every source within the situation in which he finds himself, so too, for the one who is called in the Church, his obedience is clarified again and again by every aspect of his existence in the world and in the Church, if only he retains the character of true acceptance which marks out those who have offered themselves for God's disposing.

3. Such readiness to put oneself at God's disposal, to do his work in the world, cannot simply be comprehended in terms of the categories of turning to the world—turning away from the world, remaining in the world—separation from the world. On the one hand, all Christians have died to the "world" through baptism and live in anticipation, in hope of the coming aeon, no matter how much they may have to remain in this our present world (Jn 17:15; 1 Cor 5:10), and indeed have to fulfil decisive tasks for this world (Phil 2:15; Mt 5:13–16). The tension between "in the world" and "not of the world", which is something felt by all Christians, is heightened for those who have been specially called out: they are in a most radical sense completely set free from the world in order that they may be just as radically thrown into action, be used by God for the world. Only Christology can shed light on this mysterious dialectic: Jesus is the one who in complete freedom ("I consecrate myself", Jn 17:19; Heb 7:27; 9:14) has been "offered" as "ransom money" (Mk 10:45) and as a "living sacrifice" (Heb 10:10); he is the one who denies himself all, who separates himself from everything only in order that he may be the more effectu-

ally thrown into action, distributed for all. It is to this law and to no other that the man who has been called by Jesus to offer up his life to an existence governed by the counsels is subjected. As such it only condenses and intensifies the christological form of existence of all the baptized; it bears witness to the meaning of the tension which there is in such a life. There is little profit to be gained from continual reflection on the relation of baptism (at least where it is lived out to the full) to the "consecrated life" of the counsels, whether one attempts to approximate them so closely to each other that the "consecrated life" appears as a *mere* intensification of baptism (but that is not to do justice to the element of the particular calling by Jesus), or whether one contrasts them to such a degree that one speaks of two "states" within the Church (and then the danger arises that two categories of Christian are created, which does not correspond to the model of the apostolic Church). Special vocations have never had the character of privileges in the Church; one should never claim them for oneself and for one's "state", nor should they be brandished in argument against another "state". The more deeply a man is dispossessed, the more deeply he must serve: that is the fundamental law of Christ, and blessed the Church whose life is conformed to that law.

There is consequently even less justification for creating a gulf within the "life of the counsels" in the Church between those who "are separated from the world" (which would be the old monastic orders and, to a lesser degree, also the apostolic orders and congregations) and those who, while "consecrated to God" and living out the counsels, yet "remain in the world" (which would be the so-called secular institutes or worldly communities). On the basis of what we have said, such a gulf would be artificial and could not theologically be justified. The element of separation from the world may have been one-sidedly emphasized, either verbally or indeed in practice, by the old orders: today the orders are seeking to give expression to the balance between the two elements which has always been part of the Christian task, to give expression to it both verbally and in their form of life. Thus, for the secular institutes to accuse the orders of unworldliness, and thereby to attempt to establish themselves more firmly in their own worldliness, would be an unworthy kind of polemic. Qualitatively the emphasis may be set differently, but the basic structure can only be the same. This will become still clearer if we allow Christology to be transparent to its ultimate mystery: the trinitarian love. In Jesus there appears to us a love of the Father which precisely, in so far as it wills the incarnation of God in the world, is a love which most deeply and most radically denies itself. The Father renounces for the sake of the world that which is most dear to him, his Son; he does not spare him (and consequently does not spare himself); he gives him up into abandonment. This element of divine renunciation is reflected in all aspects of Jesus' existence. It is precisely because he loves the world and men that he offers up his life for them. And this certainly not only in the latter stages of his life as something forced on him by the failure of his active mission in Israel. If this were so, then all the books of the New Testament would have given us a falsifying interpretation of the phenomenon of Jesus. Rather the meaning and purpose of the incarnation, according to the texts which give a definitive interpretation of Jesus, is the Cross "for us" and the Resurrection equally "for us". According to the same texts, the act of the Son in allowing himself to become man (of the Son who as the seed of the Father is carried by the Spirit into the womb of the Virgin) is already an act of self- emptying love. Thus in this sense Jesus' whole existence would be the function of his prior, all-embracing readiness to put himself at the disposal of the saving will of the Father (one could speak of an *oboedientia antecedens et determinans existentiam*), and the first disciples on whose act of existence Jesus will found his Church would then be seen as those who have been called, as far as it is humanly possible, to be conformed to his own prior readiness for service. Seen from another, more interior point of view, the prior redemption of Jesus' Mother would again be the condition of the possibility of a word of acceptance which undergirds the whole existence of the handmaid of the Lord. Those are things which apparently fade away into the mists of theological obscurity, but for the one who listens sensitively and hard to the origin of the Church in his call to discipleship, they stand illuminated in a bright light.

Everything in the Church is subject continually to decay, to decline, to faithlessness, to falsification of its very essence. The more demanding and the more difficult therefore a Christian witness is to live out, the more disastrous are the consequences of its failure. The criticism of the life of the evangelical counsels will never be silenced so long as weak, fallible men attempt to live it out. They must listen again and again to such criticisms, must recognize what is justified in them and attempt by renewed efforts to show them to be wrong. But against the particular calling to such readiness for total service itself there will never be a justified criticism, for without such readiness there would be no gospel and no Church.

The Christian and Chastity

There is no ethic in the world which in matters of chastity is less prudish and more whole-heartedly demanding than the ethic of Jesus and his disciples. Nowhere is there any trace of antagonism toward the body, nowhere any trace of Manichaeism; for how could it be otherwise in a religion centered on God's coming in the flesh? But, equally, there is nowhere any trace of that kind of misguided casuistry which, it is claimed, is invented for the benefit of weak men, but which for the most part has the effect of sapping the springs of moral action. Jesus withdraws from the casuistry of divorce which Moses allowed in certain cases "because of the hardness of your hearts" into the pure air of the origin, of the pure will of God, "in the beginning of creation God created men as man and wife ... both will become one flesh. There are therefore no longer two but one flesh. What God has joined together, let no man put asunder!" (Mk 10:5ff.). The clause in Matthew, which again permits a ground for divorce, must be taken to be an addition by the theology of the Early Church. The one spirit uniting two hearts corresponds, according to the original will of the Creator, to the "one flesh". "Whoever looks on a woman with the intention of desiring her has already committed adultery in his heart" (Mt 5:28). That is quite simply the norm. And the love which is necessary for there to be "one spirit" to correspond to the "one flesh" is brought anew by Jesus.

It is a love which loves the whole physical spiritual man wholly, with body and soul, loves him and gives himself totally for him. The high demands made by Jesus are backed up by his own total self-commitment. Again and again he works precisely with his flesh. It is his flesh which is crucified for me; his flesh is prodigally given to me in the Eucharist in order that in this way and no other (Jn 6:53f.) I may attain to eternal life. His flesh is concerned with my flesh, that is to say, with me, the whole man, with all my physical strength and drives. "The body is not there for immorality but for the Lord and the Lord for the body." Indeed, precisely in so far as Christ has in his flesh borne all my spiritual and fleshly sins, he has, as it were, expropriated me; we all "no longer belong to ourselves but have been bought for a high price"; we are physically incorporated into the body of Christ. "May I then take the members of Christ and make them members of a prostitute" with whom they will then become "one flesh"? That runs not only contrary to the law of creation which Jesus re-established in a purified form, but contrary to the much more sensitive law of redemption according to which flesh was offered up for flesh. "But he who is united to the Lord" (more properly: "who is fused together with the Lord") "is one spirit with him", concludes Paul (1 Cor 6:13ff.), and he could just as well have said: one heart, one flesh. It is from this point of view that he illuminates created marriage: he places it expressly under the norm of Christ's love for his bride, for humanity redeemed by him. The man, even and specifically in the sexual act, must show perfect, loving self-giving, which at the same time takes up the self-giving of the woman and gives it form; the wife is the one who allows herself to be formed, without setting inner limits on the love which she has received. In the opposition of the sexes, which in none of its aspects is simply physical but which always leaves its imprint on personal attitudes and responses, lies the possibility of a perfect mutual interpenetration which opens up the way to a unity of love and to a fruitfulness which transcends the two individual partners. "This is a great mystery and I take it to mean Christ and the Church" (Eph 5:25–32 RSV). Now it is no longer simply the individual Christian in his physicality who is expropriated (as before), nor is it simply that in marriage the man belongs to the woman and the woman belongs to the man in such a way that neither has any longer the power of disposal over his own body (1 Cor 7:4); rather, both are now in the interaction of their love again expropriated and taken up into the absolute love of God (in Christ) for mankind ("Church"), and this love is a nuptial love. Human sexuality is precisely created by and for such love.

For many this will doubtless all sound terribly exalted, and they will be thinking that it is all too far removed from life, too impracticable. Let us leave such reservations aside for the moment and simply make the point again that, whatever it is, such a train of thought is at the very least inimical to physicality. Men have often accused Christianity of anathematizing the sexual, of Manichaeism, and so on. However, the kernel of truth which such accusations contain cannot be urged against the New Testament, but at best against certain views of the late classical world which find their way into Christianity at a later stage. In its origin it presents to man and woman a glorious picture of sexual integrity: the Son of God who has become man and flesh, knowing his Father's work from inside and perfecting it in the total self-giving of himself, not only of his spiritual but precisely also of his physical powers, giving not only to one individual but to all. What else is his Eucharist but, at a higher level, an endless act of fruitful outpouring of his whole flesh, such as a man can achieve only for a moment with a limited organ of his body? And the man soon withdraws again into himself, and it is only rarely that his heart fully achieves the meaning of the physical act: the letting oneself go completely, the handing over of oneself totally in a love which "does not seek his own", which seeks neither pleasure nor gain for itself. It is only rarely that he understands that the mark of his sexuality in his body is a reminder of his own dispossession: You are there in order that you may become fruitful beyond yourself, in an act of self-giving which alone reveals what you can properly achieve: namely, procreation in the freedom and power of your Creator. The physical is only a pointer to something which equally determines his whole personality, his spiritual life. "Husbands, love your wives as Christ loved the Church and gave himself for it" (Eph 5:25).

Now one can see that in the New Testament the Christians truly stand alone with their picture of love. The whole heathen world around them thinks quite differently. Paul sees it as dominated by two major sins, covetousness and lechery, and considers that they both spring from the same root. Lechery *is* covetousness, the perversion of love whose essence is to let itself go, to renounce itself for the sake of the other, into a grasping speculation concerned only with its own pleasure and advantage. It is really of very little significance whether this covetousness is lived out in the form of a marital or extra-marital egoism *à deux*, whether it is lived out with the opposite or with the same sex or indeed alone, whether normally or perversely; neither Jesus nor Paul enters into the casuistry of such egoism. They simply warn the Christian not to allow himself to be impressed in the least by statistics about practices in his contemporary world, by reports and behavioral studies. Where Christian faith is concerned, statistics have never proved anything; at the very most they have shown that those who truly believe, who take their faith seriously in this life, are a very "small flock" (who however "should not be afraid"), much smaller than the numbers of the ecclesiastical fellow-travellers might lead one to believe. For the non-Christian, "morals" can change depending on the cultural constellations obtaining at a particular time. On one occasion it is the fashion to erect great taboos around sexual covetousness, consequently making the matter more adventurous and interesting; but then there comes a time when one destroys the magic of these taboos with a great shout of triumph, and this gives men a sense of enormous freedom, of being very enlightened, but the thing itself becomes much more boring and eventually one is completely fed up with it. The shorter the skirts, the less exciting the legs. Fashion designers will have to bring out something new if they are to turn up the thermostat on our eroticism. But can this merry-go-round impinge in any real sense on the Christian, if he truly knows what he believes: God's infinite self-giving for him on the Cross and in the Eucharist? "*Scio cui credidi*, I know to whom I have entrusted myself" (2 Tim 1:12). His own sexual behavior would then be for the world around him a witness equally as remarkable and offensive as his faith itself; for both are part of the same indivisible whole. His sexual behavior is a part of his faith, which is to be incarnated and which only so can become credible.

Of course there are a whole host of questions still to be answered in this area, questions, problems, causes for concern which cannot be swept away with a motion of the hand, which cannot be solved by casuistic distinction and which equally cannot be allayed and set aside by a "generous" permissiveness. The norm, the norm toward which we strive, has been set up like a trigonometrical point on the top of the mountain, and it is by this point that we must and can take our bearings and make our very complicated cartographical calculations. You do not belong to yourself but to God and to your neighbor; you have no right of disposing over a physical function which has its meaning only as an expression of truly selfless love, of love which is ready for service. One should start on one's journey with one's eyes fixed on this point. And further, your body is not a matter of no importance, of no concern in the religion of the incarnate love of God. On the contrary, the whole matter of the body receives the greatest emphasis. There is no need here to discuss the question of deadly sins and venial sins. We only have to think of the fact that in the light of the Cross and the Eucharist the Christian body "is a shrine of the Holy

Spirit who lives in you and whom you have received from God so that you now no longer belong to yourselves". Mortal sin, venial sin, that too often smacks of casuistry. Let us say simply that from the Christian point of view it is a serious matter. And it becomes no less serious by virtue of the fact that it is embedded—for the Christian is a being who shares common humanity each in his own particular age—in a multitude of sociological problems which must be thought through responsibly and which are in no way to be equated with the sexual egoism which we have mentioned above. The question of the norms which are to be established both for the state and for the Church within such a system of co-ordinates is not something which can be in any sense easily and quickly decided. What is demanded of the Church is simply that she, as well as the individual Christian, should keep her eyes fixed on the content of the evangelical, primitive Christian faith. There are here matters of greater importance than making statistical analyses and judgments. It is indeed more important to keep alive in the heart of Christians the dynamic which drives them to follow the simple, shining, and demanding ideal of faith at a time when their small boats are threatening to capsize in the heavy seas of our time, when the Christian voice becomes almost inaudible against the background of the hellish screeching of the mass-media and the glaring lights of films, of magazines and advertisements, of the whole pornographic industry.

We said at the beginning that Christianity was not prudish. Jesus offended the Pharisees by sitting in a pub with collaborators and prostitutes. And he saw these people going into the kingdom of heaven before the religious dignitaries. Why are there so many dubious women in the Gospel? The Samaritan woman with her five or six husbands, the weeping sinner, the Magdalen with her countless devils, the adultress, and doubtless many others? There are a number of things to notice here. In the first place, prostitution is the most important Old Testament term for referring to the abandonment of the true God, who is Israel's rightful husband and who accuses Israel of opening her legs for a strange god under every bush and, moreover, of even paying him for the privilege instead of charging him for it (Ezek 16). Jesus has come to seek what was lost. But then we have to notice the care and tenderness with which the lost sheep, which can scarcely walk, is lifted onto the shoulders of the shepherd and carried home. It is his nature and manner which draw the lost ones to him—"my sheep know my voice"—and that is true of Jesus and the company he kept. The woman with her box of ointment would never have forced her way through to the dignified Pharisee, for his stony heart would never have brought hers to the point where it could melt. She weeps because she knows she has sinned, and she is dismissed with the words "Go and sin no more!"; but in the encounter of these two the miracle occurs. Jesus' pure fire distinguishes in her soul between that which is impure desire and lust and that which was the hidden willingness for self-giving; and this willingness is fanned by her into a burning love: "Because she has loved much, much will be forgiven her." A distinction is made in the prostitute. Her attempts at true love and self-giving are stripped of their soiled packaging, are recognized, purified, and borne home into their land of origin, which is love. The terminology cannot deceive the one who knows men's hearts for a moment. What men call "love" can be the crassest egoism, a business which one carries on for one's own advantage, whether spiritual, sensual, or financial. It can also be the "weakness of the flesh" (Mt 26:41), while the spirit was willing to commit itself in a more powerful manner; the Lord knows that too and turns to it not in fierce anger but with a quiet, sad reproach and the exhortation "Be on your guard and pray that you do not fall into temptation."

Christian sexual ethics is best advised to keep to the quite simple outline of the New Testament. For this is as unchangeable as the nature of the divine love which has become flesh in Christ. This is unalterable because a "greater love" than the one shown to men in Christ is not conceivable, not in any phase of our evolving world. So long as the Christian's heart and mind are spellbound by this humble and totally selfless love, he has in his possession the best possible compass for finding his way in the fog of sexual matters. With the image of this love before him he will not be able to maintain that the ideal of self-giving—of true self-giving, not of throwing oneself in front of people—is unrealistic in our world and impracticable. It demands a very great deal: namely, to subordinate everything to the love which does not seek its own; but it gives a great deal more: namely, the only true happiness. One can use sex, like drugs and alcohol, to maneuver oneself into a state of excited, illusory happiness, but one is merely transporting oneself into momentary states which do not alter one's nature or one's heart. The states fade and disappear, and the heart finds itself emptier and more loveless than before. It is only when the innermost heart of a man is opened that the sun of love can penetrate into it. "*Fili, praebe mihi cor tuum*, Son, give me your heart" (Prov 23:26).

Am I a Sinner?

I

The word *sinner* no longer has any meaning for me. Among the general public it has a slightly comical note: it is used in the title of sex films as a means of attracting attention, but its effectiveness in that respect is much reduced. It is a word which comes to us from a lost world where there was a whole range of instruments of torture designed to inculcate the delinquent's conscience with a sense of his sinfulness and then to exorcise it by means of confession and imposed penances, while at the same time repeated applications of the treatment were designed to keep alive the general feeling of being a sinner and continually to bring it to a head. All this was performed with regard to a divinity supposedly hurt in its love, effectively represented by an official priesthood which possessed the power of working on a man's conscience till he considered himself to be "the greatest living sinner" and, equally, the power to save some magical entity from the mire and to endow it with the innocence of the loving child of the God of love—at least till the next fall from grace. It is, then, hardly surprising that men gradually lost patience with these hot and cold baths which the priests prescribed for them and avoided undergoing their cures by the claim that one was all the time always both "sinner and justified at the same time". That certainly made a substantial dent in the authority of the priestly office and the sacrament; but, on the other hand, the withdrawal from their authority had taken place quite honorably. Such an insistence on the simultaneity of the states was the consequence one might logically have expected of the practice of alternating between one and the other. In the long run no man can put up with that, the extremes fuse together into the average, mean consciousness of life. And why should one, so long as one felt oneself to be a Christian, not confess both simultaneously before the just and merciful God: namely, that one feels oneself to be a total failure and does not claim to measure up to God's standard and that one nevertheless knows oneself to be wrapped in the cloak of the redeeming love of the Son in which, in spite of the filth of sin which still attaches to one, one can appear decently clothed in the presence of the Father in heaven?

It is a consequence of this coincidence of opposites that our present sense of indifference has developed. For it contained in itself the principle of a democratic levelling—we are all together sinners and all together justified: the particular percentages in any given case are no longer of any fundamental importance. If, then, on top of that particular emphasis is given to man's consciousness (as in pietism and idealism) and, finally, if general sociological psychology claims this consciousness as its object, then factors within one's family background (Freud) and in the structures of society (Marx) can contribute to an illumination of that *mixtum compositum*. Thus the psychoanalyst and the social psychologist make their appearance apparently as the legitimate heirs of the one-time confessors, spiritual directors, and inquisitors. They have the "authority" which is now scientifically accredited to excise men's consciousness of sin by explaining its natural causes; at least they can perform this operation with so much success that men can now take their place within the average collective of humanity and there behave according to average norms and can join in the general swim without attracting attention.

The standard which is now applied is that of the collective. It is the task of scientific tests and reports to determine the state of a man's consciousness. Thus general and average behavior become the norm; a doctor may advise a neurotic youth to indulge in sexual intercourse *in order to* rid himself of his complexes and *because* all normal young people behave in this manner. The collective is the fig leaf behind which the individual may hide his feelings of guilt. It is true that in some respects the collective still feels slight after-pains of a former Christian dialectic, but scarcely more clearly than the first pains were felt in the pagan pre-Christian world. Humanity as a whole stands in an impenetrable twilight confronted by the gods and subject to the powers of this world. Both exist simultaneously: salvation, grace, fortune, all of which are received from individual gracious divinities and, at the same time, the disastrous, jealous, wilful, and spiteless onslaughts of other, darker powers. These two elements do not simply coincide, nor can they be equated. Man still knows that there is such a thing as guilt and atonement and still pleads his case at his altars with all kinds of offering, asking for signs of God's favor; but the wind of fate which bends over all trees in the same direction—in the direction of disillusionment—is stronger than both and has the last word. Today the gods and powers have other names; the benevolent ones are called "hope", "progress", "evolution"; the malevolent ones are called "the self-destruction of technological humanity", "the atom bomb", "the spiral of power", "the dialectic of aid to underdeveloped countries"; and the impenetrable twilight between day and night moves, as in the ancient world, toward night. The twilight itself is completely mysterious and strange. And this terrifying strangeness which envelops us on all sides is so powerful that even those forces which in an earlier age, as Christian "sin", seemed to lay upon us a weight of final responsibility are now resolved into the mystery of that for which we can bear no responsibility. One symptom of this is the trend toward the abolition of Christian private confession and toward its replacement by cumulative absolution. Just as I as a sinner am only a small part in the collective, so too when I have received absolution I am no different. And, for the rest, do we not all travel along the same path of fate together in solidarity? What meaning can we attach today to the old pictures set over the porches of cathedrals where humanity is finally divided into two parts, on the right heaven, on the left hell? Is there anyone among us who does not stand both on the left and on the right at the same time? Are we not all, as the thief on the cross said, "in the same condemnation", and do we not all share the same "unobjectifiable", utopian hope? So that it is our consciousness, admittedly a split, schizophrenic consciousness, but nevertheless our consciousness, which receives this eschatological blow of the sword, endures it, and survives it.

II

If there is any way back from here, it could only be a narrow mule track which, so faint that strangers can scarcely follow it, winds its way through the scrub of the individual conscience. The first sinner was quick to hide himself in this scrubland, but the voice, whose speaker he did not need to see, nevertheless reached him: "Adam, where are you?" A question which presupposes that the man who has hidden himself hears it, recognizes that he is not where he should be, that is to say, that he is not out in the open and visible where conversation would be possible. Yet the voice reaches him in spite of this barrier.

In the next episode the question which rings out takes another form: " 'Where is your brother Abel?' He replied, 'I do not know. Am I my brother's keeper?' " The question is more pointed, more accusing than the first; the answer is aggressive and rejects provocatively what he has been accused of. In this he dissociates himself from his fellows as a consequence of an attitude and deed which have drawn the line of division between himself and his fellows all too finally. "Whoever hates his brother is a murderer ... like Cain who was a child of evil and who killed his brother. And why did he kill him? Because his works were evil and those of his brother were just" (1 Jn 3:15, 12). Here we have got back behind the great solidarity of collective guilt and atonement to the origin of such guilt, and the question which rings out so sharply and penetratingly finds each one of us not as a member of a collective but in our isolation, an isolation which is so terrifyingly lonely precisely because in our hatred we have maneuvered ourselves into it. The gesture with which Cain shrugs off his responsibility for his brother (although it lies all too heavily upon him) is no accidental gesture which he can forget or come to terms with; from now on it will permanently mold the form of his conscience and consciousness. *L'enfer c'est les autres*: but it is I who have in the first place made the others into a hell, I myself experience them as hell: in me, in my hellish inside.

There is yet a third story where a man tells another of a scandalous affair, a deed of crass selfishness, and where the one who listens becomes terribly incensed. His moral sensitivity is aroused and the narrator interrupts him with the statement "You are the man" (2 Sam 12:7). In effect those words contain the death sentence for King David which he himself has passed on the common adulterer and murderer. Cain's gesture disclaiming responsibility for his deed is superseded by the unconscious act of self-condemnation. There is no question here of exculpating David by allusion to the case of Oedipus, because David himself knew very well what he was doing when he took Bethsheba and ordered Uriah to his death. He himself has dug out his evil deed from his "unconscious". Of him it can be said, "Out of your own mouth will I condemn you" (Lk 19:22).

These three stories have this much in common: on the one hand, the attempt to hide, to escape, to bury the deed in the forgotten parts of one's mind; and on the other, the word which confronts these men, like Hamlet's sword, pierces through the curtains and penetrates the heart, "living and active, sharper than any two-edged sword, piercing to the division of soul and spirit, of joints and marrow ... all are open and laid bare" (Heb 4:12f. RSV). So much of course is true: if Adam, Cain, and David had not been spoken to by the voice, then they could have so enmeshed themselves in the wilderness of their consciousness that they would gradually have become inextricably intertwined, caught up in a thicket of threatening fate or, in more general terms, in the "fallenness of existence", in a tragic sense of life, relieved from time to time by an attempt at religious escape. Fortunately for them the sword catches them, as it were, red-handed, when the glowing coals of their sin have not yet completely turned to ash. The sword addresses them as thou. It attacks the person, it throws it sharply into light; it is only the person who is addressed, the person who, as it were, has been purely and cleanly prepared, carefully separated from all social involvements, from all psychological and sociological generalizations (which distribute guilt and divide it by the number of individuals). There is this terrible and yet blessed moment when it is I and only I who am addressed, when the voice summons me to its presence, as it were produces me as a person; there is this moment when I am compelled to give it the answer which I was unable to give to myself, or which I had put off till later or had allowed to sink without trace in the deep well of the past. Perhaps indeed under these circumstances I do not even need to answer. The very words addressed to me present me with the answer in its finished form, like the image in the mirror, so that I would have to invent a barefaced lie in order to find any other answer than the one which is demanded from me. The person is taken seriously, is stripped of all outward covering and confronted with the word which speaks to it personally, over and above all the horizontal laws which enmesh individuals.

III

This protest is perfected in the New Testament. The word has become flesh and taken the form of the word of eternal love to sinners. The term "sinner" is found everywhere on its pages, cannot be avoided. It is from this encounter that it receives an acute and virulent sense: all previous meanings are taken up into this dramatic action. "If I had not spoken to them, they would be without sin". Or, more clearly, "This is judgment, that light has come into the world, but that men loved darkness rather than light, for their deeds were evil." And this, although shortly before we read: "God has not sent his Son into the world, in order that he might judge the world, but that the world through him might be saved" (Jn 3:17ff.). It is a new, definitive "Adam, where are you?" which gives him the opportunity either of being found or of hiding himself more deeply in his wilderness. "For everyone who does evil hates the light and does not walk into the light lest he be convicted of his deeds." The voice which addresses the one who hides himself is pure love. It is that which challenges him. He is not condemned but asked whether he will not step into the light of love. The light itself gives him the possibility, which of himself he would not have had. He must decide, he must open himself to its light. And this always in a final loneliness, alone with the light. Perhaps as a consequence of a question put by one's fellow men—whether the question was itself actually intended selfishly or not. But it is a question to which he alone can give the answer. There are no general absolutions anywhere in the gospel. Every individual must step into the light alone, in isolation. The Samaritan woman is questioned in a private conversation where her past and present are examined, put under the light; it is the light itself which gives her the courage to capitulate: "Lord, I see that you are a prophet ..." Peter has to appear alone, is examined, scolded, praised, then warned again, looked at with deep sorrow, and finally confronted with the unanswerable question "Do you love me more than these?" He is presented with a task which he has to carry out completely on his own, which he may not delegate to anyone else, because personal love has entrusted him alone with it. Thomas has to appear alone, to step out of the circle of the disciples who surround him; he alone has doubted; he must put his hand into the side; he and no other must here cease to be unbelieving and become believing. Many can find edification and strength in these examples, for good reproduces itself no less than evil; but just as everyone dies alone, so too everyone must answer for himself alone before the word of God.

And yet this word has not come into the world to judge but to save. It would judge if it only spoke to us and attacked us from above and from without. But it has died for us and descended into our hell and has shared with us the power of its light, the Holy Spirit from within. And so the matter does not remain hanging in mid-air, with a question mark posed against the word, whether it has power enough to penetrate the thicket in which we are caught and to free us from it. We no longer stand in the Old Testament. We have been caught up. We can, if we will, give ourselves up. "Everything stands ready."

But the advent of the one who saves us intensifies the danger. For are we not all redeemed, has not the love of God in Christ shown itself to be catholic, for all, and does this not mean that in consequence the isolation of the Old Testament has been superseded? But this is to raise again the specter of a levelling psychology and sociology, and to raise it this time from within the very heart of Christianity itself. Here one has to hold fast to the gospel, which says two things to us. Jesus Christ confronts every individual with the lonely choice between discipleship and rejection, faith and denial, between giving God the honor by keeping the commandment of love and seeking one's own honor. The great judgment scene in which those on the right are divided from those on the left means quite simply this, that the personal reaches down into the very depths of our being. No one is automatically swept along in the crowd toward the gates of heaven. And the second thing is this, that the word which calls us out is spoken in the name of God's love. That love alone is the content of what is called out. The love of the Father waits for the lost Son. The love of the Father in the form of his Son seeks the lost sheep. And the total love of the Father concentrates its attention on the one individual to such an extent that the nine and ninety must now stand in the shade. It is always a particular person with whom God deals. And it is only when the man who is thus caught in the light of God's love notices what kind of a light has been waiting for him, for him in particular, that he can say in simple truth, "Father I have sinned against heaven and before you, and am no more worthy to be called your son" (Lk 15:21 RSV). Is there anyone who dares to smile condescendingly at this Lucan parable? If not, then people will have to be content to allow the word "sin" to stand here. The father and the son stand alone on the dusty track, the son broken, making his way home, humbled and small. Nothing could be farther from the son's mind than to start pleading mitigating circumstances. What earlier appeared as the penetrating sword of the word—"Adam, where are you?"—has now become the silent waiting of the Father and his silent kiss. What point is there now of trying to escape from love, instead of confessing to its face that one has sinned? The bright mirror of this love reveals in sharp contours what sin was, but it reveals it now as something that is already in the process of disappearing, of breaking up. The man who has been uncovered is already, as it were in advance, wrapped in the protecting cloak of his Father.

But if the image of the waiting Father is obscured, then the consciousness of sin will itself begin to disappear into the twilight. Perhaps simply because we stand helpless before the enormous mountains of refuse of worldly injustice which tower above us like a natural phenomenon; or because we are often naïve enough to think that one could perhaps gradually deal with evil by means of increasingly developed technology or by means of alterations in the structure of society. Of course we should do what we can in order to alleviate injustice in the world. But this should not distract us from what is most important, that I, and always I, am the sinner in the sight of that love which calls me out and in whose sight I always fail so miserably.

The Church as "Caritas"

Caritas is the word for "Christian love", and something is called "Christian" in so far as it is derived from the man Jesus Christ. The "Church" too is not an association which has been arbitrarily provided with statutes by men, but a society which has gathered around the event of the man Jesus Christ. But is there any point in seriously considering for ourselves today a society like this which ultimately cannot determine itself but whose very lines were laid down at the point of its origin? At least it would be fair to try to get a clear picture of the laws which govern its structure by looking at the first clear spring rather than at the muddy canals which have been tapped off the main stream.

The Church, the society gathered around its center, Jesus Christ, stands at the intersection of two lines; both are statements about love. The first: "Herein is love, *not* that *we* have loved God, but that *he* has loved *us* and given his Son as a sacrificial offering for our sins" (1 Jn 4:10). The second, on the other hand: "If you love one another, then you will all know that you are my disciples" (Jn 13:35). That means to say that the criterion by which we can judge whether the Church is indeed the discipleship of Christ is truly the love of the disciples for one another; no other distinctive mark of the "true Church" is envisaged. But the first statement sets up a powerful barrier around this criterion, namely, the condition which must be satisfied if we are to speak of Christian love, "not that *we* ... but that *he*. ..." Love must first be received, from an unexpected, because superhuman, realm, from God himself; and it is received in an unpredictable manner because God gives his Son for us men who do not love him. It is this love which falls into our realm from above and which provides the standard, the law, and the form of that which in the Church has to be love in discipleship: "By this we know love, that he laid down his life for us; and we ought therefore to lay down our lives for the brethren" (1 Jn 3:16). How are we to explain this "therefore"? Is there, as it were, an appeal here to our moral sense of propriety? Not simply to this; according to the understanding of Christians, it is a much closer bond which holds both together, at the intersection of which we spoke earlier. The fact that God allows his Son to make expiation for our, for your and my sin, that Christ takes on himself my and your guilt in his death in abandonment by God, receives final, concrete, and yet ever-present form in the fact that God offers us as our food of bread and wine his Son, given for us—one can say his substantial love for us. We take his love to ourselves, we assimilate it, or rather it penetrates and assimilates us. And we all who "partake of the one bread" henceforth form "one body" (1 Cor 10:17) whose "members" have for one another a much more intimate and substantial love than men who are linked together by natural sympathies, by blood relationships, or by common interest. This needs close inspection. Who am I to receive this gift of God in the circle of the brethren (for it is only there that it is offered)? I am the one whom

God has so loved that he gave his Son for me who took my guilt upon him and took it with him into his death and in return made the gift to me of his love. It is because of that, and not because of what I imagine myself to be, that I am marked out ultimately for God by God's love. And the same is true of the brother. He is not the imperfect, unredeemed man whom he perhaps seemed to me to be; in truth he is the "brother for whom Christ died" (Rom 14:15; 1 Cor 8:11). As such I must look at him in a quite different light and, equally, love him quite differently because again of a quite different principle of loving than the limited, self-dictated principle which has its source in me alone. Only then will he become my companion at table in the Church and I his.

At this point an objection will be raised. It will be urged that this love of the God who gave his Son for us is a universal one. Is it not intended for all men? What, then, is the point of this particular Church? Does she not narrow the horizon of the love which should be as widely open in us as the love of our Father in heaven, who allows his sun to rise on all men, on all just men and on all sinners? If there has to be something like the Church, then at best she should be the denomination of those who *know* about this universal love of God but who, far from relating it to themselves, or indeed from limiting it to themselves, go out to all men proclaiming this love in deed and word. The Church then would only have her justification in so far as she was involved in a movement away from herself toward the others. It is with this great mission that the whole gospel ends, and the Acts of the Apostles report the first steps of the young

Church which are to lead her "from Jerusalem and all Judaea through Samaria to the ends of the earth".

That is true, provided that this Church which packs her bags and sets off on her journeys exists in the first place. You are the "salt of the earth", the "light of the world", the "city on a hill". All that has to exist. As a reality, and that means, of course, much more than a mere "knowledge" of something. For God's love is a deed, an ultimate committing of himself. And this is not something which one can teach others about, as one can a theoretical truth. But is it not enough, then, for everyone in his personal individual engagement in the world to point to God's engagement in the world? Then Christianity would consist of any number of scattered individuals, who have convinced themselves of the truth of this saving deed of God. (The manner in which they have come to conviction is left unspecified, perhaps as a result of an accidental encounter with Christ, as the result of reading the New Testament.) But that will not do under any circumstances. It needs a real *society of love*, as it were, a real *model* of that which humanity is to become, if the members of this community are to be able to communicate to the world from their own inner experience what the meaning of the message is. And this community is formed around the table of the Lord where the love of God is *received* in the first place as *his* practice, in order that it may then be converted into the practice of those who have received this gift, who have been joined together already by this love. It is the common belief of those who share in this table fellowship that they do really receive *his* love, a belief whose essential content is nothing but the reality of this love. Without this unity of belief, from which unity then proceeds the transformation of belief into the love of the Church, there could be no Christian proclamation in the world. The Church in God's plan is the indispensable link between the love of God and the love of mankind. Jesus' great prayer of farewell is constructed precisely along the lines of this plan: the unity of faith and love of the Church *as* the mediating link between the unity of love in God and the unity of love of all men in God which is yet to be created.

Christ knows therefore what he is doing when he in the first place calls his disciples into a total engagement, "Leave everything", "Follow him alone", in order that as a society they may become "yeast" and multipliers for the world. And wherever we can get some picture of the Church in action, as for example in the Epistle to the Ephesians, it is clear that according to the will of Christ, of the exalted Christ, provision has been made in the Church for particular forms of engagement—"apostles", "prophets", "evangelists" (catechists), "pastors", "teachers" (Eph 4:11)—all entrusted with the task of assisting in building up the Church of the believers as an organism of mutual serving love, which Church has then to stand in the world unmistakably and effectively as the model of true love. Those particular obligations are a service to the service of love. They demand themselves therefore especially an intensified love in order that by them that Church may be built up which can then work in the world as a multiplier of such love.

There is a second objection. It is urged that the Church does not give the appearance of being what is claimed for her. She is bourgeois, sleepy, full of organizational fury signifying nothing. In so far as this objection is justified (but of course love cannot be comprehended by statistical methods) the answer may run like this. Then see to it yourself that she becomes different; commit yourself to the cause of love, and that can only be done by committing your own love fully, a love which, in so far as it is thought of as Christian, must see itself first as a love that has been received. "In this is love, not that we ..." Any man who wishes to reform the Church must first allow himself to be stripped of any sense of superiority, of knowing better, in order that he may be molded by the form of the love of Christ, and that love he will only receive in the—ecclesial!—society of the Lord's table. Whoever wishes to mold the Church must first allow himself to be molded by her in so far as she is the "body" and the "bride" of Christ. Then he may be seized and consumed by the zeal that the Church should become more and more what she *is*. Anyone who wishes to raise the Church's potential for love, in order that through the Church the world's potential for love may be raised, must imitate and make his own Jesus' humble attitude of love, not only externally but in his heart of hearts: an attitude which finds its expression in Jesus' washing his brothers' dirty feet. "Do you understand what I have done to you? ... If I, your Lord and Master, have washed your feet, then you *must* wash one another's feet. The servant is not greater than his master" (Jn 13:13ff.). There is no selection for the feet washing; each of these brothers with his dirty feet is "the brother for whom Christ died". Whether he is sympathetic or not.

Whether he is progressive, reactionary, or Lord knows what else. Only love—the love which is instituted by the Lord but which now is to portray itself—"edifies", whereas the sense of knowing better (*gnosis*) destroys (1 Cor 8:1). The continued existence of the Church in the present and in the future depends on whether we understand this sentence and realize it.

Love and Congregation

I

The Quarrel

The Ecumenical Movement was initiated by men for whom the contradiction between the Church and her division was something that had burned itself intolerably into their consciences. For them the Church denied her own very essence in such divisions and lost all credibility in the eyes of the world, which could then only shrug its shoulders and turn away from the message which the Church herself failed to realize, to look for a more enlightened religion or ethic of humanity. The Movement has slowed down, indeed in many places has come to a halt, because the inter-confessional quarrel has meanwhile broken out within the individual Churches, and this most noticeably within the Catholic Church (which until now has been more or less spared such quarrelling), and has now further robbed even the individual Churches of their credibility. Or should one not rather say that the sickness, which previously was most noticeable in the inter-confessional organism—with its symptoms of alienation, enmity, slandering, malicious misrepresentation—has now spread inexorably to the internal organs of the individual confessions and so revealed the true source of the evil:

> Where there are sins, there is multiplicity, there are divisions, there are false doctrines, there are disputes

> [remarks Origen, who continues], but where virtue rules, there is oneness, there is union, as indeed then all the faithful "were of one heart and one mind". Or to put it more clearly: the ground of all evil is the falling apart of things, the ground of all good on the contrary is the joining together, the bringing back of confused masses to unity; for if we are to be saved, then such salvation must lead to unity, so that we may become "perfect" in a single mind and view of things, may become "one body and one spirit". But if, on the other hand, we behave in such a manner that it is not unity which characterizes us but rather that men can say of us, "I belong to Paul, I, on the other hand, to Apollos, I to Cephas", if, that is, we are torn apart and divided by our jealousies and ambition, then we shall never reach the place where men are who have been joined together in unity. For just as the Father and the Son "are one", so too those who have the same "Spirit" will be fused together in union (*Hom. on Ezekiel* 9.1).

None too late the old teacher of the Church presents us clearly with the two simple, basic directions which we can take, the centripetal and the centrifugal, that which builds up and that which destroys the Church, and he is not to be distracted by objections of any sort, by appeals to the legitimate pluralism of our time. He would have disposed of this objection with the same serenity and the same facility for drawing clear distinctions; for he does not speak of the multiplicity of the members, which is indeed an expression of the unity of the living body, but of the sinfulness of heart whose fruit is division and strife. And, indeed, is it not the case that the strife which dominates all that we do, the aggressive, cutting, mocking, supercilious, self-justifying tones of all our discussions and publications, leads us very naturally to the conclusion that somewhere quite definitely there is sin here? For whatever else sin is, it is lack of love, and as soon as we think of that, no one will be able to be the first to cast the stone at others, but will be compelled to examine himself. The need for such a self-examination is more than urgent; it is five to twelve. It will not be easy, because it has become part of our accepted social *mores* to strike a rather bitter note.

And indeed it is very difficult not to become bitter when one sees that the principle of the unity of the Church, the unity of the Father and the Son who give us their one Spirit, the faith, that is, that Jesus Christ is not only one of us, but is also on God's side in order that he may give us the Spirit of unity from within the divine unity—when all that is put in question. How can I ultimately be one with the man who disputes the very ground on which I would be one with him? And who proposes to me another rendezvous and insists upon that as a *conditio sine qua non*, namely, the unity of man or the union which has still to be created among men? This other man, with whom I cannot agree on the question of unity, calls himself a Christian, appeals consequently to Christ, who according to him can only have intended that our present divisions and their causes, namely, the crying injustice of the division of goods, should be ended. For what good will all the transcendental "reconciliation of the world with God" do us, if Lazarus is dying of hunger at our gate, yours and mine? What price orthodoxy, praying, and running to church, if we do not change the world?—But why can he not make his case calmly, why does he get so roused? Clearly, my orthodoxy casts such a shadow on his view of things that he will only be able to follow it through if he has first pushed me out of the light. And so it seems that the closer our disputes about the nature of unity come to the very point of unity itself, the more irreconcilable our strife becomes. It is at this point that the role of the congregation assumes concrete form.

II

Love and Help

We have no intention of speculating now on the question of what changes the parish principle will undergo in the next decade, or indeed whether it will not be abandoned altogether. Not only because there will be too few parish priests left, but also because there will be a definite division of opinion among those who do remain. We want simply to take as our starting point the fact that the Church, if she is to be visible at all, must always be realized as a church in a particular place, as a concrete group and congregation. A congregation is constituted, in the view of the first Christians, as "one heart and one mind", and this through the two actions of the common breaking of bread (with which a love feast, especially for the poor, was associated—or should have been associated) and by the mutual help and support of the members of the congregation for each other. The *caritas* which the Christians received, and which by virtue of their participation in the "one bread" flows from Christ into all their hearts and minds, flows on through them in the practical exercise of *caritas* between Christians. And it is not so much the *caritas* which Christians have received, which lends itself as little to apologetic use as do all the "mysteries" of Christianity, but the charity which is exercised by the Christians which is intended as an exemplary sign by which men may know that here "truth" is present: a truth which fulfils man's nature at the very point at which perhaps it desires to achieve fulfilment but is powerless to do so. It is in this way therefore that it reveals a more than human power. Faith and the sacrament do not have practical effect spontaneously, but only if the Christian recognizes the demand which they contain and overcomes the resistance of his own sloth. And so one can say without reservation that it is up to Christians whether or not they make credible in their practice the truth of the mystery from which they take their name. For the first Christians the congregation, by virtue of the mutual selfless help which members gave to one another, was to be for the world a model of what being a Christian really means.

This closed model was only a starting point; today the Christian attitude can indeed be exercised in a manner which is thoroughly open to the non-Christian world, can be exercised together with non-Christians without, if it is so exercised, becoming any the less credible. (One might think, for instance, of the manner in which Paul VI attempts to bring his personal interest to bear at all places where men are concerned with making peace and avoiding political crises.) But this activity which is open to the world is none the less best inspired by the life of the congregation, inspired, activated, and over-arched; this of course not so much in matters which demand the kind of special technical knowledge which can only be had in specialized, extra-parochial commissions, but in matters which, if they are to be received and tackled practically at all, demand a Christian eye and a Christian sense. The problems which are encountered within the narrower sphere of the parish itself: uncared-for poor people, spiritually abandoned people, broken marriages, neglected children, problems connected with living conditions or with wages, the mass of hidden misery, in the Church and outside her boundaries. How much more important it would be to consider problems like this in one's church meetings (with due discretion) and to seek for means of overcoming them, than to be perpetually concerned with organizations, appointments, and questions of parish finance! One would then gather round the table of the Lord in a common caring love now realized in a very new kind of attitude. There might even be a possibility of bringing together different views of the Church, even perhaps of overcoming the apparently unbridgeable gulf between a notion of unity which is to be found in Christ the "God-man" who, really present among the gathered congregation, offers them his flesh and blood, and the notion of unity as something to be realized by those who are inspired by Jesus as the exemplary man in whose memory we now celebrate our brotherly meal: even this gulf could, even if it could not be completely closed, nevertheless be in a manner bridged. But it would be a necessary condition of such a coming together that there should be a general recognition that the name under which we are gathered, which we bear as a name that distinguishes us and describes us, cannot simply be exchanged for the name of other great philanthropists, but that its bearer has given us originally something which we would not have had or have of ourselves and that it is on the basis of this gift that he can make the demands of us that he does. It is this gift which provides the help which in turn sets us free to help others; we do not wish to separate these two elements from each other (even if, perhaps, we would emphasize the relationship between them in different ways): that we receive help as we are allowed to help, that we have received help and consequently may help.

III

The Encompassing Love

Under this sign, which gives expression to our primary concern, the secondary questions which are today inflated, and which threaten to tear the Church apart, ought to fall back into place and cease to have such divisive effect within the Church and the congregation. The bitterness which in wider areas has become the basic characteristic of church fellowship, the divisiveness which assumes many kinds of masks and titles in order to justify itself, is continually showing itself to be unchristian and consequently putting the speakers and the matter to which they are so much attached in the wrong.

The "one heart, one mind" of the Early Church was, even at the very beginning, never something which could be achieved without stern self-discipline: even in the very earliest days in Jerusalem there is a sharp confrontation between Jewish Christians and Hellenists over the question of actual or supposed discrimination in the distribution of alms; attempts were made to overcome the grievances by creating a new institution. The properly dogmatic struggles were the occasion of a still sharper confrontation: questions about how much of the Old Testament tradition should be taken over into the Church and how much should be discarded, questions about how far one should think of oneself and behave as one who is "risen with the Lord", a "pneumatic", a brother of the free spirit, or whether one must be brought back to the folly of the Crucified, questions about the extent to which Christians as "free men", as spiritually "strong men", should impose their own views on the congregation or if they should act more out of consideration for the spiritually "weak", for those still tied to elements of their past, perhaps even to the extent that they would have to renounce some of their privileges as strong men ("to me everything is permitted") for the sake of other brothers. All these matters are treated at length in Paul's epistles; all this still sounds familiar enough. If people had only listened to what Paul had to say and taken this as a decisive norm of their behavior within their congregations, then things in the Church today would look very different. Instead of mutual suspicion, recrimination, scorn, and complaint, our mutual love for one another would lead us together to turn our eyes upward, and the vision which would meet us there would condemn the fraternal hatred in our hearts, no matter where the haters and despisers take up their positions within the Church. The intransigence which is becoming more and more the accepted style of our dealings with one another, no matter whom it may be turned against—the Pope and the bishops or the progressives—places those who speak and think in this manner automatically outside the Christian brotherhood. Anyone in whose ears there still rings something of the echoes of the Christian gospel and its joyful message can sense immediately that this is the wrong key.

The self-denial which is demanded of men so much in the New Testament is very hard; in practice one must give up everything, even one's favorite views, whenever the encompassing love of the congregation is at stake. It has become a popular rallying call that faith without love is dead and that it must prove itself in right practice. Well and good: here then, precisely, is its first and indeed last test. For the man who makes it his aim to pursue his own separate actions of love somewhere in the wide world while still at odds with the congregation might perhaps be a philanthropist, but not a Christian who is always a member and representative of his Church; he would be like a member of a religious order, carrying out his apostolic work in disobedience to his superiors. The Church test is the decisive one. No matter how wonderfully Paul had spoken to the Christian pagan congregation about love, if at the same time he had lived in a state of war with the Jewish Christian congregation at Jerusalem, the whole construction would have been erected on a lie. He survived the real test when (in Acts Chapter 21) he is asked by James to undergo a Jewish custom in the old Temple and submits to the request without demur. The unity of the Church, realized in the unity of love, which abandons its own standpoint for the sake of the wider, encompassing community, is the first concern: it is here that we find belief in Jesus Christ, who by his self-denial has redeemed the world, assuming concrete form. The unity of the Church has its origin in the participation of the community in his self-emptying: in the Eucharist and at the same time in the active frame of mind which the reception of his Eucharist should effect in us. From the start in the primitive Church, poor and rich alike were expected to bear with each other in the same congregation, under their common Lord, who became poor in order to enrich all men with his goods. Even at that time the apostolic letters take up the cause of the poor against the indifference and hard-heartedness of the rich or against the flattering of the rich by a majority of the congregation. The letters make their protest in the name of Christ, in the name of love. They do not condemn wealth; they do not plead for a congregation consisting exclusively of the poor. But abundance of wealth is given to men for them to share, and God's blessing is given to such sharing, a blessing which takes visible form in the fact that such sharing produces gratitude both to God and to love. The things that Paul (2 Cor 9) worked out on the small model of the exchanges within a congregation or between two congregations are indeed to be tested at precisely this point and not in the large-scale, world-embracing, and consequently rather abstract social and political models which are sometimes suggested. At least this is so for the majority of Christians.

Of course it is true that the relationships between Corinth and Jerusalem can be reflected today in those between a European and a Bolivian congregation or some inter-church aid project in that country, at least where such relationships are guided by those whose task it is to ensure that such monies are properly and usefully applied. But such a relationship ought to be founded on the true character of the European congregation as a congregation, that is to say, on the mutual love in the peace of Christ which is to be found in it—notwithstanding the fact that this peace and unity may again be furthered by their common action in helping those outside. But the danger will never be far off that such attention paid to those outside may be an attempt to create an alibi for one's failure to undertake the very concrete acts of renunciation which are demanded by one's own place within one's own congregation, which is not infrequently composed of very unlovable neighbors. Even the world of ecumenical action can (though it must not) become such an alibi. Even more dangerous are the numerous conventicles which are formed within congregations, but also across the boundaries of several congregations, in the name of some slogan or other of supposedly charismatic character, and which then dissociate themselves from the meetings of the congregation. Ignatius of Antioch has said already all that needs be said on the subject of the formation of such sects ("heresies" in the original sense of the word of "splitting off"). The celebration of the Eucharist by such a group is for them a confirmation of their partial program, a program which sets itself up polemically against other church programs and is therefore consequently anti-universal, anti-catholic. Such celebrations profane the Eucharist in the deepest sense: the sacred sign and event, whose very purpose is to incorporate all that is particular within itself and to subject it to the Father, is here itself misused by being subjected to a particular program and principle (particular, and consequently profane).

IV

Conversion and Prayer

The congregation meets together for communal acts of eucharistic prayer, and it is out of this "vertical" praying community that the "horizontal" community of discourse, dialogue arises. This has its origin in prayer and always leads back into prayer. One should never utter a word in dialogue which one cannot relate to prayer and which one would not own to in prayer.

But let us first say something about prayer itself. There are many today who do not know what to say or to think about it; their own words seem not to carry to God; their relation to the prayer and worship of the congregation remains external, both things because they are estranged from the origin from which both arise, namely, Jesus' prayer to his Father. It is not only that Jesus' whole existence (and consequently the center of Christian faith) is grounded in this permanent communication, but also that in that communication every individual Christian truth which one is wont to speak of abstractly as a dogma or "articles of faith" comes to life, becomes verifiable. Jesus is himself precisely the identity of prayer and conversation, his mission to the world is what he receives, once and for all and yet continually anew at each moment from the Father; it is that of which he receives continual confirmation in the instructions of the Holy Spirit, and his attention to God is the guarantee of the rightness of his execution of his task. Everything is spread out before the Father, just as the Father openly displays his will to the Son (Jn 5:19f.). All the cares and tragedies of the world are borne up in the word which travels between the Father and the Son, receive in that word their place, their proper weight. And everything which the Son will do in obedience to his Father's charge, even his going to the Cross and his descent into death, even his Resurrection, which opens a way to God for the world, everything which is drawn into this event becomes expressible, receives a share in the eternal word. For it is thither that men's works, if they are to embrace the whole truth, must be translated. The Christian ought to know that and ought to hold his speech to God and his speech to men closely together. In the middle, mediating, stand the words of the Church; it is the Church which allows words from God's realm to pass over into the realm of men and vice versa. If I am told, "Our Lord Jesus Christ pardons you, and I, by virtue of his authority, absolve you from your sins ...", then the first part of that saying of the Church refers to something which has been spoken to me from heaven, while the second part addresses that saying to me personally in the power of heaven, and the third part, which in this case has not been formulated but which follows directly from what has gone before, entrusts me with this saying so that

I may pass it on to others and allow it to prove itself in me, "as we forgive our debtors". Those words can be prayed, they can—spoken or unspoken—be done, they can also be presupposed and active as the background in every apparently quite worldly conversation. And they imply, when seen in the light of the primal conversation between the Father and the Son, that there is within that conversation the process of "representation, substitution". One does not take part in the conversation, as it were, from behind fortified positions, but one must show oneself, one must allow oneself to be put in question, perhaps to be deeply wounded. One must take upon oneself the questions, burdens, and accusations of the other and thereby allow him entrance into oneself. But I can only seriously do that if behind me stands the one who has already taken me upon himself and has carried me through all things. Because we are all carried men, we can bear one another's burdens, having all the time in mind what we are giving to others to bear.

It is important that the Church, to speak in concrete terms the congregation, stands at this point as a mediating link. It is true, of course, that Jesus prays alone on the mountain and also teaches us to pray to the Father in our own "chambers". But the true participant in the words of prayer between the Father and the Son is "his bride", "his body", the Church. Her word is secret and public, personal and social, prayer and conversation, both at the same time. The individual aspect may and must find expression in individual acts with their different emphases, but everything must have its validity in its mutual coherence, each aspect must lead over into the next, must be felt to be insufficient and in need of supplementation in so far as it is isolated. The way from communal prayer to communal conversation about the daily concerns of members of the congregation or of those for whom a member feels himself responsible should not be very long. What one has said communally to God will prevent lovelessness and alienation from taking a hold in the divisions of opinion which will certainly occur. The distinction between the different gifts of the Spirit serves, according to Paul, only to hold the living whole more strongly together. The multiplicity is the unfolding, the mediation of the unity, and in this it is admittedly also the test and trial of such unity. The word, whether it is prayer or conversation, will as it passes around the circle, like a ball in a game, be caught and thrown back by very different hands, but it is, seen in terms of its origin, always the same word. The ball is the focus of the group at play, it holds them together. So too the one word, whether it is prayer or conversation, is the uniting center of the congregation. It is active, incarnate word, a word which always wants again to become flesh in the congregation as it is created in its activity. And so it is said, "Bear one another in love, be zealous in preserving the unity of the spirit in the bond of peace: for you are one body and one spirit" (Eph 4:3f.).

The Boundary Line

I

The most difficult question which confronts us today with respect to the Church is the question of her boundary. Has she got one at all? It would seem that the slogan "opening up the Church to the world" would suggest that she has, but even that would leave the question open as to whether the boundary which today is to be opened up ought to have existed previously or not. It is possible that the Church might have shut herself up in a ghetto, against her own nature; and such suspicion is strengthened when we consider that the Church was, from the very beginning, sent out by Jesus Christ into the highways of the world to proclaim the salvation which God has made known, not exclusively to the Church, but to the world. That might lead us to suppose that the Church, if indeed she has any nature of her own at all, is a space whose nature is always to extend beyond its own limits, a permanent crossing of its own boundary, pure transcendence. And the axiom which appeared early on the scene, "outside the Church no salvation", and which in the course of the long history of its interpretation has today—and indeed long ago—been dropped in its literal meaning, would on such a view only have been possible as a result of a deep misconception of the nature of the Church.

The question has received a new urgency as a result of the tragedy of the large and smaller divisions within the

Church. Today the Catholic Church recognizes that other Christian churches, in differing degrees, deserve the name of "churches" if they preserve more or less central elements of Christ's Church. In so doing she recognizes that the Church's self-transcendence to the world occurs, as it were, in the form of waves, even if the wave-crests have in each case to be traced back to unchristian troughs, to rejection and fraternal wars. But perhaps the fact of the divisions, which we are working to overcome, has at least one positive side. It may help to give us practice within the Christian sphere in the dialogue which we are to pursue with the world, as we learn to recognize what each "Church" possesses and preserves of the true Christian heritage, as we learn, that is, how far the one Lord of the Church stands supreme above all Christian denominations.

When the frontiers become as unclear as this, we are compelled to look back to that area which was for us, in some mostly rather unreflected manner, traditionally marked off by a boundary: namely, the area of one's own Church. Can her boundaries be determined? And is what is determinable the really important thing about her? Augustine was fond of pointing out that there are many who seem to be outside the Church who are in truth within her, and what is worse, vice versa. Translated into the modern idiom, many heterodox Christians, many anonymous Christians are better Christians than many orthodox Christians who practice in the Church. This is not simply, as we suggested at the beginning, to set the Church moving toward her self-transcendence, because something of what she has to bring the world is already present in the world, but here the Church becomes so transcending that one no longer sees *what* it is at all that transcends or what it is that is immanent to itself. Has she an "in herself" which is actuated in her "for the world"? If so, then it will certainly not be easy to define. Is the interior of the Church bounded by a particular confession of faith? But what would such faith be without love, and is not the love of those who believe differently or not at all often in every way as living as that of church Christians? And, in any case, what form of confession of faith would a Catholic Christian own to today? Is there not increasingly a wealth of different interpretations attached to the same words of the Apostles' Creed, attached to every article, and opposed to each other pluralistically, to the point of irreconcilability? Or is the interior bounded by the sacraments? But there are sacraments which are validly administered in other confessions, there are *sacramenta in voto* in the sphere outside Christianity, and there are sacraments which are received fruitlessly and unworthily within the Church. Is that to say that being in the Church means, Christianly speaking, nothing more than an external mark of identification, even less than a passport?

Before one asks oneself *whether* a boundary can be drawn and *where* it ought to be drawn, one ought to establish the fact *that* in the New Testament such a boundary line was indeed drawn, and not without pain and struggle. For the Old Testament the boundary consisted quite simply and unproblematically in one's membership in the chosen people; proselytes, as the word suggests, were people who had come in additionally. But if the people become the "new", "spiritual" Israel, if "the scattered children of God are brought back" into the fold, the problem of where to put the boundaries then becomes more serious. In their letters the apostles, the primitive Church, do indeed draw such boundaries under the inspiration of the Spirit. Paul "in the authority of our Lord Jesus Christ" (1 Cor 5:4) throws a sinner out of the congregation as intolerable (cf. 1 Tim 1:20). In the Matthaean community-rule Jesus himself instructs the Church to apply the power of loosing and binding in this sense (Mt 18:17f.). The man who did not wish to obey the author of 2 Thessalonians is reproved in a brotherly manner, but nevertheless other Christians are to avoid intercourse with him (2 Th 3:14f.). Titus is instructed to warn once or twice anyone who is separated in the faith (*hairetikon anthropon*: one who produces separatisms, believing cliques in the congregation) and then to avoid him (Titus 3:10). Similarly we read at the end of the Epistle to the Romans: "My brothers, I exalt you to take care with those men who cause divisions and scandal concerning the teaching which you have learned; avoid them" (Rom 16:17). By contrast the "strong" and the "weak" brothers in the Church are to bear with one another instead of mutually estranging one another (Rom 14:15; 1 Cor 8:7ff.). The Johannine epistles continually underline the boundary line with high seriousness and reduce the criteria which Paul applied to a double statement: faith in the love of God which appeared in Jesus' atoning death, and life in the exercise of this love. It is here that the division occurs between Christians and anti-Christs. The latter "went forth from our midst, but they did not belong to us. If they had belonged to us, then they would have remained with us" (1 Jn 2:19). There is no question of going beyond the doctrine contained in that double statement. "Whoever goes beyond [*pro-agon*] and does not remain in the teaching of Christ, does not possess God ... if any man comes to you and does not bring this doctrine with him, then do not receive him in your house and do not offer him any greeting" (2 Jn 9f.). Whoever commits a sin which "leads to death" (and for John that is the conscious denial of the double statement about love), "of him I do not say that you should pray for him" (1 Jn 5:16). The Epistle of Jude (22f.) speaks in milder terms of two groups of people standing at or perhaps already beyond the boundary of the Church: the Church is to have sympathy with both of them, she is to attempt to bring back the one group, of those who only doubt, but to avoid all contact with the others, even external contact with their clothing.

How could the primitive Church draw such a hard line of division? Does she not already contain a healthy pluralism of theological, christological, and ecclesiological views? Surely the Epistle of James did not beat about the bush in its opposition to the pointed formulation of the doctrine of justification in the Epistle to the Romans? Did not Paul oppose Peter to his face? And does not *Peter* complain at the end of his second letter about the obscurity of the Pauline writings which lead to the destruction of many ignorant readers? Or was it that during the life-time of the apostles pluralism remained within bearable bounds, but that at the end of the apostolic age the seed which had been sown had already come up so far that one could keep it under control only by drawing the boundaries in a draconian and legalistic manner—boundaries which today seem to us extraneous and outmoded so that once again the floodgates are opened to the pluralism which was present in germ in Christianity from the start, and the early Christian boundaries are superseded?

But if one pulls down the barriers, then one must at least be clear that there can no longer be anything specifically Christian "in itself", no longer anything distinct and identifiable which could give of itself "for the world"; rather, that "in itself" would be absorbed into a more general "being for". In a "being for" of man for God or for the all-embracing or the absolute, as in all forms of "religion", or—if God really is dead and the all-embracing and absolute is man himself—in a "being for" of our common humanity. The being of Christians would then at best only be a subspecies, with its own particular characteristics, of such general "being for", but, for all its distinctiveness, still only a subspecies.

II

Before one adopts this solution (for there is no third, middle way), before, that is, one cuts the ties between oneself and primitive Christianity or accuses the latter of a lack of consistency, which it overlooked in its prime and which only subsequently broke out like a disease which had been lying hidden during that time; before one decides to take such radical measures which would dissolve Christianity in its very essence, it is perhaps appropriate to give some thought to the boundary which was actually drawn by the primitive Church. Appropriate, that is, in view of the primitive Church's invincible consciousness of her unity, which she never lost even when this consciousness was subjected to the severest tension, for the primitive Church was driven on by the desire to proclaim the one message in different languages (the miracle of Pentecost!) and was conscious all the time of circling round this one point, of always trying to grasp with all available intellectual means that which in its essence was simple and yet ungraspable. If it was in Antioch that believers were first given the name of "Christians" (Acts 11:26), then this name must give expression to their essential concern, namely, that the rabbi Jesus of Nazareth was the Christ, the Messiah, the fulfilment of all God's promises to Israel and to the world. For the Christians the emphasis in this synthetic proposition lies on the predicate (for otherwise they would have had to be called Jesuans). But the predicate makes it clear that here God has not given men "something" but everything, has not made him a penultimate but an ultimate gift. In Paul's words, "He who did not spare his own Son but gave him up for us all, will he not also give us *all* things with him?" (Rom 8:32 RSV). This God is love both in the giver and in the one who is given: "Who shall separate us from the love of *Christ*?... neither...height, nor depth, nor anything else in all creation, will be able to separate us from the love of *God*, in Christ Jesus our Lord" (8:35, 39 RSV). And the same teaching is to be found in John; "*God* so loved the world, that he gave his only begotten Son" (Jn 3:16 RSV) and, "as the Father has loved me, so have *I* loved you" (15:9 RSV). For both the love of Jesus Christ, proven in his giving of his life and his Eucharist, is the proof and the substantial presence of the love of God the Father. To allow oneself to be given this, to allow this to be true, to believe this is to be a Christian, and "to believe this" means in turn, without further reflection or deduction, to respond to it with the answering love of one's whole existence.

Here, in the spaceless transition from belief to love, in this primal reaction to God's extreme, eschatological love in Christ (a reaction which precedes any theological reflection), must lie the basic formula which expresses the center of Christian being and therefore also, in an elementary manner, the distinctive boundary of Christian being. There is such a formula. Paul, when he had finished dictating, added to the conclusion of the first Epistle to the Corinthians a greeting in his own hand: "I, Paul, write this greeting with my own hand. If anyone has no love for the Lord, let him be accursed [*anathema*]" (1 Cor 16:22 RSV). The formula is probably not his own invention but most likely comes from a primitive Christian liturgy. It expresses not only the essence of Christian being but also its distinctive mark. "The Lord" is of course Jesus Christ, and for Paul there is no question that "the Lord", that is to say, the exalted Lord, could be any other than he who was crucified for us all: for it is only as such that he is unconditionally worthy of love. The gnostic "moderns" would have liked a Christ without the historical Jesus, and as a result enthusiastic shouts of "Accursed [*anathema*] be Jesus!" were to be heard in their services (1 Cor 12:3). But Paul, as he says at the beginning of his letter to the Corinthians, wants "to know nothing among you except Jesus Christ and him crucified" (1 Cor 2:2 RSV), to proclaim nothing but the "word of the cross" with its divisive power: for all who do not accept it, it is "folly", for us "the power of God" (1 Cor 1:18), for them "the stench of death", for us "the fragrance of life" (2 Cor 2:15f.). What does "accursed" [*anathema*] mean here? It means to be put under a ban which excludes one from the community. In this sense Paul says of himself, "I could wish that I myself were anathema and cut off from Jesus Christ" (Rom 9:3), if by that means he could undo Israel's exclusion from the community of Christ. No one is excluded from this community who wishes to belong to it; but to belong to it means to love the love shown to us by God. "We love [God], because he has loved us first. ... Herein is love, not that we have loved God, but that he has loved us and has sent his Son as an expiation for our sin. God is love" (1 Jn 4:19, 10, 16). Whoever feels that he cannot share the Church's understanding of herself has by that very fact, perhaps to his regret, announced his non-membership of the Church, so that his removing himself or being removed from the Church is now no more than an act of honesty on both sides.

"If anyone has no love for the Lord," we read, "he should set himself apart." It does not say, if anyone does not find Jesus of Nazareth religiously interesting or sympathetic or in some respect (perhaps as a rebel) exemplary. Nor does it say, if anyone has difficulty in believing a particular dogma (only the one dogma is presupposed, the dogma which provokes this love). It does not even say, "If any man has no love for his brother" (even though this, for Paul and John, is the inevitable conclusion which has to be drawn from the former statement and is indeed the criterion for that statement). It only says, "If anyone has no love for the Lord". The Lord, that is to say, who is the risen, crucified Jesus of Nazareth. If one asks—although one should not ask—why it is so necessary that he should be loved by those who are gathered together in the congregation, the answer is, because he "has loved me and has given himself *for me* [on the Cross, as he casts himself into abandonment by God]" (Gal 2:20). This, of course, is only valid if this Jesus is not just any one of a hundred thousand crucified men but the one who is the "only beloved" of God (Lk 3:22; Jn 1:18), whose ultimately effective love for me and for all men in his representative suffering for me and for all men has been confirmed by God in his Resurrection. Whenever I cast doubt on this one thing, then my love wavers, perhaps not my love of God, perhaps not my love of my fellow men, but my love of the Lord. Belief—which lies at the center of the synthetic proposition "Jesus is Christ"—is only the starting point of this love, and without this point love in its Christian understanding cannot exist. The first Epistle of Peter speaks of "Jesus Christ, whom you love, without having seen him" (1 Pet 1:8), that is to say, by virtue of faith. And the conclusion of the Epistle to the Ephesians gives the positive form of the anathema of the earlier Pauline epistle: "Blessed be all who love our Lord Jesus Christ" (Eph 6:24).

That is the kernel. Everything else is, as it were, the fruit and the husk which lies around it, both our love for the Father who showed his love for us in the gift of his Son, and our love for the congregation of those who believe and love, that is, for the Church, and also our love (in the spirit of love of the Church) for all our human brothers. And this includes all dogma which developed organically from the central synthesis. Anyone who, taking the spirit of the Church for his guide, attempts to penetrate into the internal presuppositions and consequences of that synthesis will see that the statement of the "tri-personality" of God, of the divinity of Christ, of the Holy Spirit, of the Church as the body of Christ, of the Eucharist, of the resurrection from the dead (to mention only the most important), are mere explications and definitions of the statement "Jesus is Christ". He is the Lord (one of God's names), he must be loved, because he "has first loved" us and me, because in him the absolute love and faithfulness of God the Father have been revealed, God who has fulfilled his promise by giving up his only Son into death and into the depths of hell for the sake of our guilt. And the Spirit is the love of Father and Son, which is given to us so that we may, through God, learn to understand that God is love. And the Eucharist is the incomprehensible, re-presentation of God's loving self-giving. Why should a Christian go to church on Sunday (cf. Heb 10:25) if not to encounter God's giving to himself for us again and again, to encounter it and to incorporate it into himself? And what point would there be in referring to oneself as a member of a Church if she were not the "body" of love, where eternal, more than human love for the world takes—or at least should take—bodily form? Of course this "body" consists of sinners, that is to say, those who do not love, and will therefore till the end of the world be subject to the most radical criticism. But if this criticism does not consist primarily in the example of a greater love, then it will heal no wound; the critic without love resembles rather a man who scratches himself all the more furiously, the more fiercely he itches, a process which of course can only result in exacerbating and spreading the inflammation. The great saints were reformers of the Church, but they were edifying reformers. Not all great reformers were saints, that is to say, those who truly loved; many of them destroyed more than they built up. The fierce acids which today are dropped into the hearts of millions from the pulpit, from the press, radio, and television, or which are prescribed as medicine for man's enlightenment, in the interest of progress in accordance with the natural sciences and with the most recent exegesis, as medicine to enable man to turn (or indeed to convert himself) to the world, have hardly been brewed up by those who love the Lord.

Even in the Old Testament and in Judaism the command to love God, the Lord, with all one's strength was the central point of the law. This love demanded the whole man for itself and was to be tested by man's conduct toward his neighbor; but this test was no substitute for the thing itself. In the New Testament God becomes man: the Lord in heaven becomes our "Master and Lord" on earth (Jn 13:13) and at the same time our "slave" and "neighbor"; as a result the connection between love of God and of neighbor becomes even tighter, becomes indissoluble in him. But "was Paul [or Mr. Smith] crucified for you?" (1 Cor 1:13). Or to put it another way: Is our neighbor Christ simply identical with any other neighbor, once I know in faith who he is? That he condescends to receive the gift which we give to the least of his brothers as a gift made to him does not in the least alter the fact that he is the "only beloved Son" of the Father "full of grace and truth", that he is *in himself* and *for me* in no sense comparable with any other man. It is he whom I have to thank for what I am in the sight of God: a child of the Father and therefore an "heir of God and fellow heir of Christ" (Rom 8:17). No one can compel me to accept that and to regard it as valid, but it can very properly be proved to me that the acceptance of this faith and of this love justifies one's bearing the name of Christian, whereas the rejection (perhaps on grounds of conscience) of any intention of loving the Lord is logically equivalent to non-membership in the community which is constituted by such love.

There are many kinds of excuse which can be offered for the man who declares that he is unable to love in such a way. Above all, it may be urged that such loving is impossible because what is conceived of here is something superhuman and consequently apparently inhuman. It is probably that which above all passes understanding, for who could think anything greater than that God himself is "love" and, while remaining what he is, gives himself for the guilty lost creature into the hands of death and lostness? That is not only the greatest thing that can be conceived, but "greater than anything that can be thought" (Anselm). For the man who assumes that the horizon of our thinking reason is the horizon of truth, it is at best "too beautiful to be true" and consequently, presumably, an imaginative creation, a "myth", a product of religious fantasy. That it is so can be seen from the fact that it cannot be incorporated into human plans for the future and is consequently incapable of effectively changing the world. For the person who refuses to go along with such a myth in the name of reason, of a general human understanding of reality, the less one takes over of the myth the better; he is attracted to the human form of the myth and attempts at best to build this up from within. And, as a result, his sympathies will be with those exegetes who treat the synthetic judgment "Jesus is Christ" as an a posteriori judgment and who trace it back to its historical origins, thus distancing themselves from the self-understanding of the primitive Church and from her way of loving the Lord. Whether in spite of this they still retain the right to call themselves "Christians", as many indeed do, depends on the propriety of changing the meaning of a name after nearly two thousand years, a name which was originally coined for this and for no other purpose. It would be permissible if the synthesis which was then created was unconsciously a product of the same critical reason which today reflects critically on its action then. And we can leave aside for the moment the question of whether its reflection is the result simply of its theoretical or also of its practical and dialogical use, because what confronts it in the Christian synthetic proposition itself transcends every situation in the relationships between men.

Ultimately such decisions are not taken in the field of exegesis, for exegesis is in every case guided by a prior decision as to whether critical reason should be regarded as the final court of appeal or not. Sir Edwyn Hoskins and Noel Davey in *The Riddle of the New Testament* have described the situation of exegesis today as follows: "It is a strange paradox that precisely as the critic grows in confidence in the adequacy of his method, so he becomes increasingly diffident of his ability to catalogue 'assured results'" (p. 10f.). That this is so is because critical reason is confronted by something which transcends it and consequently sees itself, even if this is not always openly admitted, as permanently confronted by a fundamental decision. In spite of this, there is one possible way of retaining certainty of faith and consequently the Church's "love of the Lord" and still taking part honestly and humbly in theological research, namely, by allowing that synthesis the chance of proving itself to be the formative principle of unity, and consequently the principle of intelligibility, of the Christian revelation (theoretically, practically, and aesthetically in a unity of all three approaches), by allowing it at the same time the chance of measuring itself against all actual and possible products of human reason.[1] What, however, must emerge from these controversial struggles is above all the powerlessness of the Christian principle—the sighting of the unity of the love which gives itself up into death—because this is

[1] Cf. on this point my work *Herrlichkeit* (1961ff.); English edition: *The Glory of the Lord.*

something which lies outside the range of human possibilities, a grace which the heavenly Father gives to the simple and to the children while hiding it from the wise and the understanding, of whom the Church today is all too full. Jesus dares to thank him for this (Mt 11:25).

III

Has this then provided us with a solution to the question of the boundary which we should draw? Yes and no. Yes, in so far as this allows the Church to sight the glory of the eternal love in the light of grace and to affirm this love with her faith and her whole existence. No, in so far as she can never lay claim for herself to the principle on which she is founded, can never control it, can never master it. The Church can say with certainty that this love is unique and without competitors; she can say more, that it is precisely to the Church that this love has revealed its light, that it has moreover given the Church the eyes to see it. And so Paul can speak of "the" mystery—the mystery of God's love to the world in the Cross of Jesus Christ—which had remained hidden to men all down the ages and is now revealed through the Church, through Paul "to the children of men" (Eph 3:1ff.; Col 1:26; Rom 16:25f.). There is here something which has truly an existence "in itself" and which in and through the Church is to become something "for all"; the Church, as the place of illumination and of assent, belongs to this "in herself", but is at the same time set in motion toward this "for all": it is what she is, as she transcends herself. But because it is not itself the principle of her transcendence, but has to be first formed and furthered by this principle in order that she may then in obedience be sent out into the world, because of this the field of operation of her transcendence (or of her mission) is not identical with the field within which the principle is itself at work. Ultimately it is the head of the Church, in his unfathomable judgment, who determines who on earth, both inside and outside the visible Church, has responded to and corresponded to the demands of divine love. Peter's question, the question of the official Church, as to what shall happen to the disciple of love (who represents the loving Church) remains unanswered: "If it is my will that he remain until I come, what is that to you? Follow me!" (Jn 21:22).

So there is indeed a boundary to be drawn, and the Church is in no way permitted to blur it over or to minimize its importance; and at the same time there is no such boundary, because the Lord of the Church, who himself orders the setting up of such boundaries, is not himself tied to this order: "If it is my will ..." Such a boundary exists not only as a juridical boundary stone, but as a theologically inescapable fact, because in Christ God has entered into the realm of visibility and of human fate, not as an individual lost in the history of the world, but as one received into the womb of a particular mother, in a particular people, and as the founder of a particular congregation, which believes him and loves him. It is to this congregation that he entrusts his authority, his tasks, that he leaves the legacy of himself in his Eucharist. The marriage feast which finally will bring all men together in his Father's hall is now already in process in the Church. And the Church is to go out into all the highways and hedgerows, to invite men into the center of the feast. And she must do this in a manner which allows something of the festive spirit to pour over into the everydayness and difficulties of our world.

And yet the Church can never know how genuine, how deep or how superficial is her own answer of love which she speaks to the Lord. Only the "handmaid of the Lord" in the heart of the Church has lived out such a response immaculately. And it is only in so far as the Church has been called to be the "spotless bride" of her Lord by his own deed, and in a sense as she transcends herself, that she can by anticipation be the eschatological "spouse of the Lamb". Where, in which members, in which acts of belief, of love, of hope, this is realized is something which is not revealed to her. The Church travels on the way to her own realization in the dark; she has been given the task of realizing herself, and she fulfils this task always at the same time as she transcends herself and moves out into the world, to make her proclamation in word and existence. Much in the outer rooms which she enters has already been touched by the grace of her Lord; she will encounter much which does not properly understand itself and which can help to give itself a name which she can recognize as already a part of herself. But she must leave the final judgment on such matters, as indeed on herself, and as on the world, to the Lord. "This is how one should regard us, as servants of Christ and stewards of the mysteries of God. Moreover it is required of stewards that they should be found trustworthy. But with me it is a very small thing that I should be judged by you or by any human court. I do not even judge myself" (1 Cor 4:1–3 RSV). Paul no more allows the possibility of judgment on himself before the last judgment than he allows men to dispute his own stewardship. It is precisely in the distinctiveness of her service that the Church becomes credible.

Christianity as Utopia

Assuming that the fact on which "Christianity" rests is a reality, it nevertheless remains very difficult to conceive of the possibility of this reality. The point is this. Even if we allow the fundamental paradox that God has become man to stand as such, if we take it as given, if we "believe" it as a real fact, then our difficulties are only beginning. For this paradox remains so inaccessible to the average man, it is with all its implications so unique, unrepeatable, and inimitable, that one cannot see at all what consequences it should have for our task of changing the world. It is one of the principal implications of God's incarnation that thereby humanity as a whole and every individual is redeemed from his sin and estrangement from God: such an act can (such is the Christian view) only be performed by one who as a man identifies himself with all sinners; but the readiness of a man to "represent" another who is under the same guilt, is, of course, not a sufficient condition of the fulfilment of such a deed once and for all, fully, effectively, for all men: such a man must "really have been God's Son" (Mt 27:54).

Assuming then that this is true, there only seem to be two ways open to one. First, the way of the extreme orthodox Protestants (which can claim support from certain aspects of the New Testament, in particular of Paul), asserting that this fact must be *believed* before one can proceed to consider all its consequences. This unique event performed by God is something which, within the world of human thought and action, could not even be suspected, let alone constructed. It can only be accepted as the absolute gift offered to us by God; it is on this paradox that we must, in an act of courage, build our existence; and our loving behavior toward our fellow men will be a sign of our doing this and of our attempt to show ourselves grateful for it.

And secondly, there is the extreme liberal way which regards the theological fact as the inner fulfilment of the anthropological sphere. Man's readiness to exist for his fellow man, to stand in for his fellow, is precisely the characteristic of humanity to which belongs creative powers which are in some manner divine, which are able to change his existence. Perhaps Jesus was the first man to develop such powers in their true freedom and purity; since then the way of discipleship, of sharing in his work and redemption, has been opened up; it is not orthodoxy, as in the first case, but orthopraxis which shows that we move within the sphere of the Christian fact, that we have made its cause our own.

It is easy to see that both ways foreshorten the paradox with which we started: the first because here (general) human action remains at best an echo of the lonely deed of the God-man, with the consequence that this deed clearly never truly penetrates to the (general) human plane; the second more clearly because the uniqueness of God's deed in Christ is reduced to the level of a supreme example and consequently turned into a mere model of ideal human behavior. It might now seem easy to demand at this point that one should make a synthesis of the two one-sided ways, as indeed the old conciliar theology always did. Christ is true God and true man, one person in two undivided and yet unmixed natures. But it is much more difficult to draw the consequences which would lead us on beyond this fixed paradox with which we started (and which, as we said, does not concern us thematically here). Can there be a discipleship of that which is inimitable, because essentially unique? Are we drawn into and related to this event internally, in such a manner that we do not merely respond to it as a subsequent echo (love as the echo of faith), and yet on the other hand not so related to it that we ourselves (secretly or openly) do that which was done for us, indeed have always done it for ourselves (faith as the pointer to life which, as it points, makes itself superfluous)?

One can see the problem more clearly if one pays attention, within the fundamental paradox of the God-man, not only to the incarnation and the passion, but to the third reference point which belongs internally to this "fact", namely, the Resurrection from the dead. For this is clearly unique and inimitable for mortal men like ourselves, whereas the redeeming effects of the Cross were unique only in a hidden sense, only for the believers. And if the Resurrection was the conclusion and justification of the whole event which, in the Christian view, was to give meaning to the world and to human existence, then the question can be put much more sharply: Now what follows? Should we emphasize the reality of the Resurrection? Then it remains the hoped for goal of faith, and our earthly action remains again an echo (within the sphere of mortality and utility) of the "eschatological" fact which stands at the end of and above history. Or can one emphasize the repeatability of his Resurrection, its implications for our existence (particularly since Cross and Resurrection are indissolubly united)? Then one will say that we are "risen with him and transported with him into the heavenly kingdom" (Eph 2:6; Col 2:12; Heb 12:22). But how, then, can we avoid the view of the Corinthian Gnostics that the Resurrection is to be understood in a spiritual and present sense, that a future resurrection no longer concerns us? One can only escape from this fault by insisting again that it is not a question of either–or but of both–and, or more precisely by insisting on the simultaneity of the "not yet" and of the "and yet already", an insistence which will be seen by many as a poor compromise on the part of the Christian, an artificial, existentially ineffectual synthesis. Nor will there be any difficulty in sustaining such a charge, for the sad history of Christianity condemns it clearly enough. Orthodoxy, with its faith in the Resurrection of Christ and its constant peering into the future to the coming resurrection of the dead and the transcendental transformation of heaven and earth, has always hampered the true work of orthopraxis and the immanent transformation of the world. The history of Christianity is itself the disproof of the possibility of that paradox (of the incarnation of God and the redemptive deed of Christ) and consequently, of course, of its reality as well. And so it is of no great importance how one moves from the proof of its impossibility to showing its unreality; perhaps the easiest way is to show how that apparent synthesis, which subsequently proved to be impossible to live out, can be traced back to temporally conditioned circumstances (the encounter with differing Jewish views of hope, in Judaism and Hellenism, and so forth).

Viewed in this light, Christianity with its claims, which have been unmasked, is in a pejorative sense utopian, without purchase on the world. By contrast one can regard the two alternative forms, from which Christianity has historically distanced itself, namely, Judaism and (ancient) paganism, as "topian", having a purchase on the world. Paganism in this context means an existence lived out within the boundaries of death which are affirmed as such, an existence which offers an individual prospect of immortality of the soul and makes the political, social claim to represent the "divine" order of the world in the social community. Judaism, however, means the drive—starting with God's promise to Abraham and with the promises made to Israel at the giving of the covenant and through the great prophets—to move on beyond all static, figurative, and "categorical" realizations into the future, toward a kingdom of God which is breaking in, in whose coming man as he engages himself politically, socially, ethically, is to have a decisive share. Today this Judaism (from Marx through to the more recent Jewish "utopians" who now dominate all German thinking) has made a logical alliance with the liberal Christian wing, has forced that wing to show itself in its true colors, and has taken over the leadership. It can claim to possess a spirit of utopia which is characterized by an absolute imperative which transcends the limit of death as it moves into the future (where such a characterization is based on the dynamism of the promises). Moreover, this spirit is not encumbered with the Christian fact which apparently fetters Christianity's ability to advance unreservedly into the future, because of the schizophrenia which it induces between the this-worldly ("not yet") and the other-worldly ("and yet already"), a schizophrenia in which one is never certain whether the decisive act has already been achieved (by the God-man) or still waits for achievement (by man).

The vital conflict in our present culture, despite the noisy posturing of a pseudo-pagan atheism in the foreground, is in fact being fought out in a renewed struggle between Judaism and Christianity. And if that is the case, one can say from the start two things. If the Jewish principle of the "Old Testament"—in the Christian view of things—runs out into its fulfilment in the "New Testament", then the latter, albeit in an eminent way, will always embrace the former. And further, if in its present form the Jewish principle conceives of itself as utopian (because by some dialectic or other the kingdom of freedom must "spring out of" the kingdom of necessity), then on these grounds one will not be able to reproach Christianity with the element of (perhaps intensified) utopianism which it contains. Rather it can be "fulfilled utopianism", precisely because its utopianism is not an out-moded form but rather the "perfected, unsurpassable utopia".

In order to substantiate that, one would have to be able to show two things. In the first place, that there is a genuine utopian element in Judaism, but that the condition of its possibility is to be sought not in Judaism itself but in the fulfilment of its promise, namely, in Christ. And secondly, that the utopian possibility opened up by Christ is not, as it seemed at the beginning, an impossible possibility, but one which can be realized by men and which would then as such show the true meaning of the Jewish utopian hope.

The first point can indeed be made by pointing to the fact that Judaism, whenever it attempts to exalt its (truly!) utopian dynamism to the level of an absolute, independent principle, must necessarily negate its own foundation, namely, Yahweh's promise. The furious war of destruction which Ernst Bloch wages against the tyrannical Father God and which, out of sheer hatred for this God who is eternally set beyond men, drives him into an alliance with an atheistically understood Jesus and moreover with a radically dualistic Gnosticism, is a clear proof of this fact. And he must pay this price if he wants to erect the Jewish principle into a purely human "principle of hope". But even such a price gets him no more than the self-destruction of man and of his history. Precisely *because* both man and history in such a view transcend themselves absolutely in their movement into the future—and *even if* they are to be understood on the basis of this essential self-transcendence—they cease as a result of this act of transcendence to have any pictorial form, any shape, any outline, any definition, any conceivable nature at all. And as a consequence neither the individual nor humanity as a whole can be fired by the vision of any ideal or goal as they embark upon the absolute adventure of constructing the future. That which is totally inconceivable cannot be striven for, whereas ancient Israel at least received a large number of images and figures which accompanied it on its way but which, admittedly, were all to be transcended: "Messiah", "mediator", "servant of God", "prophet", (Danielic) "Son of Man", and so on. As long as the frontier of death stands, these images cannot achieve any unity; and as long as this frontier holds sway over life, so long will all attempts to storm it fail which are merely inspired by an imageless pressing forward into the future. What kind of offensive shall they mount, in which direction shall they go?

It is here that the Christian understanding begins to show its superiority. The Jewish "images" converge precisely on that point at which man steps over the barrier of death in the Resurrection of Jesus. Man, not merely an "immortal soul". Paul shows how, behind all the Old Testament images, the first promise (and consequently the dynamism which that unleashed) was always directed toward this dissolution of the barrier of death (Rom 4:17ff.). But the fact that it is precisely here that the point of unity of all promises is to be found is of importance not only within the biblical conception, but unconditionally of importance for anthropology, for our total understanding of man. For what we are concerned with here is the promise of a way out of that dilemma which runs through all human nature, namely, the dilemma which is posed by the contradiction of death, with a promise which shows such a way out to be not only possible but finally also to be real. And the contradiction lies in this, that life promises the individual more than it can keep, that hope for one's children and one's children's children is not an adequate substitute for personal fulfilment, particularly in view of the fact that one's children and children's children will themselves in their turn have to live in this hope. Admittedly, the "resurrection of the dead", or, to put it more soberly, the gathering up of man's total existence, body and soul, in its temporal and transitory form into eternal love, remains an "idea surpassing reason", which can no more be constructed out of a general view of humanity than it can be out of the images of the Old Testament. But with the Resurrection of Jesus Christ, this "idea" becomes *real*, it is made present (that is the meaning of the post-Easter encounters) as a reality which from now on can become the *real, utopian* goal of man's life and of the world's history. "Ascension" and the promised "coming again" are precisely the necessary transporting of the fact of this breakthrough—which cannot be given a lasting place within history, which must remain u-topian—to its only possible place, to the eschaton or the omega point. Is this not precisely what man and history have been looking for, what they desire, what they are prepared to give themselves for, to contribute their inmost and their utmost for, and that which at the same time they know they cannot of their own efforts ever achieve? The individual can of his own efforts "perfect" himself only by withdrawing into a spiritual realm, by resigning himself to a certain distancing of himself from the concrete and material form of his life. And history can "perfect" itself of its own efforts only by (at best) striving toward a final generation which will live in a humanized world, and by sacrificing the whole concrete, material course of the history of the generations which lead up to this final stage, by sacrificing them and putting them behind itself. One simply lets go of all that has been. But in the Christian experience the very gesture of "letting go", of acquiescing, becomes the gesture of gathering in: the cross, pain, renunciation, abandonment, and death are essentially transvalued into means of expression and effective signs of the love which overcomes death: the love of God of course, but in the man Jesus Christ.

And so again we are confronted with the dilemma which we faced at the beginning. In what sense is this unique event, the divinely human, of use for all men; how can it be imitated? If Jesus Christ is the name for God's dealing with us, how then can he be the name for our dealings with him? The answer can only lie in the fact of the God-man himself, who is the concrete perfection of the "covenant" between God and man, God with us. In the plural "us" resides the solidarity, which not only explains why he can "bear our sins", but also why we in this event cannot simply be passive subjects, swept along by a one-sided action of God. Every man receives, otherwise he would not be and he would not become a man. Even the God-man permits himself to be carried out, to be born, to be fed, to be brought up, to be educated in the religion of his fathers, to be told things, to be given advice, to be baptized. And all this not on the purely human level but on his divine-human level, in matters which are of importance for his own unique mission. The gulf between "law" and "gospel" is not so deep that the *faith* of Israel in its promises could not be enlarged into Mary's faith and into the faith of the "bridegroom's friend", who in gratitude "decreases" once the fulfiller arrives and is "given up" (Mk 1:14) in a manner which preserves the internal continuity between the faith of the prophets and of Jesus himself. But did not Mary's faith always have its source in God's promise, and is not the name of this promise Jesus? Is there not here a vicious circle? Circle, yes; vicious, no. The mother bestows on her child what she can only receive in fulness from him (even though this of course is hidden to her). And yet she gives it really, and the child receives it really. Otherwise the whole relationship would not be human, and God would not seriously have become man. It is here, in the heart of mariology, that Jewish dynamism, the belief which transcends all images, receives its irreplaceable setting within the Christian economy. Man's contribution is assumed and used in the divine human task, which could not be executed without that contribution. The "images" receive their definitive reality only as they are transcended and taken up into Christ. Thus after Christ the reality of Christ can submerge itself in everything that assumes the name of discipleship, that wishes to make its contribution to the redemption of the world. He can use everything that is built on his foundation (1 Cor 3:10ff.), on faith, on self-giving, on selfless service: whether it be serving the human community in one's daily work, in mutual support, or whether it is a service given by renunciation, by suffering and dying. Obedience to the will of the Father, the admission that we are not ourselves the principle of hope, but that God gives a justified hope, can make us mothers and brothers and sisters of Jesus (Mk 3:35). And so man has to abandon any attempt to get an oversight of the synthesis between his contribution and God's work in Christ. He (in every case as an individual part of the whole of the world's history) provides what he can and must—*terra dedit fructum suum*—in the consciousness that his own strength is something that he must receive (in faith in a surpassing promise) and that he has to yield up the fruits of such powers (to a surpassing, eschatological, and real utopian fulfilment). Given this condition, then, not only man and humanity, but also its personal and historical work, will rise up on the other side of the judging fire of death (1 Cor 3:15).

Temporary Christians

I

It began with the notion of "temporary monasteries". One can attach a certain sense to this, either on the grounds that there are "temporary vows" which are designed to lead up to the "permanent" vows, or because there are lay people who desire to share for a time in the life of a monastery and who are allowed to participate in this way. They are inspired by a similar desire to that which, in the third orders, leads many men in the world to give their life a sense of direction by setting it in relationship to the central focus of a monastic life and by accepting a measure of order imposed upon their life by that focus. Admittedly the notion of "temporary monasteries" obscures something decisive: namely, that, while one can "participate" in something "in one's life in the world" which in an eminent sense is "not of this world", such participation does not of itself constitute "entry" into the monastery, membership in a strict sense. One could learn something here from the philosophers of participation, from the Platonists, for whom it is generally true of the thing in which one participates: *amethektos metechetai*; one might even translate, with a slight Christian bias: that which gives itself to be shared is not as a consequence shared out, split up; it can only allow men to share in itself because it remains a whole, indivisible.

The notion of "temporary monasteries" was followed by that of "temporary abbots" and of "temporary bishops"; and today we not only have the postulates of "temporary popes" (after all, why not?), but, quite openly, even of "temporary priests", "temporary marriage", and of course "temporary monks and nuns". That those who have important offices within the Church should give them up after a certain period, at the latest when they have reached a certain age, is something against which one can certainly raise no objection. But the question becomes acute in the case of the priesthood, of marriage, and of "professions" (if we may refer to an intended engagement for one's whole life with Christian virginity, usually connected with a vow of poverty and obedience, in such simple terms). For here the very basic act of the Christian life is put in question, namely, that God in Jesus Christ can dispose of a man's life once and for all and that this man is enabled to ratify that act of God's disposing.

The fundamental Christian facts are all distinguished by this "once and for all". Paul himself formulated the concept when he said of Christ that he had "died once and for all to an existence under sin" (Rom 6:10), "Christ died once for all for sin" (1 Pet 3:18); in the Epistle to the Hebrews the phrase becomes a *Leitmotiv*: Christ made his sacrifice "once and for all, when he offered himself up" (7:27), he broke through "once and for all the dividing wall between God and man" (9:12), and so "we are sanctified once and for all by the offering of the body of Christ" (10:10), and so on. It is a mark of the eternal God's acts of promise and reconciliation toward men that they are "without regrets" (Rom 11:31): God's definitive act has found adequate humanized expression in Jesus' self-giving and at the same time received a genuinely human response. For it is of the very essence of man's nobility, it is a decisive mark of his similarity to God, that he can respond with a supratemporal freedom in which he disposes of his whole temporal existence—always as an answer to the incalculable decisions of the divine grace. The Church which is built on the twelve foundation stones of the first disciples is based, as a result, on vocation and decisions which are unconditionally final. "Do you too want to go?" "Lord, where shall we go? You have words of eternal life" (Jn 6:68). He not only has them, but he is the very essence of these words, which as God's words are for the Bible always at the same time his decisions and his deeds. "What I say, I do." And corresponding to this deed-word there is the answer, "Lo, we have left all and have followed you" (Mt 19:27); and even if this statement was formulated in the post-Easter period, nevertheless Jesus' command to leave all and to follow him holds in any case for the period before Easter, and the answer follows at the very latest with the knowledge of who Jesus was and is in reality. "Feed my sheep": for the rest of your existence, which includes the foretold crucifixion in the discipleship of the good shepherd, not temporarily. The man who feeds the sheep temporarily is the hireling. One should try the experiment of applying the word "temporarily" to the phenomenon of Paul. This man is once and for all an uprooted tree, transplanted to another spot. The sharpness of his word and his action which founds congregations, judges them, changes them, stems from the indivisibility of his existence. It is identical with it. He is conscious, it is true, of the special nature of his own calling, which makes him forget everything which lies behind him. But he anchors his unique mission in the law which is valid for all Christians and which demands that men should make the same unique act of decision which God has made in Christ by an equally unique and all-embracing act (2 Cor 5:14f.; Rom 6:10f.). Christian existence and the Church as a whole are "eschatological": we could perhaps render the word best by "de-finitive": that is to say, unsurpassable and in its essence inalterable. Both, Christian existence and the Church, are not temporary but eternal, and they are the sign in the midst of the passing ages that the definitive future of God has already begun here and now.

II

The fact that the Church, following her Lord, is to be merciful to the weak and the sinners, that she should free men from burdens which have become intolerable for them, that she is not to reject with a formalistic harshness and to break those who are in danger of breaking down under the task which they have assumed, all this is another matter. It may be that today, when the ground under so many people's feet has become uncertain and treacherous, such cases are on the increase. But we are not here concerned with that. What we are concerned with is the fundamental questioning of the act in which the free man, in his answer to God, disposes freely of his whole existence. That is the most noble act which can be his. The act by which he outreaches in advance every "if" and "but" which may occur in the future. By which he makes a wholeness and a unity out of his existence so that he may order its ultimate meaning in an act of total freedom. Such an act is already possible in that human love which is rooted in the divinely ordained origin and which makes of two people one flesh: "What God has joined together, let no man put asunder" (Mk 10:9). In this order of creation God allows the persons who join together into "one flesh", one fruitfulness, one child, to share something of his eternal definitiveness. And the man who leaves mother and father in order to hold his wife knows, no less than the wife, that this departure is not intended as a "temporary" measure. And so it is only in the light of what was originally intended that developments which were not intended, and which are yet brought about by the weakness and "hardness of heart" of men, can be regulated. If the limiting case becomes the norm, then it is all up with the essence of the Christians and the Church. Then there can no longer be any "sharing" in the one who cannot "be shared out, split up". The latter then disappears like an abstraction into heaven. Then there is neither incarnation nor apostleship nor Church, but the most one could hope for would be a continuing series of avatars, without binding force, without permanent form.

The definitiveness of marriage which is laid down primordially in creation is confirmed in a manner which surpasses all expectation in Christ: he shows why man has been given so much eternity by the Creator to accompany him on his temporal way (Eph 5). Jesus' definitive self-giving to his "bride", to mankind gathered together into the Church, has its origin in that first covenant and now, as he sets his seal on it, makes it into a definitive covenant. According to the two-thousand-year-old tradition of the Church, which here looks back to her origin, it is into that definitive covenant that the priest too is sealed. It would be a scandal if, after the total self-giving of Christ for mankind and after the lifelong decisions of the apostles to consecrate their existence to the gospel, one were to wish to fall back into a merely sociological and functional understanding of the priestly ministry. There are many functions in the service of the Church which do not demand the totality of men's lives, and these can certainly be extended today. But if one were to understand the ministry which represents the unity of the Church and her eschatological character merely as a temporary office, then the countenance of the Church would be turned into an undecipherable hieroglyphic.

The same is true of those who are eunuchs for the sake of the kingdom of heaven (Mt 19:12). The comparison with those who are born without powers of procreation and with those who are artificially castrated itself shows that we are concerned here with something definitive. If "temporary vows" are permitted in the Church, then only as a stage on the way to and a training in unconditional self-giving. In the same way that engagement precedes marriage. And just as the man and woman who become engaged know that their love is intended as a definitive one, and just as they take upon themselves the duty of allowing such love, with God's help, to endure beyond all temporal and passing enthusiasms, and perhaps at the cost of great effort and self-denial, so too the novice who embarks on his way to his "permanent vows" knows that he is casting himself on Christ's grace, for better or for worse, which is to say, to be used or to be used up, without insuring himself against any possible disaster. "This is the proclamation of the kingdom of God: it is into this kingdom, as the kingdom of love for God, that man has to transport himself in such a manner that he casts himself directly into this truth" (Hegel). And this act alone gives Christian existence—whether in the state of marriage or within the priesthood or in the life of the counsels—its inner and even its outer fruitfulness.

The fear of lifelong decision gnaws today at the marrow of the life of society, most dangerously in the Church. Perhaps young people speak about commitment so much today because they are frightened of the "once and for all" character of decision. They seek refuge in provisional commitments which for their limited period are meaningful (a spell of work in overseas development), which hold open the possibility of changing over to something else later. They imagine that they are being serious about it, but in truth, a truth which is hidden to them, they are only flirting like half-virgins who have all kinds of experience but not the decisive one: namely, that of finally giving oneself.

There may be many sorts of sociological reasons why men today are so reluctant to commit their whole existence, and Christians will naturally be affected by these reasons. But if they see that in this the axe is laid at the roots of their existence as Christians, then they have cause for reflection. For ultimately what stands behind these three programs, "temporary marriage", "temporary priests", "temporary vows", is the unsaid "temporary Christians". A Christian, as long as I feel I can responsibly continue to recognize the increasingly questionable faith (and what after all does that mean?) of the Church (and what does that mean?) as my own. Or else: a Christian, for the time being, with many, perhaps very many reservations, until such time as I can see more clearly whether I must move toward a more definite faith or toward a more definite unfaith. The much discussed partial identification which, according to the results of statistical surveys, is gradually becoming the norm. What indeed would the present-day normal Christian have answered to Jesus' question: "Do you too want to go?" Probably, "For the time being we do not know." They would have put off the hour of decision which Jesus set and consequently have missed it and turned it into an hour over which they themselves wished to have control. Perhaps they are excusable. But they are letting down the Church which stands or falls with the definitiveness of her own calling and response. Perhaps they will have to be subjected to the earthly *auto da fé*, in which there are only two answers to the question: Are you a Christian?—Yes or no. Perhaps then they will receive, in their hour of decision, the grace by which they will suddenly see the indivisibility of Christianity, as God's decision for men and man's decision for God. Perhaps they will then realize, beyond all the changes of temporality, the definitiveness of the gospel and will again learn what Christian witness is.

III

All this is not in the least affected by the knowledge that Christianity has never existed as a substantial unity and essence in itself which has to prove itself only accidentally in the particular world and time in which it happens to find itself, but rather that it is in its very essence dependent on the world if it is to achieve its own true being for itself in its ministry to the brothers, to the hungry, naked, prisoners, sick, tortured, and to the structures of society which further rather than alleviate suffering. One might perhaps be tempted to think that this openness to the world, this mission to all people which exists from the very beginning, but also this quite individual, unobtrusive pointing of each individual Christian to the brother who suffers alongside him, was itself the true process of Christian decision. That is to say, it is never the case that one *is* from the outset a Christian; one only *becomes* a Christian as one proves oneself to be such in the worldly realm of common humanity. I am only a Christian when, through me, the Christian cause is credibly presented to the world, and that occurs, as long as I live, never once and for all, but always only now. Perhaps today I shall succeed for once, but what ground have I for believing that I shall succeed tomorrow and the day after?

It is, I suspect, precisely in this consciousness that Christianity must always first prove itself as such in the public sphere of our shared humanity and of society that the real pathos of the new political theology lies. And since we are here concerned with human commitments that retain their human dimensions as advances into the world and as individual moves on the chessboard of our social conditions, such acts of commitment are finite, are spacially and also temporally limited, and must under changed circumstances be thought out anew. And so one is led to a temporary commitment which, in such a concrete manner of looking at things, seems to gain the ascendency over abstract and dramatic decision made "once and for all". On the other hand, even in political theology, the temporal commitment, in time and for a time, is relativized by the two points of origin and of destination which control every commitment. The origin of such action remains the total and definitive commitment of Jesus even to death on the Cross (and to the Eucharist of the supratemporal and de-finitive distribution of himself to all men); the destination of all commitment which is dependent on such an origin remains the coming of the kingdom of God, which is more than all that can be achieved by united efforts of men to push into the future; and this is the reason for the "eschatological reservation" (Käsemann) in all political Christian action. Now these double brackets around all conditional verifications of Christianity in action, which relate such action to their alpha and omega which is Christ, show that Christian action, if it is to be recognizable as such at all, must be borne along by an unconditional force which has its origins beyond all human initiatives and which also reaches out beyond all human goals. The difference between Christian commitment and all other forms of commitment, which may themselves humanly speaking be of a remarkable character and may indeed often put the Christians to shame, is that the former is the response to an all-embracing prior and later commitment on God's part to men. The response to that is the ratification of the claims which God has established upon us; it is called faith. And it is this faith which in the spirit of Christ undertakes whatever is possible in a particular worldly situation, limited as it is by time and space. And consequently any political theology which wants to call itself Christian is always, as it were, moving from one confession to another; the first confesses its acceptance of the deed, the last is its confirmation. The way which lies between the two, our mission to the public world (and every man, even the most insignificant, lives in some sort of public world), is not optional. It cannot be omitted. Otherwise one would stand at the end before one's judge and would only be able to plead "Lord! Lord!" But the situation can arise where this essential mission and political action consist in witness itself. And this will be all the more credible, the less a man presents himself as a "temporary Christian", as "one who is taking Christianity on approval", but as one who has built his house on the rock and who is able to strengthen his brothers.

The *auto da fé* of political theology will be the Prague situation, for it is here that it will emerge clearly enough what price one is ready to pay for being present when the structures of society are changed. It is in such a situation that that eschatological decision, which for us in recent times, although scarcely for much longer, has been so difficult to achieve, occurs almost, as it were, of itself. And it is in such a situation, under such an eschatological light, that we can see clearly where ultimately the greater "political" effectiveness lies.

Why Do I Still Remain in the Church?

Why do I remain in the Church? In any case not because I am able to read off from any kind of indicator that the Church corresponds (a) to my expectations or (b) to God's expectations. For where (a) is concerned, the question in fact lies the other way about: whether, that is, I correspond to the expectations of the Church; and where (b) is concerned, even the dimmest of men can see that the Church as the collection of sinners which she is can never correspond to God's expectations. The last fact is, of course, in no way altered by those who, laying all true wisdom aside, are confident with a comic seriousness that they are indeed capable of such a correspondence, which they define in their own particular way, as they turn up the heat by throwing a few switches in the Church's system. The collection of sinners in the Church, to which we all belong, has acted more or less idiotically in all ages of the Church, most notably when it acted under the impression that it was able to conjure up by wily manipulations a present or future approximate kingdom of God on earth, and rarely more idiotically than today when everyone, with his eyes glued to the switchboard, waits for the point when the structures of the Church have been altered to such a degree that finally the engine of the coming kingdom will spring into life. "They know not what they do."

And why do I (despite all this) still remain in the Church? Because, remarkable though it is, not even all that we idiots with all our measures can do has yet succeeded in destroying the Church. Indeed, almost the opposite seems true: the more one violates her, the more clearly appears her inviolable virginity. The more one humiliates her, the more clearly one can see that the Church is in her own, proper place. That is, of course, in the "last" place. The saying about the last place is found on Jesus' and Paul's lips. What people outside the Church get up to need not worry us, but there are very many within her who think that they are doing God a service by belaboring the Church like a dusty old mattress; and indeed why not, if only they would not forget at every blow to identify themselves with what they are beating, and so were really to beat their own ancient and ailing breast. But as soon as they leave off doing that, then I cannot understand why they should be able to maintain that they have remained *in* the Church, that they are not kicking at her from without. However, let us leave them to their fate, or rather to a gentle providence, in the hope that it may one day open their eyes to the fact that a pure Church which imagines she knows better than other Christians and which belabors the old dusty Church is not a Church at all but a Montanistic-Donatistic-Pelagian sect which it is not worth belonging to because it has nothing whatsoever in common with the Church of Jesus Christ. But we must leave it to them to draw this simple conclusion while we move on to the positive arguments.

1. I remain in the Church because the old *Catholica* still resembles to a large measure the formation which crystallized in the day after Jesus' Resurrection and of which

the Pauline epistles and the Acts of the Apostles give us a sufficient idea. It is a remarkable and indeed very strange fact that, on the one hand, Paul refers to the same Corinthians as "enriched in every gift of teaching and in all knowledge as the preaching of Christ has taken such firm root in you, so that you are lacking in no spiritual gift" (1 Cor 1:5ff.) and at the same time that he, from chapter to chapter, lays into them with increasing fierceness for their cliques, for their overbearingness, for the loveless disorder of their "eucharistic party" (the expression comes from a Swiss clergy journal), and finally for the fact that they have put the Resurrection of Christ behind themselves by their enlightened re-interpretation of it. This congregation, which the apostle wanted to "betroth as a pure virgin to Christ", has overnight become in every way a respectable little popsy. And what does Paul hold up to it to call it back to order (to its true nature)? Of course Christ's Cross, God's folly. And as well as that, in an almost embarrassingly pushing way, embarrassing because he makes too much of it, his own portrait: the picture of *the humiliated office of the Church*, in which Christ's Cross and God's folly remain concretely visible. It is for this reason that the congregation should look at it, in order to see their own true face, however unwilling they may be to see it. One ought really to quote the whole chapter, but here at least a few snatches: "For I think that God has exhibited us apostles as last of all, like men sentenced to death, because we have become a spectacle to the world, to angels and to men. We have become stupid simpletons for Christ's sake. You on the other hand are supremely wise in Christ; we make no impact on men but you on the contrary push on strongly, you are held in honor but we in disrepute ... we have become and are till today, the refuse of all the world (which runs off when you wash yourself), everyone's rubbish" (1 Cor 4:9f., 13). Notice here the "till today". "We proclaim not ourselves, but Jesus Christ as the Lord, ourselves as your slaves for Jesus' sake ... at all times we carry around in our bodily life Jesus' death, in order that Jesus' life too may become visible in the life of our body ... so death is at work in us but life in you" (2 Cor 4:5, 10, 12). His bitter irony is overlaid by his sober statement of the rule. That is the definitive structure which has been established "till today". On the one hand, what the Church ought to be (and in the gift of God's grace also is); on the other hand, what she de facto makes of this gift and, mediating between the two at the bottom of the rubbish heap, the humiliated office of the Church. It may well be that Paul was not a particularly sympathetic man and that his excessive insistence on his official capacity was one of the factors which encouraged the charismatic progressives to move into opposition to him. But if he had not polarized everything in Corinth relentlessly about his office, if he had not insisted on the fact that all charisms had to find their fulfilment as they transcend themselves and take their place in the unity of the love of the *whole* Church in her conformation to Christ (1 Cor 13), if he had not staked his life on the preservation of the unity between the congregations of the diaspora and their mother congregation, then at least, as far as one can humanly see, the *Catholica* would never have come into being.

The question at issue today is not one about the limits of the Pope's or the bishops' jurisdiction, but about the established structure which persists (not of its own strength, for it is weak and "crippled", but because it has been established) precisely at the point where it is humiliated. In the gospel Peter is often in the wrong, and every occasion is taken to reprove him in order to train him in the true position of an office-bearer. It is edifying that Boniface VIII "deserved" to be so demonstratively humiliated. And if today [1971] Paul VI is, in the eyes of the world, as a result of so many mistakes which today are inevitable as a consequence of the absurd overloading of the papal office, a deeply humiliated man, then I can only breathe a sigh of relief as I catch a scent of fresh air. For this makes him to me far more credible than the pontificating cardinals, whose democratic ecclesiastical politics earn them the plaudits of the masses (headed by the theologians).

One speaks of the visibility of the Church, but one should take care, for the apostolic "structure" of the Church is always only visible together with her humiliation. And it may be that, in an age where both inside and outside the Church structures are built up, pulled down, and reconstructed with an increasing ease and speed, that in such an age the structure, the form of the building, may not be able to attract attention to itself, that this element may perhaps be reduced to a minimum while the other side, the humiliation, precisely because of this shrinking process, may shine out all the more brightly in its mysterious visibility and thus may show us *which* of the many possible structures is really and truly intended.

Indeed it might perhaps be very much to the point if the Pope were to turn the Vatican into a museum and were to take up his seat in one of the many administrative buildings of some pious society at the gates of Rome, buildings which were superfluous when they were built and are now ready for sale. It could be a sign; and Paul VI has already given many such signs. At any rate it is not of great importance. But it might also happen—and this would be more important—that, as a consequence of the humiliation of the *Catholica*, the apparent sublimity of her structures would show themselves in their true lowliness and that thereby the unification of the divided Christian denominations, under the archetypal image of the crucified Lord and the humiliated apostles, might be brought nearer. It is, I think, correct to say that in recent times nearly all attempts to reach a closer agreement have come actively from the side of the Catholic Church, whereas the others have looked on more or less curiously, if not with a certain maliciousness (how far will she condescend to abandon her position of supremacy in her diplomatic moves toward unity?); but it is also correct to say that such "condescension" will only achieve true credibility for all if it can show itself unambiguously to be humiliation, at least for those who are prepared to see it (for there will always be the others). There will be those who will laugh, but for the others it will then be high time to examine themselves and the manner in which the head of the Church and the serving office of the Church exists.

2. Why do I remain in the Church? Because she alone, as the Church of the apostles which knows what is meant

by a commission from the Lord and by service to the Lord, can offer me the bread and wine of life. "Truly, truly, I say to you, if you do not eat the flesh of the Son of Man and do not drink his blood, you have no life in you." I am not going to be put off with assurances that there are condensed substitute foods, above all love of one's neighbor, without which the aforementioned food is of no nutritional value in any case. But I want to receive the blood of life as the offering of God, who in his Son sets before me his total love, which is poured out really in history, irrespective of any attendant circumstances and regardless of the attitude which I as the receiver may assume. God is not love in itself, in principle, in general; it is not we who, unworthy as we are, can take to ourselves the Johannine statement, but rather such a statement, together with the message of the Cross and of the Resurrection of the historical Jesus, must be placed in the mouth of the receiver, unworthy as he is. For all my love of my neighbor and for all my futurological fantasies there is still no comparison between me and him, there is simply no possibility of a gradual transition between a man's love of his neighbor and the eucharistic love of God to us. One only needs to pick up and read through a Greek tragedy in order to have one's confused standards put back into their proper perspective. Just as man can never master his "fate", no matter what attempts he may make to humanize the world around him, so too human love can never approach the love of God which is man's very foundation and which ultimately judges and saves him. There is no question of him approximating to it asymptotically, no question of forming a "synthesis" with it, in such a way, for example, that the two together might form, in the divine-human love which is founded by Jesus Christ and then continued by us, a higher *tertium quid*.

It is consequently, from a Christian point of view, a piece of grotesque bad taste to imagine that when a group of people sit down for a meal and are very fond of each other and share their rolls and wine and whatever else with each other, and at the same time among other things think very hard of their big brother Jesus, that he will then suddenly, as it were, coagulate out of their common love and be materialized on their plates. Either the whole thing does not go beyond a mere remembrancing or, if it is more, then it is a magical, spiritistic left-over which one should exorcise. (I say this in spite of the logion, "If two or three are gathered together in my name ...", for that stands in a quite different context: the reference is to unanimity and to corporate prayer, both of which can only be achieved and can only be successful in the presence of the Lord.) No, the only thing which can offer me the body of the Lord given for me is that thing which in the Church is more than the sum of her gathered members, which relieves me once and for all of the necessity to calculate whether enough love has been collected and invested in this congregation for Christ to become present, that thing which cannot be set up and delegated even by the authority of faith and the good intention of the congregation, but which principally, from the beginning and to this very day, transcends all relativities of individual subjects, and that again is the office of the Church. That is something which the Eastern Church knows very well, as to a large extent does the Anglican Church. And it must be clear to anyone who gives thought to these matters that it is only in this way that the worm of sectarianism, namely, of subjective, self-judging charismatics, can be kept out of the wood of the Church. This worm ravages her interior until it reaches the point when the gift of God, the peace of Christ which passes all understanding, is overcome by the quarrels and controversies of the charismatic. By their fruit ye shall know them.

3. Why do I remain in the Church? Because she is the Church of the saints, of the hidden saints and of a few who, against their will, are pushed out into the light of day. They disprove the absurd objection that Christians are only interested in receiving the God who has offered himself to them, forgetting in the process that they should have the courage and the imagination to go beyond themselves in the unknown adventure. The saints know that God is never strange, other. He is, when he calls me, closer to me than I am to myself. They are spurred on by his self-giving to attempt and to realize things which those who remain tied to their own resources could never have dreamed of. The only man who is estranged is the one who refuses to listen to the call or who only follows it half-heartedly. The saint is the proof that Christians can become whole people, out of grace better than nature; he is wholly aflame, but he does not need other men for kindling before he starts to burn, and he does not, like Nietzsche, leave them behind in ashes. He burns with an absolute fire; like the salamander, he inhabits it; he is selfless and is yet wholly a self, a man; he

ıers plan to do or deliberately forget: Peter
Casas, Philip Neri, Don Bosco. (I would
plea for an end to the attacks on those who
...othing but expose themselves to the fire, have burned for the sake of burning, for if the absolute fire takes responsibility for the world, it is surely enough to burn with it for the world. De Foucauld, and those like him.) They are the true realists; they take seriously the hopelessness of man as it is and do not seek a refuge from the present in the future. They are the true utopians: they get on with the job in spite of everything and hope against hope. They are clever but not calculating; they live out of a desire to squander themselves which stems from God's eucharistic love.

And they are humble, that is to say that the mediocrity of the Church does not deter them from joining themselves to her once and for all, for they know well enough that without the Church they would not find their way to God. They do not attempt to get on good terms with God on their own initiative, leaving Christ's Church on one side. They do not fight the mediocrity in a spirit of contestation, but by spurring on those who have quality, by inspiring them, by igniting them. They suffer at the hands of the Church, but they do not become embittered, nor do they stand sulkily aside. They do not set up their own conventicle alongside the Church, but they throw their fire into her very center. And if they are genuine, they never point to themselves; they themselves are only a reflection; it is the master of the flame who is all-important. This pointing away from themselves is an exact criterion: "He was not the light, but was only to bear witness of the light." But it is also said of the same man that he was a "light to those who sit in darkness and the shadow of death" (Lk 1:79). Is it not true that such pointing away from oneself occurs uniquely within the Church, which is more than a "congregation", a sociological unit, which is, that is to say, the "handmaid of the Lord" who points away from herself (and the humiliated office of the Church is precisely related to the handmaid), who is herself fulness, but not a fulness which is full of a sense of its own superiority, but "the body and fulness of him who fills all in all" (Eph 1:23)?

Why, then, do I remain in the Church? Because it is the only chance to escape from oneself, from this curse of one's importance, of one's own gravity, from the role which is identified with my own person, so that if I lost my role I would end up falling in love with my person: to escape from all this without becoming estranged from man, because God has become man, not in a vacuum but in the community of the Church. I do not doubt for a moment that God's incarnation is intended for all men and that he is sufficiently God in order to reach all whom he will. But he has set up, in the middle of the history of humanity with all its terrors and hells, a marriage bed, splendid and untouchable—it is portrayed in the Song of Songs—and even the endless problems of the Church cannot create a fog so thick that it cannot from time to time be penetrated by the light of love which shines from the saints: a love which is naïve, which cannot be suspected of any ideological bias, which cannot be taken over and built into any program.

There is a counter-test, and this is, unfortunately, the most irrefutable experience that I have had in my life in the Church. Nobody need attach to it any greater importance than that of a report based on experience. There are vocations in which men are called into the sphere of the fire. They always demand the whole person. And such vocations are refused, though one can only speak of refusals where men consciously resist the call (for a thousand unimportant reasons). Such refusals are more numerous than one might think. Those who have said "no" remain marked. They burn, but they consume themselves. They become cynical and destructive, they smell each other out and hold together. It makes no matter whether they officially leave the Church or remain within her. Anyone who has some facility for discerning spirits can recognize them. They are, of course, not identical with the so-called "enemies of the Church", nor with what Ida F. Görres has referred to as "God's demolition-squad in the Church". These latter can perform the rough but necessary tasks; unsentimental, straightforward. The work of the former is much more insidious, and I do not wish to portray it here; enough to say that its negative form provides the irrefutable, because involuntary, witness for the positive form of what may be called election and sanctity in the Church. In the desperate exhibition which they make of themselves, those who have rejected their call show what disappearance into pure service could have been.

Of course the Church "should" ... She "should" do everything and much more than she ever can. I would simply like to know whether all those who leave the Church because she does not fulfil their expectations of her find satisfaction elsewhere. Whenever I hear, "the Church should", then that simply seems to say to me, "I should". The more so because I receive so much more from the Church than I deserve. More than ever a man or a human society could give. It is up to me, up to us, to see that the Church comes closer to that which in reality she is.